TeeJay Maths

CfE Second Level
Book 2C

Tom Strang, James Geddes, James Cairns,
Dr Naomi Norman and Catherine Murphy

HODDER Education

Although every effort has been made to ensure that website addresses are correct at time of going to press, Hodder Gibson cannot be held responsible for the content of any website mentioned in this book. It is sometimes possible to find a relocated web page by typing in the address of the home page for a website in the URL window of your browser.

Hachette UK's policy is to use papers that are natural, renewable and recyclable products and made from wood grown in well-managed forests and other controlled sources. The logging and manufacturing processes are expected to conform to the environmental regulations of the country of origin.

Orders: please contact Hachette UK Distribution, Hely Hutchinson Centre, Milton Road, Didcot, Oxfordshire, OX11 7HH. Telephone: +44 (0)1235 827827. Email education@hachette.co.uk Lines are open from 9 a.m. to 5 p.m., Monday to Friday. You can also order through our website: www.hoddereducation.co.uk. If you have queries or questions that aren't about an order, you can contact us at hoddergibson@hodder.co.uk

© Thomas Strang, James Geddes, James Cairns 2023

Special thanks to Dr Naomi Norman and Catherine Murphy for their significant contribution.

First published in 2023 by

TeeJay Publishers, an imprint of Hodder Gibson, which is part of the Hodder Education Group

An Hachette UK Company

50 Frederick Street

Edinburgh, EH2 1EX

Impression number	5	4	3	2	1
Year	2027	2026	2025	2024	2023

All rights reserved. Apart from any use permitted under UK copyright law, no part of this publication may be reproduced or transmitted in any form or by any means, electronic or mechanical, including photocopying and recording, or held within any information storage and retrieval system, without permission in writing from the publisher or under licence from the Copyright Licensing Agency Limited. Further details of such licences (for reprographic reproduction) may be obtained from the Copyright Licensing Agency Limited, www.cla.co.uk

Cover illustration by Ai Higaki/D'Avila Illustration Agency

Illustrations by Ai Higaki/D'Avila Illustration Agency and Aptara, Inc.

Typeset in FS Albert 16/20 pts by Aptara, Inc.

Produced by DZS Grafik, Printed in Slovenia

A catalogue record for this title is available from the British Library.

ISBN: 978 1 3983 6327 4

Contents

Introduction		6
Chapter 0	**Revision of Book 2B**	8
Chapter 1	**Multiples and factors: Solving problems**	19
	Multiples and factors problems	19
	Revisit, review, revise	23
Chapter 2	**Decimal fractions 1: Decimal fraction calculations**	24
	Multiplying decimal fractions	24
	Dividing decimal fractions	28
	Decimal fractions: a mixture	31
	Revisit, review, revise	34
Chapter 3	**Money 1: Solving money problems**	35
	Money calculations	35
	Best buys	38
	Money problems: a mixture	41
	Revisit, review, revise	45
Chapter 4	**2D shapes: Circles and polygons**	46
	Circles	46
	Quadrilaterals	49
	Polygons	53
	Revisit, review, revise	57
Chapter 5	**Percentages: Finding percentages of quantities**	59
	Simple percentages of quantities	59
	Other percentages of quantities	62
	Percentage word problems	66
	Revisit, review, revise	70
Chapter 6	**Perimeter and area: Rectangles and triangles**	71
	Perimeter and area of rectangles	71
	Area of a triangle	75
	Revisit, review, revise	78
Chapter 7	**3D objects: Volumes and nets**	80
	Volume of a cuboid	80
	Nets	84
	Revisit, review, revise	88

Chapter 8	**Whole numbers 1: Multiplying and dividing by multiples of 10, 100 and 1000**	**89**
	Multiplying whole numbers by multiples of 10, 100 and 1000	89
	Dividing whole numbers by multiples of 10, 100 and 1000	93
	Revisit, review, revise	97
Chapter 9	**Statistics: Representing data and interpreting graphs and charts**	**98**
	Pie charts	98
	Representing data	102
	Interpreting data	106
	Revisit, review, revise	109
Chapter 10	**Whole numbers 2: Order of operations**	**112**
	Working out calculations using the order of operations	112
	Using order of operations to solve problems	114
	Revisit, review, revise	117
Chapter 11	**More symmetry: Symmetry and coordinates**	**118**
	Symmetry	118
	Coordinates	121
	Revisit, review, revise	127
Chapter 12	**Time: Measuring time and calculating distances travelled**	**129**
	Measuring time	129
	Distance and time	132
	Revisit, review, revise	135
Chapter 13	**Decimal fractions 2: Decimal fraction answers**	**137**
	Dividing that gives a decimal answer	137
	Revisit, review, revise	142
Chapter 14	**More angles: Angles and scale drawings**	**143**
	Finding missing angles	143
	Compass points	147
	Using scales	150
	Scale drawings	153
	Revisit, review, revise	156
Chapter 15	**Money 2: Cards and credit**	**158**
	Cards	158
	Revisit, review, revise	163

Chapter 16	**Negative numbers: In temperatures and on number lines**	**164**
	Negative temperatures	164
	Negative numbers on a number line	168
	Revisit, review, revise	172
Chapter 17	**Algebra: Forming and solving one-step equations**	**174**
	Function machines	174
	Solving equations	177
	Forming equations	180
	Revisit, review, revise	183
Chapter 18	**More fractions, decimals and percentages: Changing between common fractions, decimals and percentages**	**185**
	Fractions, decimals and percentages	185
	Solving fraction, decimal and percentage problems	188
	Revisit, review, revise	191
Chapter 19	**Measurement: Length, volume, capacity and mass**	**192**
	Length	192
	Volume and capacity	195
	Mass	199
	Revisit, review, revise	201
Chapter 20	**Numbers and sequences: Identifying number types and patterns in sequences**	**203**
	Types of number	203
	Sequences	206
	Revisit, review, revise	209
Chapter 21	**Probability: Calculating and simplifying probabilities**	**210**
	Probability	210
	Simplifying probabilities	213
	Experimental probability	217
	Revisit, review, revise	221
Chapter 22	**End-of-year revision**	**222**

Answers online: scan the QR code or visit
www.hoddergibson.co.uk/teejay-second-level-maths-answers-2C

Introduction
Information for pupils

This book begins with Chapter 0, which is full of questions that revise maths you already know.

Each chapter is packed with lots of practice, covering all the maths you need to learn.

Each topic begins with a short explanation to get you started.

💡 I will learn how to calculate the volume of a cuboid using a formula.

There are often examples to help you understand the ideas before you answer the questions in the exercise.

Example

1 day = 24 hours $\frac{1}{4}$ day = $\frac{1}{4}$ × 24 = 6 hours

Use these questions at the end of each chapter to look back at what you have learned.

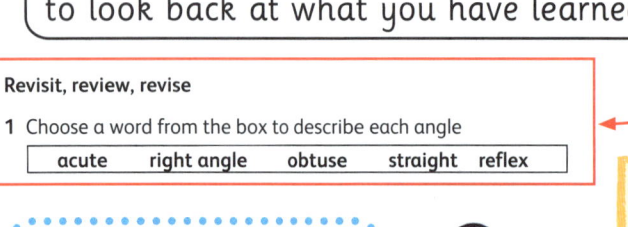

Revisit, review, revise

1 Choose a word from the box to describe each angle

| acute | right angle | obtuse | straight | reflex |

These yellow boxes introduce you to some new maths.

Now try this!
Play-based activities help you learn while you have fun.

Remember, remember
Sometimes, you need to remember some maths that you have learned before.

Review what you have learned in the end-of-year chapter at the end of the book.

Introduction

Information for teachers, parents and carers

Welcome to the second edition of a well-loved TeeJay Maths series. The Second Level scheme has been restructured so that it comprises three books instead of two, in line with curriculum structure. Book 2A covers the course for P5, Book 2B covers P6 and Book 2C covers P7.

Many of the familiar TeeJay features have been retained, including a **Chapter 0** at the start of each book, which revisits topics learned at the previous level. Additionally, each chapter ends with a **'Revisit, review, revise'** section and each book ends with an **End-of-year revision** chapter.

Progression is built into the structure of each book, with Whole Number chapters occasionally interchanging with other topics. Questions for differentiation have been flagged throughout:

- Easier questions/activities, or building blocks, are flagged by this icon 🌳
- Hard questions, or stretch, are flagged by this icon ☀️

Activities for **play-based learning** (Now try this!) have been embedded throughout to engage pupils in their learning.

Answers to all questions can be found by scanning the QR code below or online at: www.hoddergibson.co.uk/teejay-second-level-maths-answers-2C

In addition to the three second edition textbooks, new **interactive resources, editable course plans, teaching guides** and **worksheets** will be available through our Boost platform. The worksheets include **mental maths**, **practice** (to test pupils on each unit) and **assessment** (to be taken at half-term). The practice and assessment worksheets are available in digital and PDF format.

The mental maths are PDF only.

http://hoddergibson.co.uk/teejay-second-level-maths-boost

0 Revision of Book 2B

1) In your jotter, write the **first five (non-zero) multiples** of:
   a) 5
   b) 10
   c) 100

2) In your jotter, write all the **factors** of 24.

3) Finlay buys a ladder for £145.
   He sells it for £120.
   a) Does Finlay make a **profit** or **loss**?
   b) How much profit or loss does he make?

4) In the number 730 000, what does the 3 represent?

   | 300 000 | 30 000 | 3000 | 300 |

5) Copy and complete for the decimal 54.827:
   a) ___ tens
   b) 8 ___
   c) 4 ___
   d) ___ thousandths

6) In your jotter, write one hundred and twenty thousand in **digits**.

7) In your jotter, write 42 010 in **words**.

8) In your jotter, write each group of numbers in order of size. Start with the **smallest** each time.
   a) 54 603, 54 630, 54 060
   b) 1.19, 1.9, 1.09

Revision of Book 2B

9) Round:
  a) 37 412 to the nearest 10 000
  b) 761 002 to the nearest 100 000
  c) 19.74 to 1 decimal place
  d) 5.831 to 2 decimal places
  e) 0.084 to 1 decimal place.

10) Estimate the answer to 10 586 − 8914

11) Work out:
  a) 17.4 × 10
  b) 17.4 × 1000
  c) 0.8 × 100
  d) 29.5 ÷ 10
  e) 29.5 ÷ 100
  f) 295 ÷ 1000

12) Change:
  a) £37.44 to pence
  b) 7.1 m to cm
  c) 3.64 km to m.

13) In your jotter, write each division using ⌐√ ̄ ̄
Then work out the answer, including the remainder.
  a) 65 ÷ 4
  b) 104 ÷ 6
  c) 93 ÷ 8
  d) 285 ÷ 9

14) Alice is buying party invitations.
They are sold in packs of 8.
She needs 50 invitations.
How many packs should she buy?

15) Mentally work out:
  a) 1.6 + 3.2
  b) 31.8 − 0.4
  c) 5.075 − 0.01

Chapter 0 Revision of Book 2B

16) Line up the digits with the same place value to work out:
   a) 29.4 + 3.7
   b) 473.8 – 192.9

17) Work out:
   a) $\frac{1}{5}$ of 35
   b) $\frac{3}{5}$ of 35
   c) $\frac{4}{9}$ of 27
   d) $\frac{5}{8}$ of 24

18) An art club has 36 members.
   $\frac{5}{9}$ of the members like to paint.
   The rest like to do pottery.
   How many like to do pottery?

19) In your jotter, write **three pairs** of **equivalent** fractions from this list:

$\frac{4}{20}$	$\frac{6}{27}$	$\frac{9}{12}$	$\frac{2}{9}$	$\frac{2}{10}$	$\frac{30}{40}$

20) What percentage of the large square is:
   a) coloured
   b) not coloured?

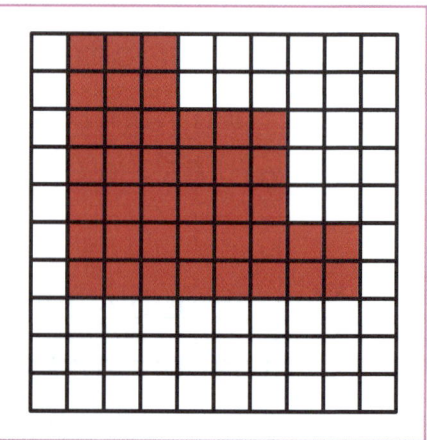

21) In your jotter, write each percentage as a **fraction in its simplest form**.
   a) 11%
   b) 50%
   c) 8%

22) In your jotter, write each fraction:
   i)   with a denominator of 100   ii)   as a percentage.
   a) $\frac{1}{50}$ b) $\frac{3}{25}$ c) $\frac{7}{10}$ d) $\frac{2}{5}$

23) The rule for a sequence is:

first term = 12

term-to-term rule = + 7

In your jotter, write down the **first five terms** in the sequence.

24) Describe each sequence by giving the first term and the term-to-term rule:
   a) 64, 32, 16, 8, …
   b) $\frac{1}{2}$, $1\frac{3}{4}$, 3, $4\frac{1}{4}$, $5\frac{1}{2}$, …

25) In your jotter, draw the next term in the sequences:

a)   b)

26) The table shows the distance an athlete runs when she completes different numbers of laps of a running track.

Number of laps	1	2	3	4	5	6
Distance in metres	400	800	1200			

a) Copy and complete the table.

b) Copy and complete the formula:

Distance in metres = ____ × number of laps.

c) Use your formula to find out how far the athlete runs when she does 10 laps.

d) How many laps would the athlete have to run to cover a distance of 10 000 metres?

Chapter 0 Revision of Book 2B

27) How many:
- a) months in 5 years
- b) days **altogether** in November and December
- c) minutes in $\frac{1}{2}$ an hour
- d) seconds in 14 minutes
- e) days between 20 March and 5 April, including both dates?

28) Here is a timetable for the Glasgow to Inverness train:

Glasgow	08:40	10:07	12:07	14:39	19:37
Stirling	09:08	10:34	12:35	15:08	20:03
Perth	09:48	11:09	13:11	15:39	20:38
Pitlochry	10:22	11:52	13:42	—	21:29
Aviemore	11:27	—	14:28	—	22:38
Inverness	12:01	13:26	15:22	19:39	23:16

- a) What time does the 12:07 train from Glasgow arrive in Inverness?
- b) How long does the 20:03 train from Stirling take to get to Pitlochry?
- c) I arrive in Perth at 11:05 a.m.
  How long do I have to wait for a train to Aviemore?

29) Mary works for 3 hours 45 minutes.
Imran works for 20 minutes longer than Mary.
How long do they work **altogether**?

Revision of Book 2B

30) a) Measure these angles and write down their sizes in your jotter.

i)

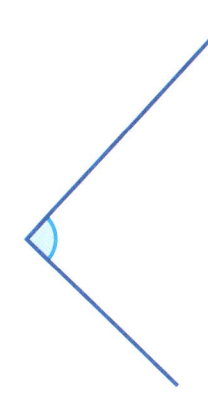

ii)

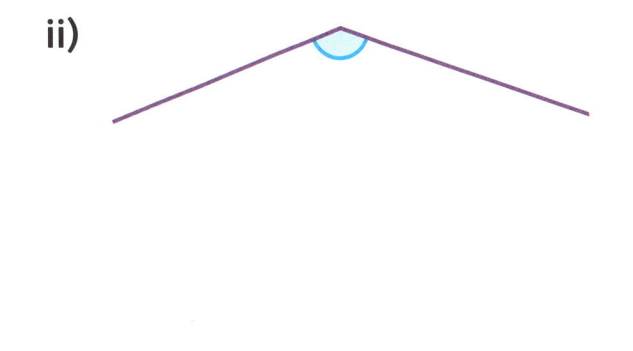

b) Are the angles in part **a** acute, reflex, right or obtuse?

31) In your jotter, draw and label these angles:
  a) ∠KLM = 62°
  b) ∠FGH = 127°

32) Choose the correct names of the triangles from the box.

| scalene triangle | isosceles triangle |
| equilateral triangle | right-angled triangle |

a) A, B, C

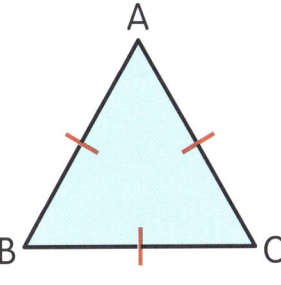

b) F, G, H

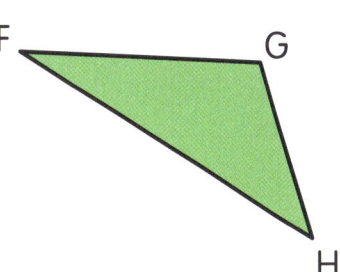

c) X, Y, Z

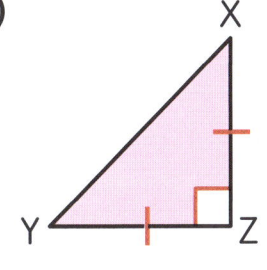

Chapter 0 Revision of Book 2B

33) a) On squared paper, draw a square with area 64 cm².
    b) What is the perimeter of the square?

34) a) Copy the pairs of calculations.
       Write the symbol = or ≠ between each pair.
       i) 18 − 0 ____ 19 × 0   ii) 12 ÷ 3 ____ 16 ÷ 4
    b) Copy the pairs of calculations.
       Write the symbol < or > between each pair.
       i) 7 × 9 ____ 8 × 10   ii) 18 ÷ 2 ____ 10 − 4

35) The symbol ◯ stands for +, −, × or ÷
    What does ◯ stand for in:
    a) 7 ◯ 11 = 77   b) 80 = 95 ◯ 15
    c) 45 ◯ 5 = 20 ◯ 11?

36) Work out what number the symbol ☐ stands for in:
    a) 56 ÷ ☐ = 7   b) 35 = ☐ × 5
    c) 123 = ☐ − 16   d) ☐ + 32 = 32

37) The total mass of 4 packets of crisps is 100 grams.
    Each packet has a mass of w grams.
    In your jotter, write an equation and solve it to find the mass of each packet.

Revision of Book 2B

38) Copy and complete these function machines:

a) 9 → ×12 → ___
___ → ×12 → 144

b) 15 → − ___ → 11
___ → − ___ → 27

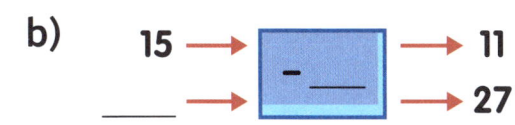

39) On squared paper, copy and complete the shapes so the dashed line is a line of symmetry:

a)

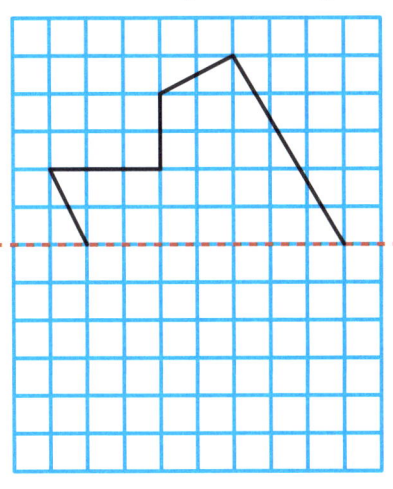

b)

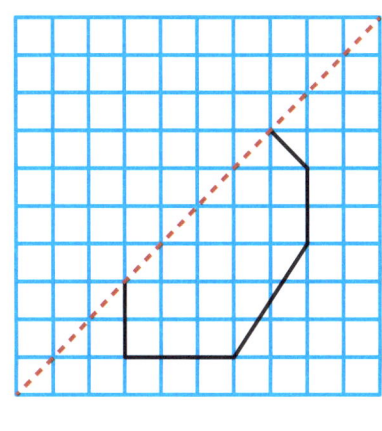

40) How many lines of symmetry does a rectangle have?

41) a) Calculate the volume of this cube.
b) Draw the cube on a piece of isometric paper.
c) Draw a net of the cube on squared paper.

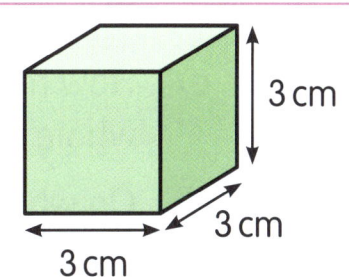

3 cm
3 cm
3 cm

Chapter 0 Revision of Book 2B

42) The line graph shows the length of time that Sita spent reading one week.

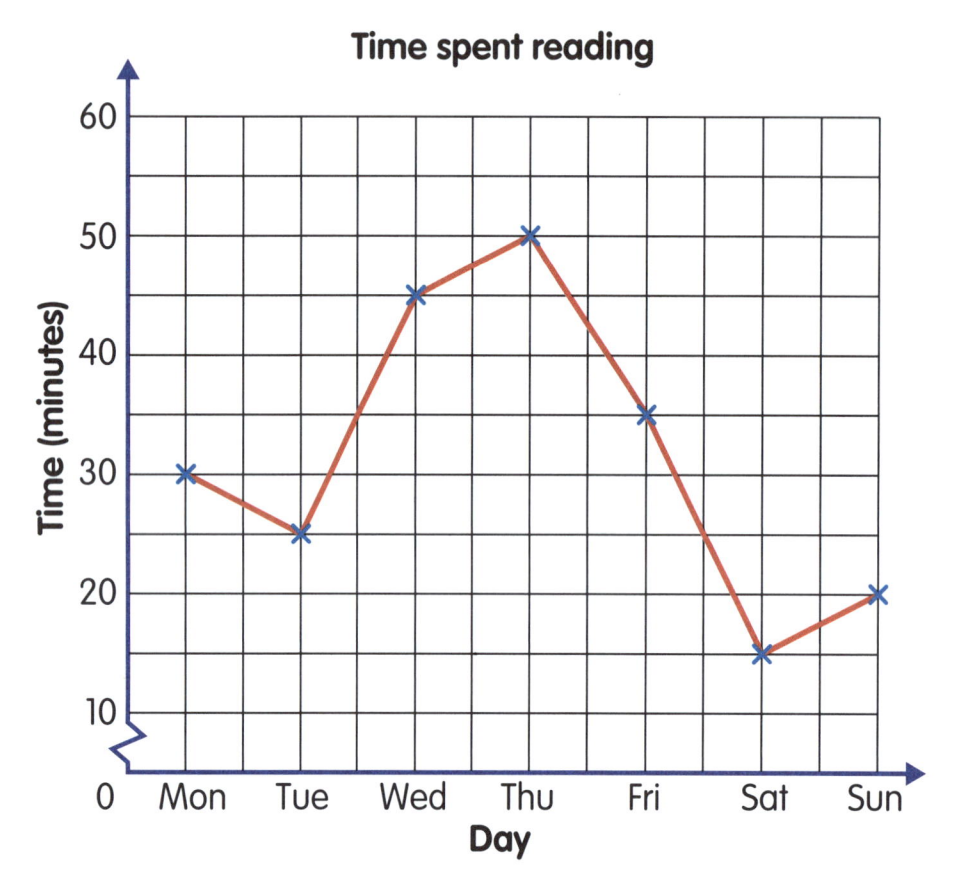

Time spent reading

(Line graph: y-axis "Time (minutes)" from 0 to 60; x-axis "Day" Mon–Sun. Values: Mon 30, Tue 25, Wed 45, Thu 50, Fri 35, Sat 15, Sun 20.)

a) How many minutes did Sita spend reading on

   i) Monday

   ii) Friday?

b) How many **more** minutes did Sita spend reading on Thursday than on Saturday?

c) How many minutes did Sita spend reading over the whole week?

d) On which day did Sita spend the **least** time reading?

Revision of Book 2B

43) The table below shows the cost of insurance for holidays abroad.

	Insurance per person			
	Europe		Rest of the world	
Duration of holiday	Adult	Child (0–15)	Adult	Child (0–15)
Up to 8 days	£55.00	£39.00	£85.00	£75.00
9–16 days	£70.00	£60.00	£102.40	£94.00
17–24 days	£79.00	£69.00	£120.40	£112.00

a) How much is insurance for:
  i) a 50-year-old going to Europe for 12 days
  ii) a 14-year-old travelling to the USA for 20 days
  iii) a 68-year-old spending 7 days in Spain?

b) Joe and Katie, both 38 years old, take their two children, aged 4 and 9, and Katie's mother to France on a three-week holiday.
Work out the **total** cost of the insurance.

44) The graph shows average house prices (in thousands of pounds) in Westfield.

a) Explain why the graph is misleading.
b) In your jotter, draw a graph that gives a better comparison of the house prices.

Chapter 0 Revision of Book 2B

45) Draw a 10 by 10 grid as shown below.

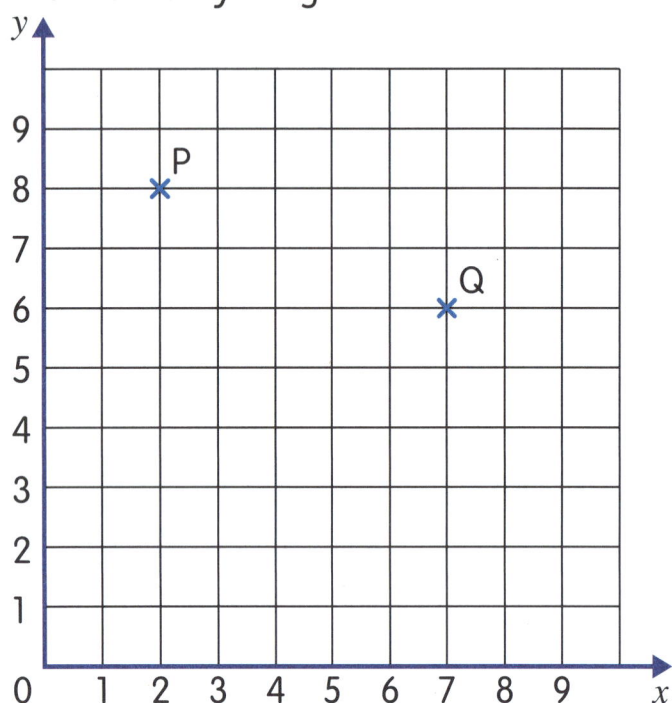

a) In your jotter, write down the coordinates of:

i) **P** ii) **Q**.

b) Plot the point **R** (5, 1).

c) **PQRS** is a square.
Plot the point **S**.

d) What are the coordinates of **S**?

46) Here is a spinner.

| certain | likely | even chance |
| unlikely | impossible |

Which word(s) in the box describe the probability the spinner will stop on:

a) 4
b) a number larger than 1
c) 9
d) a number less than 5
e) a number from 1 to 8?

18

1 Multiples and factors
Solving problems

Multiples and factors problems

> 💡 I will learn to solve multiple and factor problems.

Remember, remember

Numbers in the 8 times table are called **multiples** of 8.

For example: the first three (non-zero) **multiples of 8** are: **8**, **16**, **24**

because 8 × 1 = 8,   8 × 2 = 16,   8 × 3 = 24

Numbers that divide exactly into 8 (with no remainder) are called **factors** of 8.

For example: **1**, **2**, **4** and **8** are **factors of 8**

because 8 ÷ 1 = 8,   8 ÷ 2 = 4,   8 ÷ 4 = 2,   8 ÷ 8 = 1

and there are no remainders.

Factors can usually be written in pairs.

Factor pairs of 8 are:

1 and 8 (because 1 × 8 = 8)

2 and 4 (because 2 × 4 = 8)

Sometimes you may be asked to solve a problem involving multiples and/or factors.

Chapter 1 Multiples and factors

Example

> I am thinking of an even number between 10 and 20.
> One of its factors is 3.
> It is **not** a multiple of 4.
> What is the number?

Answer

Write all the even numbers between 10 and 20:	12, 14, 16, 18.
Cross off any numbers in the list with no factor of 3:	12, ~~14~~, ~~16~~, 18.
Cross off any number in the list that is a multiple of 4:	~~12~~, ~~14~~, ~~16~~, 18.

The number is 18.

Exercise 1

1) a) Copy and complete to show all the factors of 20:
   1, 2, ___, 5, ___, 20

   b) Copy and complete to show the first six multiples of 5:
   5, ___, ___, 20, ___, 30

   c) What numbers are factors of 20 but **not** multiples of 5?
   Use your answers to **a** and **b** to help you.

2) In your jotter, write two **odd** numbers that are a factor pair of 35.

3) In your jotter, write two numbers that are factors of 14 and multiples of 2.

4) I am thinking of a number between 30 and 40.
   It is a multiple of 6.
   What is the number?

Solving problems

5) Bailey says, 'Odd numbers only have odd factors.'
   a) Is Bailey correct? (Yes or no.)
   b) If you answered yes to **a**, then write three examples in your jotter.

6) How many factors do each of these numbers have?
   (List all the factors, then count them.)
   a) 4   b) 25   c) 9   d) 16   e) 1

7) a) Did the numbers in question 6 have an odd or even number of factors?
   b) What is the special name for these numbers: 1, 4, 9, 16, 25 ... ?

8) I am thinking of an odd number between 20 and 30.
   It has exactly 4 factors.
   It does **not** have a factor of 7.
   What is the number?

9) a) Copy and complete:
   $\frac{1}{2}$ hour = _____ minutes
   b) What numbers of minutes are factors of half an hour?

10) Aditi has a 40 cm length of string.
    In your jotter, write all the equal, whole number lengths Aditi can cut the string into without wasting any.

Chapter 1 Multiples and factors

☀ **11)** Ahmed knows there are 7 days in a week.

'Therefore,' he says, '7 must be a factor of the number of days in a year.'

Is Ahmed correct?

Show your working.

Now try this!

It takes 365 days, 5 hours and 59 minutes for the Earth to go all the way around the Sun once.

Because a year always has full days, most of the time we round down to 365 days in a year.

But every four years, we round up to 366 days in a year.

This is called a **leap year**.

This means a leap year is always a multiple of 4.

So, the year always divides by 4 with no remainder.

For example, 2020 divides by 4 with no remainder:

```
     50 5
4 ) 2 ²02 ²0
```

2020 was a leap year.

Which of these years were leap years:

1) 1746, the Battle of Culloden
2) 1888, John Logie Baird (Scottish inventor) was born
3) 1999, the Scottish Parliament was established again
4) the year you were born?

Solving problems

Revisit, review, revise

1) In your jotter, write two **even** numbers that are a factor pair of 12.

2) a) Can an even number have an odd factor? (Yes or no.)
   b) If you answered yes to a, write three examples in your jotter.

3) In your jotter, write three numbers that are factors of 18 and multiples of 3.

4) What different-size groups could a class of 32 make, without any pupil being left out?

5) a) Copy and complete:

   £1 = _____ p

   b) List all the coins that are factors of £1.

   c) Which coin is a multiple of £1?

2 Decimal fractions 1
Decimal fraction calculations

Multiplying decimal fractions

💡 I will learn to multiply decimal fractions by a single digit.

Remember, remember

10 tenths = 1 one

10 hundredths = 1 tenth

You can multiply a decimal by a single digit, **mentally**.

Decimal fraction calculations

Examples

Example 1

0.2 × 4 = 0.8   because 2 tenths × 4 = 8 tenths
                                      = 0.8

Example 2

0.5 × 7 = 3.5   because 5 tenths × 7 = 35 tenths
                                      = 3 ones + 5 tenths
                                      = 3.5

Example 3

0.06 × 2 = 0.12   because 6 hundredths × 2 = 12 hundredths
                                            = 1 tenth + 2 hundredths
                                            = 0.12

You can also use a written method to multiply a decimal by a single digit. To do this, you need to use what you already know about dividing by 10 and 100.

- When you divide by 10 digits move **1 place right**.
- When you divide by 100 digits move **2 places right**.

For example, to work out 23.18 × 4

```
   2  3  1  8  ←── Ignore the decimal point
×  1     3  4      and work out 2318 × 4
   9  2  7  2
```

2318 × 4 = 9272

Chapter 2 Decimal fractions 1

2318 ÷ ☐ = 23.18 ← Work out the relationship between 2318 and 23.18

Thousands	Hundreds	Tens	Ones	.	tenths	hundredths
2	3	1	8	.		
		2	3	.	1	8

Digits move 2 places right

2318 ÷ 100 = 23.18

So 2318 × 4 = 9272

↓ ÷ 100   ↓ ÷ 100

23.18 × 4 = 92.72

Estimate to check your answer:

23.18 × 4 is about 20 × 4 = 80

92.72 is close to 80.

So 23.18 × 4 = 92.72

Exercise 1

1) Copy and complete:

   a) 0.2 × 3 = 2 tenths × ____

   = ____ tenths

   = 0.____

   b) 0.6 × 7 = ____ tenths × 7

   = ____ tenths

   = 4 ones + ____ tenths

   = 4.____

   c) 0.03 × 5 = 3 hundredths × ____

   = ____ hundredths

   = 1 tenth + ____ hundredths

   = 0.1____

Decimal fraction calculations

2) Work out **mentally**:
   a) 0.2 × 2
   b) 0.3 × 3
   c) 0.5 × 5
   d) 0.4 × 9
   e) 0.02 × 4
   f) 0.07 × 4

3) a) Work out:

        8 7
   ×   6

   b) Copy and complete:

   87 × 6 = ____
   ↓ ÷ ☐   ↓ ÷ ☐
   8.7 × 6 = ____

   c) Estimate 8.7 × 6 to check your answer.

4) a) Work out:

      1 7 2
   ×   4

   b) Copy and complete:

   172 × 4 = ____
   ↓ ÷ ☐   ↓ ÷ ☐
   1.72 × 4 = ____

   c) Estimate 1.72 × 4 to check your answer.

5) Work out:
   a) 1.8 × 4
   b) 9.7 × 2
   c) 15.3 × 6
   d) 53.4 × 7
   e) 1.75 × 5
   f) 0.98 × 3

   Estimate to check your answers.

Chapter 2 Decimal fractions 1

6) A tile is 0.9 cm thick.
How high is a pile of 7 tiles?

7) A desk is 1.12 m long.
How long are 3 desks side by side, with no space between them?

8) A bar of chocolate has a mass of 92.4 grams.
What is the mass of 9 bars?

9) By how much is 7 × 0.82 **less** than 6 × 0.97?

Dividing decimal fractions

💡 I will learn to divide decimal fractions by a single digit.

You can divide a decimal by a single digit, **mentally**.

Examples

Example 1

0.6 ÷ 2 = 0.3   because 6 tenths ÷ 2 = 3 tenths
                                              = 0.3

Example 2

2.8 ÷ 4 = 0.7   because 2.8 = 2 ones + 8 tenths
                                      = 28 tenths
                  28 tenths ÷ 4 = 7 tenths
                                      = 0.7

Decimal fraction calculations

Example 3

$0.24 \div 3 = 0.08$ because $0.24 = 2$ tenths $+ 4$ hundredths
$= 24$ hundredths

24 hundredths $\div 3 = 8$ hundredths
$= 0.08$

You can also use a written method to divide a decimal by a single digit. For example, to work out $19.32 \div 7$

7 goes into
19 (ones)
2 times
remainder 5 (ones)

Line up the decimal points

7 goes into
53 (tenths)
7 times
remainder 4 (tenths)

7 goes into
42 (hundredths)
6 times

$$\begin{array}{r} 2\,.\,7\;6 \\ 7\,\overline{\smash{)}1^{1}9\,.^{5}3\,^{4}2} \end{array}$$

$19.32 \div 7 = 2.76$

Exercise 2

1) Copy and complete:

a) $0.8 \div 2 =$ _____

because 8 tenths $\div 2 =$ _____ tenths

b) $0.48 \div 8 =$ _____

because 4 tenths + 8 hundredths = 48 hundredths
and 48 hundredths $\div 8 =$ _____ hundredths.

2) Work out **mentally**:

a) $0.4 \div 2$ b) $3.5 \div 5$ c) $1.6 \div 8$
d) $0.08 \div 4$ e) $0.63 \div 7$ f) $5.6 \div 8$

Chapter 2 Decimal fractions 1

3) Copy and complete:

a) 2.☐☐ ÷ 3) 6.0 9

b) ☐.☐☐ ÷ 8) 3 ³0 . ⁶5 ¹6

c) ☐.☐ ÷ 6) 4 ⁴5 . ³6

4) Work out:

a) 4) 7.2

b) 7) 29.4

c) 2) 27.46

d) 8) 0.56

e) 3) 69.15

f) 9) 111.51

5) In your jotter, write these divisions using ⌐. Then work out the answer.

a) 9.8 ÷ 2
b) 0.68 ÷ 4
c) 51.8 ÷ 7
d) 9.06 ÷ 3
e) 38.34 ÷ 6
f) 143.2 ÷ 8

6) A pile of 6 books is 14.4 cm tall.
All the books are the same size.
How thick is 1 book?

7) Some raw pastry has a mass of 273.6 g.
It is used to make 8 jam tarts.
How much pastry is used for each jam tart?

8) 9 chairs are arranged in a row so that they touch each other.
All the chairs are the same width.
The row of chairs is 3.51 m long.
How wide is each chair?
Give your answer in cm.

9) Work out a fifth of 172.5.

Decimal fraction calculations

Decimal fractions: a mixture

> 💡 I will add, subtract, multiply and divide decimal fractions.

Remember, remember

You already know how to add and subtract decimals using **place value columns**.

Remember, when adding or subtracting, **line up** the digits in the same place value columns.

Example

65.71 + 23.6

	Tens	Ones	.	tenths	hundredths
	6	5	.	7	1
+	2	3₁	.	6	0
	8	9	.	3	1

23.6 and 23.60 have the same value

7 tenths + 6 tenths = 13 tenths = 1 one + 3 tenths

Carry 1 one into the one column

65.71 + 23.6 = 89.31

Chapter 2 Decimal fractions 1

Example

42.63 − 20.71

Tens	Ones	.	tenths	hundredths
4	1̷2̷	.	¹6	3
− 2	0	.	7	1
2	1	.	9	2

You cannot subtract 7 tenths from 6 tenths

Exchange 1 one for 10 tenths and carry them into the tenths column
Now there is 1 one left and 16 tenths − 7 tenths

42.63 − 20.71 = 21.92

Sometimes when solving word problems involving decimal fractions, you must decide whether you need to **add**, **subtract**, **multiply** or **divide**.

Exercise 3

1) Work out:

   a) 4 . 7 6
      + 2 . 4 2

   b) 5 3 . 5 1
      − 3 9 . 2 7

   c) 8) 3 2 8 . 8

2) Work out:

   a) 0.75 − 0.28
   b) 0.348 + 0.46
   c) 5286.3 − 4851.9
   d) 91.7 × 6
   e) 10.4 × 5
   f) 231.6 ÷ 3

Decimal fraction calculations

3) Work out the **total** height of the house.

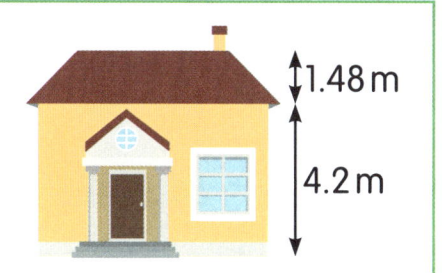

1.48 m
4.2 m

4) A pile of 4 of the same boxes is put in a van.
Each box is 19.7 cm tall.
  a) How tall is the pile?
Each box has a mass of 3.58 kg.
  b) What is the **total** mass of the pile?

5) It is 11.4 km to cycle by road from my house to the train station.
It is 8.53 km to cycle along the river.
How much **shorter** is it to cycle along the river?

☀ **6)** Ally has a square garden with sides 8.72 m.
Chen has a rectangular garden with length 7.14 m and width 9.2 m.
Who has the **larger** garden perimeter?
Show your working.

Now try this!

Digits 0 1 2 3 4 5 6 7 8 are **missing** (only once) from these three calculations.

With a partner, work out where the digits belong.

1)
```
        6□.5
     ┌────────
   8 │ 5□³6.□
```

2)
```
   6 □ 6 . 4
 − 5 2 8 . 2
 ───────────
   1 0 □ . □
```

3) 9.□4 × □ = 6□.78

33

Chapter 2 Decimal fractions 1

Revisit, review, revise

1) Work out:

   a) 3.42 + 1.64   b) 28.7 – 13.8   c) 104.78 – 73.9

2) Work out the **total** length of the screwdriver.

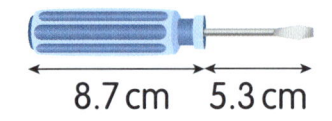

   8.7 cm   5.3 cm

3) Work out **mentally**:

   a) 0.4 × 2   b) 0.6 × 3   c) 0.07 × 7
   d) 0.6 ÷ 3   e) 4.2 ÷ 6   f) 0.24 ÷ 8

4) Work out:

   a) 3) 5.4   b) 6) 28.2   c) 9) 73.26

5) Work out:

   a) 29.4 ÷ 3   b) 141.6 ÷ 6   c) 559.26 ÷ 9
   d) 3.1 × 2   e) 2.8 × 3   f) 7.2 × 4
   g) 13.8 × 6   h) 9.17 × 5   i) 2.92 × 7

6) A brick is 6.5 cm tall.
   How tall is a stack of 8 bricks on top of each other?

7) A bag of sand has a mass of 25.1 kg.
   What is the **total** mass of 7 bags of sand?

8) What is a quarter of 285.68?

9) Jenny is at the zoo.
   Jenny is 1.64 m tall.
   She stands beside a giraffe 4.82 m tall.
   How much **taller** is the giraffe than Jenny?

3 Money 1
Solving money problems

Money calculations

> 💡 I will learn to multiply and divide money.

Remember, remember

You already know that when working with money (in pounds), you always have **two digits after the decimal point**.

You also know how to add, subtract, multiply and divide a decimal with two digits after the decimal point.

Examples

Work out 143.87 + 92.31

```
    1  4  3 . 8  7
 +  ₁9  2₁. 3  1
    2  3  6 . 1  8
```

143.87 + 92.31 = 236.18

Work out 87.63 − 12.97

```
    8  ⁶7̸.¹⁵6̸  ¹³
 −  1  2 . 9  7
    7  4 . 6  6
```

87.63 − 12.97 = 74.66

Work out 15.23 × 6

```
       1  5  2  3
    ×  ₃1 ₁1  6
       9  1  3  8
```

1523 × 6 = 9138
↓ ÷100   ↓ ÷100
15.23 × 6 = 91.38

Work out 68.32 ÷ 4

```
       1  7 . 0  8
    4 ) 6  ²8 . ³2
```

68.32 ÷ 4 = 17.08

Chapter 3 Money 1

Sometimes when solving money problems, you must decide whether you need to **add**, **subtract**, **multiply** or **divide**.

Exercise 1

1) Copy and complete:

a)
```
  £ 3 8 . 6 5
+ £     9 . 7 1
```

b)
```
  £ 1 9 7 . 0 6
- £       6 . 9 5
```

c)
```
  £ 1 2 . 4 4
×           6
```

d)
```
3 ) £ 1 9 . 5 9
```

2) Work out:
- a) £1.73 × 2
- b) £14.85 + £10.63
- c) £9.75 ÷ 5
- d) £31.26 × 3
- e) £94.16 − £13.05
- f) £28.79 × 6
- g) £206.53 + £34.71
- h) £97.65 ÷ 7

3) Husna travels to see her grandma.
She catches a train and then gets a taxi.
The train ticket costs £46.38.
The taxi costs £18.45.
How much does Husna spend on travelling to see her grandma?

Solving money problems

4) Three friends pay £289.50 each for a holiday.
How much do they pay **altogether**?

5) Alec buys a set of 4 tyres for his car.
The tyres cost him £174.48 **in total**.
What is the cost of 1 tyre?

6) Rashid has £187.93 in his savings account.
Alfie has £14.47 **less** than Rashid in his savings account.
How much does Alfie have in his savings account?

7) Florence earns £296.85 each week.
How much does she earn for working four weeks?

8) The cost of a microwave and a toaster is £328.74.
The microwave costs £275.80.
How much is the toaster?

9) A newspaper costs £3.85.
A magazine costs £2.79.
Sasha buys the newspaper and magazine for £10.
What **change** does Sasha receive?

10) Kiran and Mo have £29.80 between them.
Kiran has £1.60 **more** than Mo.
How much money does Kiran have?

Chapter 3 Money 1

Best buys

> 💡 I will learn to compare prices and choose the best value for money.

Remember, remember

You already know how to find a fraction of an amount:
- $\frac{1}{2}$ is the same as dividing by 2
- $\frac{1}{3}$ is the same as dividing by 3
- $\frac{1}{4}$ is the same as dividing by 4
- $\frac{1}{5}$ is the same as dividing by 5

and so on.

In shops, it is often useful to compare prices.
Then you can get better value for money.
You must compare the **same amount** of each item to work out **better value**.

Example

Which pack of oranges is **better value**?

£1.44   £2.20

3 oranges = £1.44   5 oranges = £2.20
1 orange = £1.44 ÷ 3   1 orange = £2.20 ÷ 5

```
    0 . 4 8                          0 . 4 4
3 ) 1 . ¹4 ²4                    5 ) 2 . ²2 ²0
```

1 orange = £0.48   1 orange = £0.44
                                 1 orange is cheaper in this pack

The pack of 5 oranges is better value.

Solving money problems

Exercise 2

1) a) Work out the cost of 1 can of orange juice in this **8 pack**. £2.64

   b) Work out the cost of 1 can of orange juice in this **9 pack**. £2.79

   c) In which pack is 1 can of orange juice **cheaper**: the 8 pack or the 9 pack?

   d) Copy and complete with 8 pack or 9 pack:

   The ____ of orange juice is better value.

2) a) Which pack of limes is better value? Show your working.

   4 pack £1.96   2 pack £1

   b) Copy and complete with 4 pack or 2 pack:

   The ____ of limes is better value.

3) The same oil is sold in two different-sized bottles.

   a) What is the cost of 100 ml of oil in the 200 ml bottle?

   £4.50 (200 ml)   £2.30 (100 ml)

   b) In which bottle is 100 ml of olive oil **cheaper**: the 200 ml or the 100 ml bottle?

   c) Copy and complete with 200 ml or 100 ml:

   The ____ bottle of olive oil is better value.

Chapter 3 Money 1

4) Super Soap washing powder is sold in two different-sized boxes.
   a) 500 g of Super Soap is £2.65.
      100 g is one-fifth of the amount.
      What is the cost of one-fifth of the amount?
   b) 700 g of Super Soap is £3.64.
      100 g is one-seventh of the amount.
      What is the cost of one-seventh of the amount?
   c) In which box is 100 g of Super Soap **cheaper**: the 500 g or 700 g box?
   d) Copy and complete with 500 g or 700 g:
      The ____ box of Super Soap is better value.

5) Gumfresh toothpaste is sold in two different-sized tubes.
   Work out the cost of 100 ml in each tube:
   a) 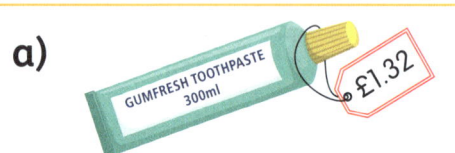 GUMFRESH TOOTHPASTE 300ml — £1.32
   b) 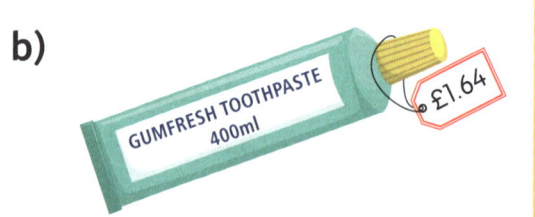 GUMFRESH TOOTHPASTE 400ml — £1.64
   c) In which tube is 100 ml of toothpaste **cheaper**: the 300 ml or 400 ml tube?
   d) In your jotter, write a sentence explaining which tube of toothpaste is **better** value.

6) You can buy juice like this:
   - 1 single carton costs 90p
   - a pack of 3 of the same cartons costs £2.61.

   How much money do you save by buying the pack of 3, rather than 3 single cartons?

Money problems: a mixture

> 💡 I will learn to use mental and written methods to work out money problems.

Remember, remember

You know a lot about money!

You know:

- The different coins and notes.
- How to add, subtract, multiply and divide money.
- Sometimes you pay more than the cost of whatever you are buying. Then you get **change**.
- **Sell** something for **more than** you buy or make it and there is a **profit**.

    profit = selling price − buying (or making) price

- **Sell** something for **less than** you buy or make it and there is a **loss**.

    loss = buying (or making) price − selling price

- If you have enough money to pay for something, then you can **afford** it.
- If you do **not** have enough money to pay for something, then you **cannot afford** it.

Sometimes when solving money problems, you must decide whether you need to **add**, **subtract**, **multiply** or **divide**.

You must also decide when it is easier to do the calculation mentally, or as a written method, or a mix of both.

Chapter 3 Money 1

Example

In a shop:
- Pairs of trousers cost £19.99 each.
- Shirts cost £12.

Toby has £50.

Can he **afford** to buy two pairs of trousers and a shirt?

Answer

You could use a **written method**:

The cost of 2 pairs of trousers:

```
   £ 1  9 . 9  9
 +   1₁ 9₁. 9₁ 9
   ─────────────
     3  9 . 9  8
```
or
```
   £ 1  9 . 9  9
 ×      1  1  1  2
   ─────────────
     3  9 . 9  8
```

The cost of 2 pairs of trousers and a shirt:

```
   £ 3  9 . 9  8
 +      1₁ 2
   ─────────────
   £ 5  1 . 9  8
```

No, Toby **cannot afford** to buy two pairs of trousers and a shirt.

You may find a **mental method** easier than a written method:

1 pair of trousers: £19.99 is £20 – 1p
2 pairs of trousers: two £20s is £40
   subtract two 1ps leaves £39.98
2 pairs of trousers and 1 shirt: £39.98 + £12
   Add £10 first to make £49.98
   then add £2 to make £51.98

No, Toby cannot afford to buy two pairs of trousers and a shirt.

42

Solving money problems

Exercise 3

1) Mhari buys 8 kiwis and 3 grapefruit.
   The kiwis are 25p each.
   The grapefruit are 50p each.
   a) How much does Mhari spend?
   b) How much **change** does Mhari get from £5?

2) Brigita buys a new TV for £399.99 and a new radio for £120.
   How much does Brigita spend?

3) Hamish earns £16.75 per hour.
   Today he works for 9 hours.
   How much does he earn today?

4) A shop sells milk for £1.10 for 1 litre.
   The shop also sells cream for £2.50 for 1 litre.
   Greta buys 5 litres of milk and $\frac{1}{2}$ litre of cream.
   How much **change** does she get from £10?

5) A pack of 6 pairs of socks is £11.58.
   A pack of 4 pairs of socks is £8.04.
   Which pack of socks is **better value**?
   Show your working.

6) Ella has £900 in her savings account.
   She uses her savings to buy a bicycle for £285 and a helmet for £14.99.
   How much is **left** in her savings account?

Chapter 3 Money 1

7) Mia buys a scooter for £1054.
A year later she sells the scooter for £995.50.
   a) Does she make a **profit** or **loss**?
   b) What profit or loss does she make?

8) Oliver sees a desk for £283.99 and a chair for £79.50.
He has £350 to spend.
How much **more** does he need to buy the desk and the chair?

desk   chair

9) Reena buys a second-hand table for £84.95.
She replaces a leg, which costs her £11.50.
She paints the table.
The paint costs her £30.65.
She wants to make a **profit** of at least £50.
What is the **minimum** (smallest) amount Reena can sell the table for?

Now try this!

Work with a partner to solve this problem.
Ibrahim buys treats from a shop for a party.
He spends £30.80 in total.
How many treats does he buy?

Treats
£1.55 for 1
Any 2 for £2.50
Any 3 for £3.25

Solving money problems

Revisit, review, revise

Work out these problems either mentally or using a written method.

1) Work out:
   a) £4.76 × 8
   b) £5.99 + £23.67
   c) £320.94 ÷ 6
   d) £5871.19 − £481.44

2) Noah earns £972.50 each week.
   He works 5 days a week.
   How much does he earn each day?

3) Which multipack of crisps is **better value**?
   Show your working.
   Copy and complete with 8 pack or 5 pack:
   The ___ of crisps is better value.

   £2.08   £1.15

4) Marta wants to buy a tent for £239.99 and a sleeping bag for £110
   Marta has £350 to spend.
   Can she **afford** to buy the tent and the sleeping bag?
   Show your working.

5) A car dealer buys a car for £10 740
   She sells the car for £12 999.99
   How much **profit** does the car dealer make?

6) A flight costs £348
   Extra baggage costs £53.60
   8 friends are going skiing.
   They buy the flight and pay the extra baggage charge for their skis.
   How much do they pay **in total**?

4 2D shapes
Circles and polygons

Circles

> 💡 I will learn the names of parts of a circle and how to draw a circle with a pair of compasses.

The **circumference** of a circle is the name for the perimeter of a circle.

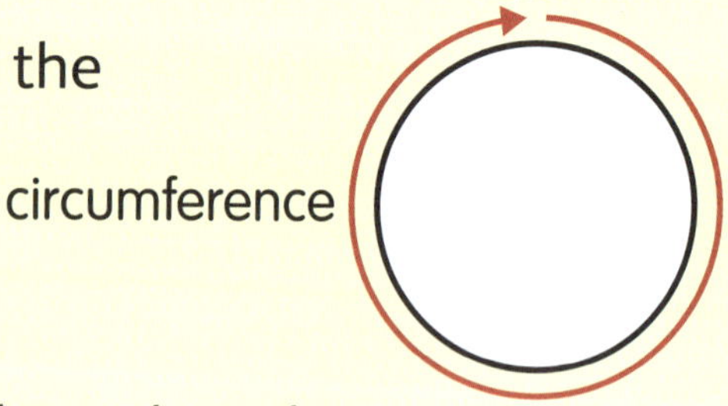

circumference

A straight line passing from one side of a circle to the other side, through the middle, is called the **diameter**.

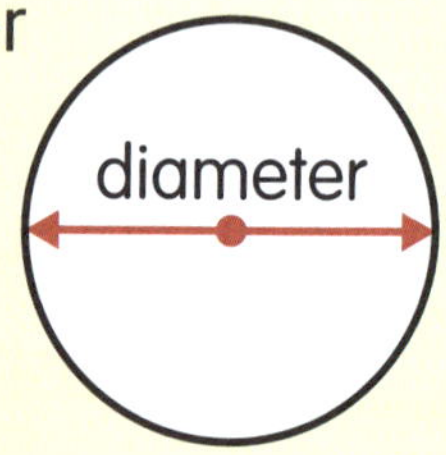

diameter

A straight line from the centre of a circle to the edge is called the **radius**.

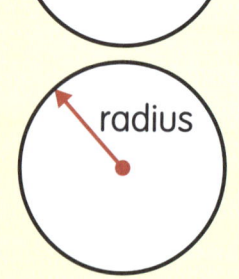

radius

diameter = 2 × radius

To accurately draw a circle, use a pair of compasses.

Example
Draw a circle with radius 5 cm.

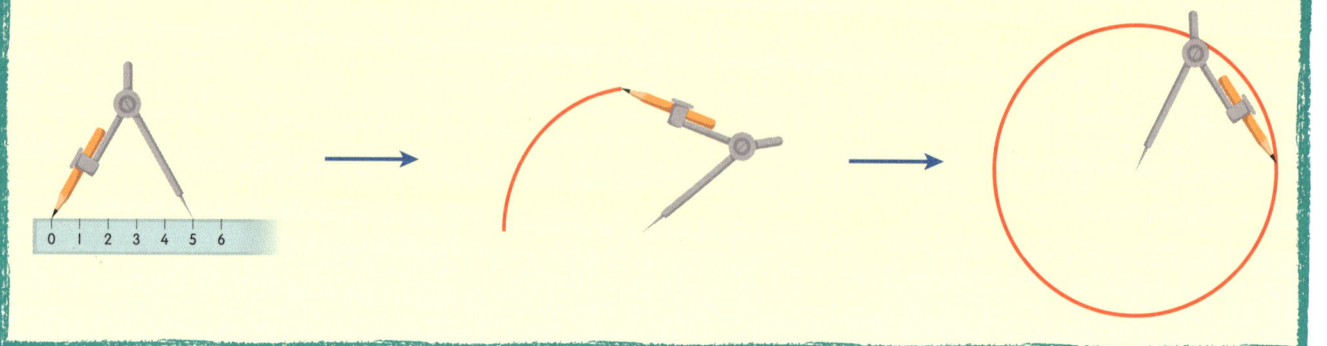

Circles and polygons

Exercise 1

1) a) Use a pair of compasses to draw a circle with a radius 3 cm in your jotter.
   b) Mark a dot in the centre.
   c) Draw a diameter on the circle and label it **diameter**.
   d) Draw a radius on the circle and label it **radius**.
   e) Write **circumference** around the edge of the circle.

2) a) What is the radius of this circle?
   b) Use a pair of compasses to draw this circle in your jotter.

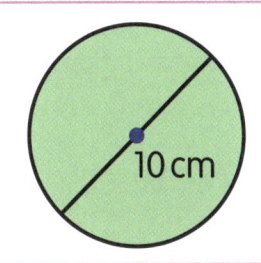

   10 cm

3) The radius of a circle is 25 mm.
   What is the diameter?

4) Draw a circle with diameter 70 mm in your jotter.

5) a) Measure the diameter of this semi-circle.
   b) What is the radius?
   c) Use a pair of compasses to draw the semi-circle in your jotter.

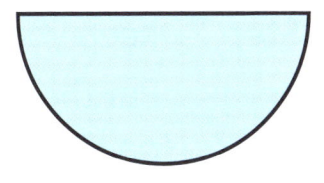

6) Here is a sketch of 3 touching circles surrounded by a rectangle.

   The radius of each circle is 8 cm.
   a) What is the height of the rectangle?
   b) What is the length of the rectangle?

47

Chapter 4 2D shapes

7) This shape is made of 4 identical semi-circles on a rectangle.

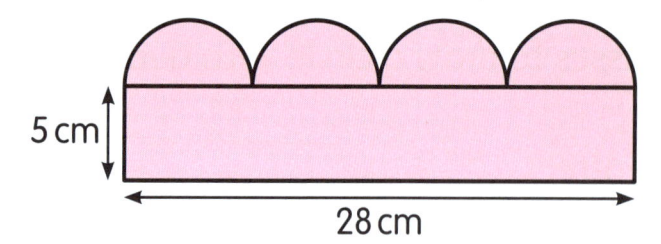

5 cm

28 cm

a) Work out the diameter of one semi-circle.

b) What is the radius of the semi-circles?

c) What is the **total** height of the shape?

Now try this!

You can draw patterns using a pair of compasses.

Step 1 Draw a circle with radius 4 cm.

Step 2 Keep your pair of compasses open to 4 cm. Put the point of the compass anywhere on the circumference and draw an **arc** (part of a circle) inside the circle.

Step 3 Move the point of the pair of compasses to one end of the arc and draw another arc inside the circle.

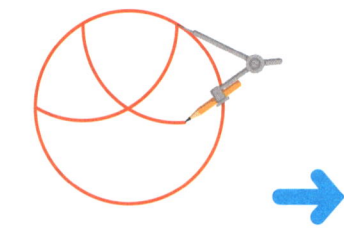

Step 4 Repeat until a flower is drawn.

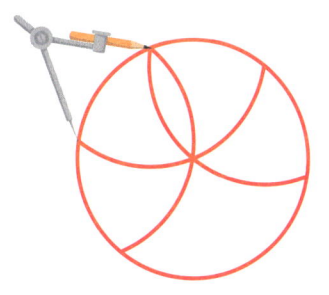

Step 5 Colour in the flower.

Quadrilaterals

💡 I will learn the properties of quadrilaterals.

Remember, remember

A **quadrilateral** is a 4-sided shape with 4 straight sides.
ABCD is a **square**.

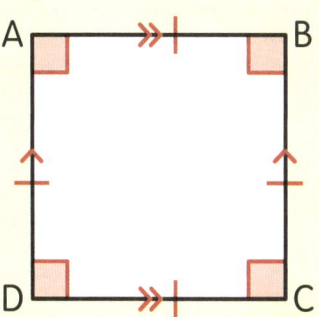

All sides are **equal** in length:
the short lines on the sides show which sides are the same length.

Two pairs of sides are **parallel**:
the arrows on the sides show which pairs of sides are parallel.

All angles are **90°**:
the squares in the corners show that the angles are right angles.

Chapter 4 2D shapes

EFGH is a **rectangle**.
Two pairs of sides are **equal** in length.
Two pairs of sides are **parallel**.
All angles are **90°**.

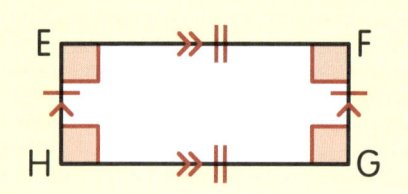

JKLM is a **rhombus**.
All sides are **equal** in length.
Two pairs of sides are **parallel**.

PQRS is a **parallelogram**.
Two pairs of sides are **equal** in length.
Two pairs of sides are **parallel**.

TUVW is a **trapezium**.
One pair of sides is **parallel**.

WXYZ is a **kite**.
Two pairs of sides are **equal** in length.

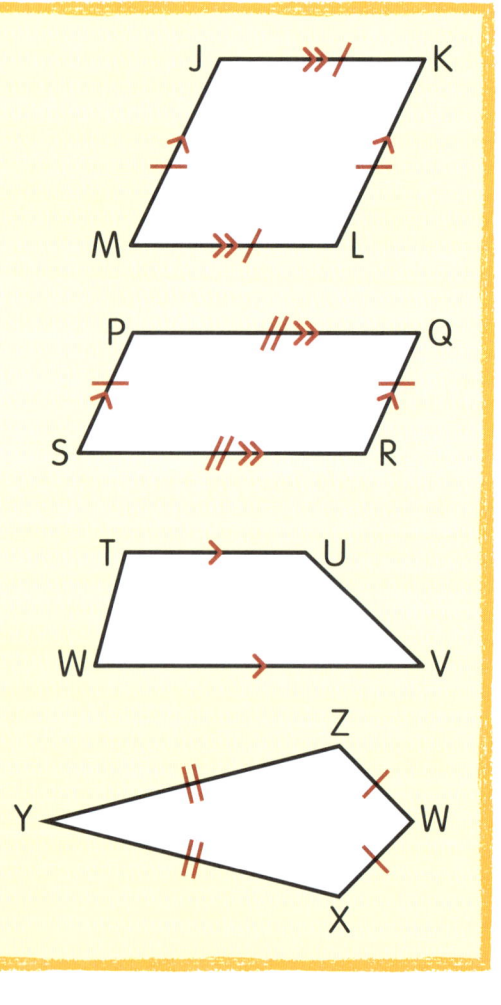

Exercise 2

1) What are the names of these shapes?

   a)

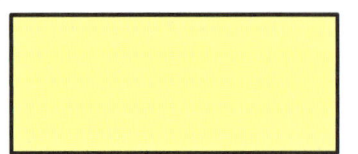

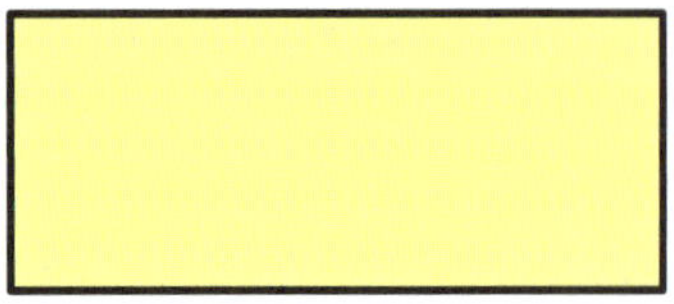

   b)

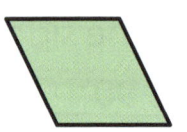

50

Circles and polygons

c)

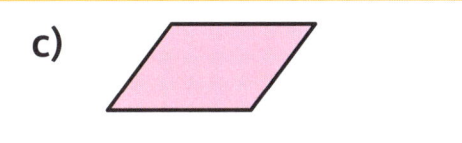

d)

e)

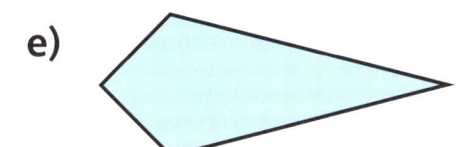

f)

2) Here is a rhombus:
   a) Trace the rhombus. 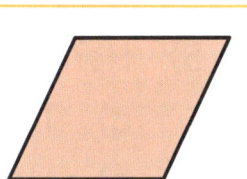
   b) Mark on any sides which are the same length with a line or lines.
   c) Measure the angles.
      Are they all the same?
   d) Write the size of the angles in the corners of the rhombus.
   e) What do you notice about the angles?
   f) Mark on any sides which are parallel with an arrow > or arrows >>.

3) Here is a parallelogram: 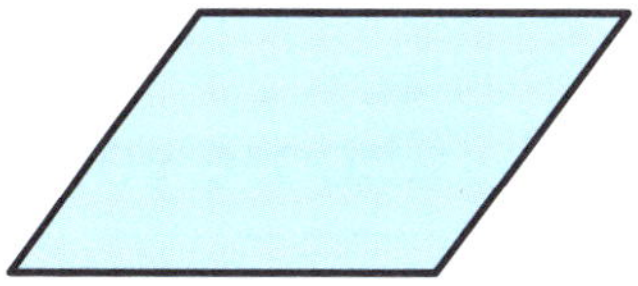
   a) Trace the parallelogram.
   b) Mark on any sides which are the same length with a line or lines.
   c) Measure the angles.
      Are they all the same?
   d) Write the size of the angles in the corners of the parallelogram.
   e) What do you notice about the angles?
   f) Mark on the sides which are parallel with an arrow > or arrows >>.

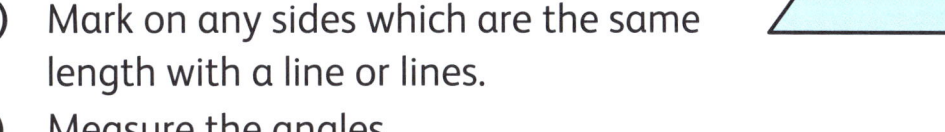

4) Here is a trapezium:
   a) Trace the trapezium.
   b) Mark on any sides which are the same length with a line or lines.

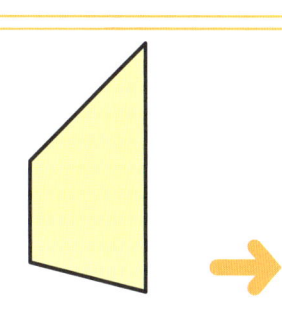

c) Measure the angles.
   Are they all the same?
d) Write the size of the angles in the corners of the trapezium.
e) What do you notice about the angles?
f) Mark on any sides which are parallel with an arrow > or arrows >>.

5) Here is a kite:
   a) Trace the kite.
   b) Mark on any sides which are the same length with a line or lines.
   c) Measure the angles.
      Are they all the same?
   d) Write the size of the angles in the corners of the kite.
   e) What do you notice about the angles?
   f) Mark on any sides which are parallel with an arrow > or arrows >>.

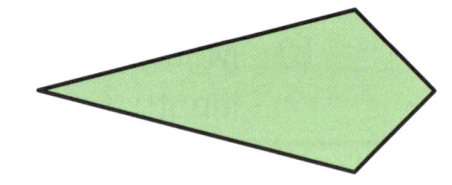

6) Choose your answers to this question from the box.

   | square rectangle kite rhombus parallelogram trapezium |

   Which quadrilaterals have:
   a) all sides equal length
   b) all angles 90°
   c) two pairs of sides parallel?

7) How many lines of symmetry has a:
   a) square
   b) rectangle
   c) rhombus
   d) parallelogram
   e) kite?

Circles and polygons

☀ **8)** Here are 4 trapeziums.
Which trapezium(s) have:
a) a pair of parallel sides
b) a pair of sides of equal length
c) a right angle
d) a line of symmetry?

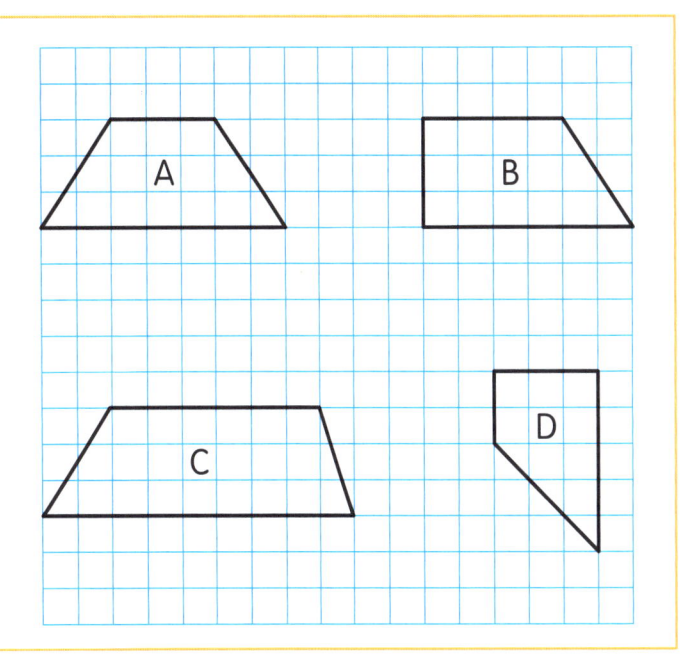

Polygons

💡 I will learn the properties of some polygons.

Remember, remember

A **polygon** is a 2D (two-dimensional) closed shape with straight sides.

Triangles are polygons.

There are four different types of triangles:

Right-angled triangle	Isosceles triangle	Equilateral triangle	Scalene triangle
One 90° angle	Two sides equal, two angles equal	All angles equal, all sides equal	No sides equal, no angles equal

53

Chapter 4 2D shapes

Polygons with different numbers of sides have different names.

Number of sides	Name	Examples
3	triangle	
4	quadrilateral	
5	pentagon	
6	hexagon	
7	heptagon	
8	octagon	
9	nonagon	
10	decagon	

Circles and polygons

If a shape is **regular**, all the **sides** are **equal** in length and all the **angles** are **equal**.
An **equilateral triangle** is a **regular triangle**.

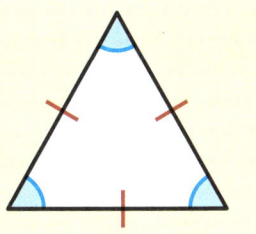

A **square** is a **regular quadrilateral**. 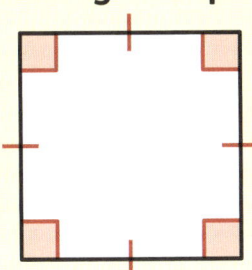   This is a **regular pentagon**:

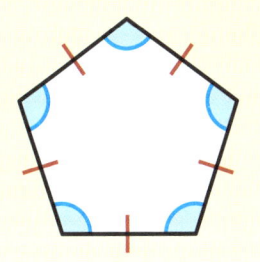

Exercise 3

1) In your jotter, write down the names of each of these shapes:
   a) 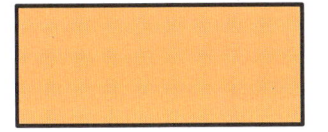   b) 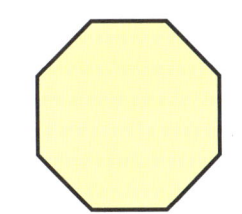   c) 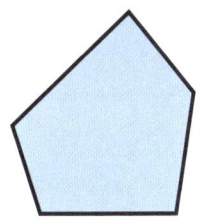
   d) 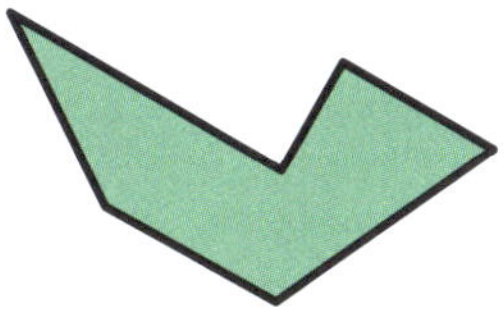   e) 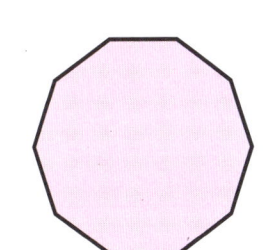   f)

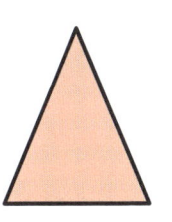

2) Which of the shapes in question 1 are **regular**?

Chapter 4 2D shapes

3) Here is a regular triangle: 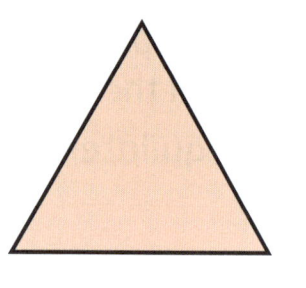
   a) What is the name of a regular triangle?
   b) Measure the angles in the triangle.
   c) Find the sum of the angles in the triangle.
      ('Find the sum' means add them all up.)

4) a) What is the name of a regular quadrilateral?
   b) What is the sum of the angles in a regular quadrilateral?

5) How many lines of symmetry do each of these regular polygons have?
   a) 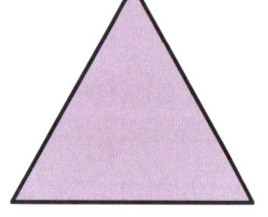
   b) 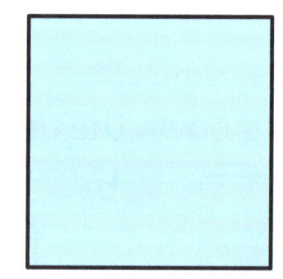
   c) 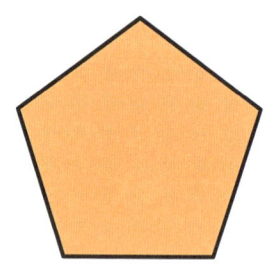
   d) 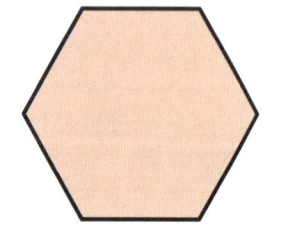
   e)

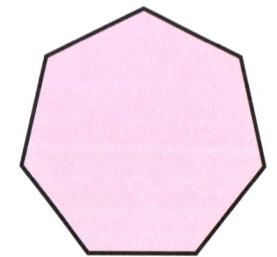

6) How many lines of symmetry will a regular decagon have?

Circles and polygons

Now try this!

You draw the **diagonals** of a quadrilateral by joining opposite corners. The diagonals of a square are drawn in the diagram here.

square

- Trace all of the shapes into your jotter.
- Draw on the **diagonals**.

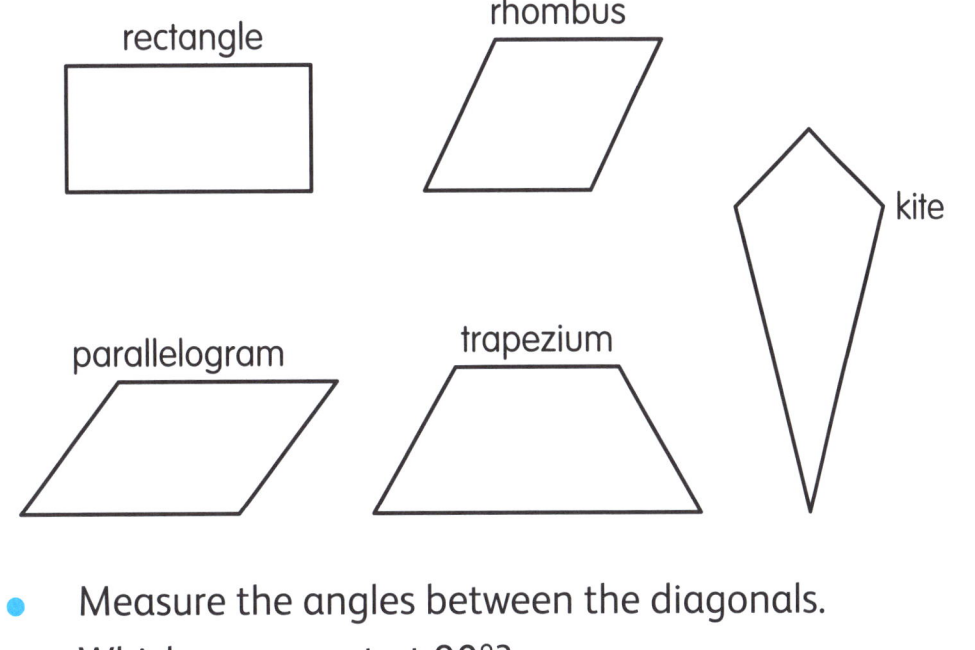

rectangle

rhombus

kite

parallelogram

trapezium

- Measure the angles between the diagonals.
- Which ones meet at 90°?

Revisit, review, revise

1) The diameter of a circle is 16 centimetres. What is the radius?

   16 cm

2) Use a pair of compasses to draw a circle with a radius of 3.5 cm in your jotter.

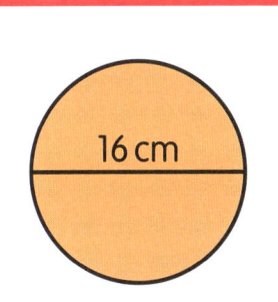

Chapter 4 2D shapes

3) This shape is made of a rectangle and a semicircle.
   What is the length of the shape?

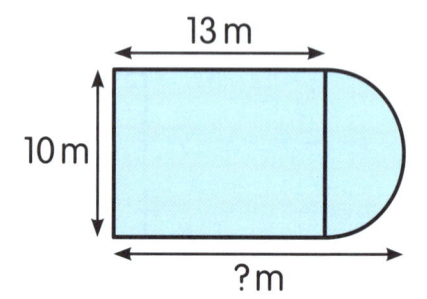

4) In your jotter, write down the names of these shapes:
   a) 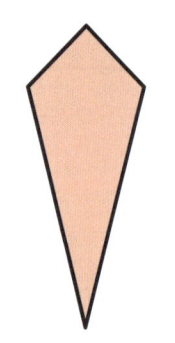
   b) 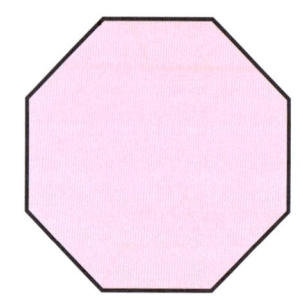
   c) 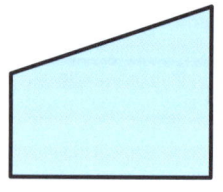
   d) 
   e)

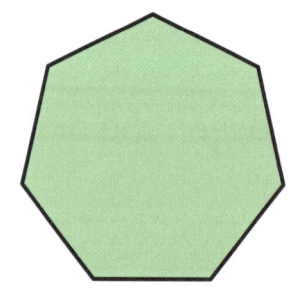

5) In your jotter, write down the names of all the quadrilaterals with **two pairs** of parallel sides.

6) Do you agree with Kemi? Explain your answer.

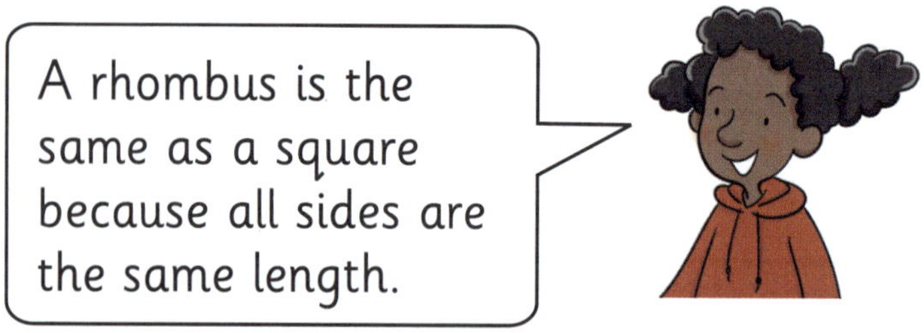

   A rhombus is the same as a square because all sides are the same length.

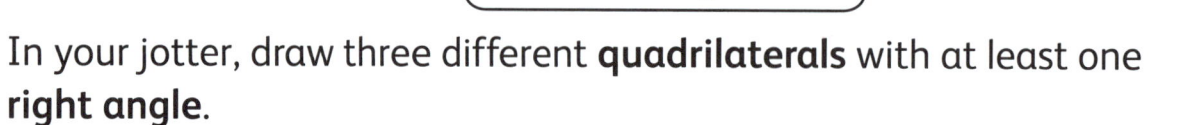

7) In your jotter, draw three different **quadrilaterals** with at least one **right angle**.

5 Percentages
Finding percentages of quantities

Simple percentages of quantities

💡 I will learn to find a percentage of a quantity using unit fractions.

Remember, remember

You already know that a percentage is:

1%

$\frac{1}{100}$

1 part out of **100 equal parts**.

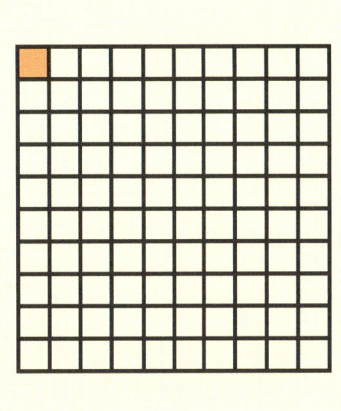

You know how to write a **percentage as a fraction** (with a **denominator of 100**), and that sometimes you may need to simplify the fraction:

$10\% = \frac{10 \div 10}{100 \div 10} = \frac{1}{10}$

You also know how to find a unit fraction of an amount by dividing. For example:

Find $\frac{1}{10}$ of 70

Divide by 10 to find $\frac{1}{10}$ (one tenth):

$\frac{1}{10}$ of 70 = 70 ÷ 10
        = 7

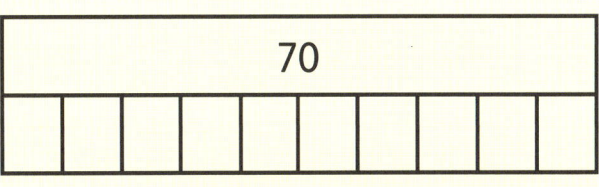

Chapter 5 Percentages

To find the percentage of an amount:
1) Write the **percentage as a fraction** with a **denominator of 100** and simplify if possible.
2) Find the fraction of the amount.

Example

Find 25% of 8.

$$25\% = \frac{25 \div 25}{100 \div 25} = \frac{1}{4}$$

You can do this in two steps if you find that easier:

$$25\% = \frac{25 \div 5}{100 \div 5} = \frac{5 \div 5}{20 \div 5} = \frac{1}{4}$$

25% of 8 = $\frac{1}{4}$ of 8
= 8 ÷ 4
= 2

Exercise 1

1) Copy and complete:

a) $50\% = \dfrac{\square \div 10}{100 \div 10} = \dfrac{\square}{\square}$

$= \dfrac{5 \div \square}{10 \div \square} = \dfrac{\square}{\square}$

b) $20\% = \dfrac{\square \div 10}{100 \div 10} = \dfrac{\square}{\square}$

$= \dfrac{2 \div \square}{10 \div \square} = \dfrac{\square}{\square}$

Finding percentages of quantities

2) Use your answer to question **1a** to help you work out:
   a) 50% of 4
   b) 50% of 12
   c) 50% of 18

3) Use your answer to question **1b** to help you work out:
   a) 20% of 10
   b) 20% of 40
   c) 20% of 35

4) Work out 10% of:
   a) 20
   b) 50
   c) 70
   d) 80
   e) 90

5) Work out 25% of:
   a) 40
   b) 12
   c) 28
   d) 16
   e) 36

6) Work out:
   a) 50% of £6
   b) 50% of 16 m
   c) 20% of 15p
   d) 20% of 30 km
   e) 10% of £50
   f) 10% of 10 ml
   g) 25% of 20 mm
   h) 25% of 24 miles
   i) 25% of £32

7) Arlo has £16 in his wallet.
   He spends 50%.
   a) How much does he spend?
   b) How much does he have left?

8) Work out these percentages.
   You may need to write the divisions using ⌐
   a) 50% of 38 m
   b) 10% of £830
   c) 50% of £32.12
   d) 20% of £18.20
   e) 25% of 10.64 m
   f) 20% of 104.5 cm

9) 25% of the animals on a farm are cows.
   There are 124 animals on the farm.
   How many are cows?

Chapter 5 Percentages

> ☀ **10)** 20% of campers on a campsite are sleeping in tents.
> The rest are sleeping in caravans.
> There are 60 people on the campsite.
> How many are sleeping in a caravan?

Other percentages of quantities

> 💡 I will learn to find a percentage of a quantity using all kinds of fractions.

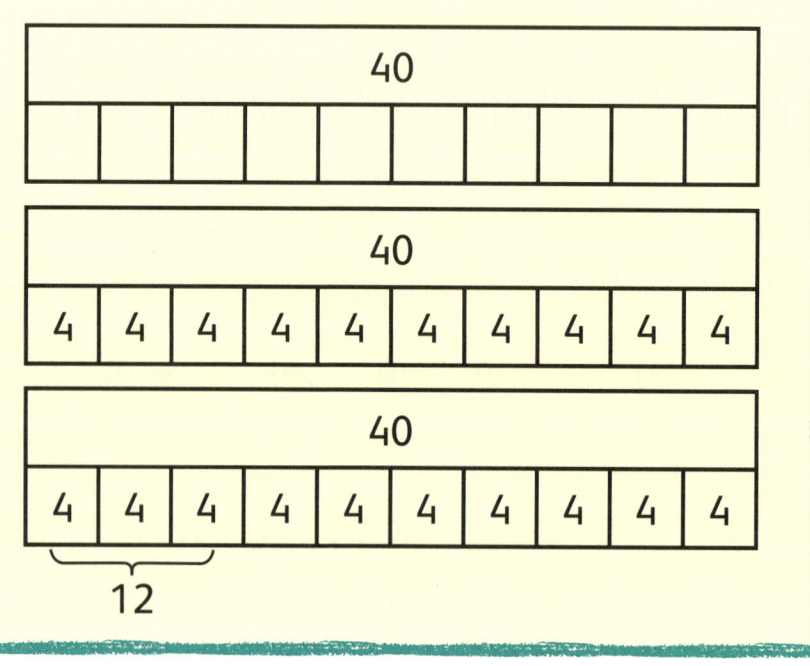

Remember, remember

You already know how to find any fraction of an amount by finding the unit fraction and then multiplying.

Example

Find $\frac{3}{10}$ of 40

Divide by 10 to find $\frac{1}{10}$ (one tenth):

$\frac{1}{10}$ of 40 = 40 ÷ 10
= 4

Multiply by 3 to find $\frac{3}{10}$ (three tenths):
4 × 3 = 12

Finding percentages of quantities

Remember, remember

You also know how to find the percentage of an amount:
1) Write the **percentage as a fraction** with a **denominator of 100** and simplify if possible.
2) Find the fraction of the amount.

Example

Find **70%** of 30.

$$70\% = \frac{70 \div 10}{100 \div 10} = \frac{7}{10}$$

$$70\% \text{ of } 30 = \frac{7}{10} \text{ of } 30$$

$$\frac{1}{10} \text{ of } 30 = 30 \div 10$$
$$= 3$$

$$\frac{7}{10} \text{ of } 30 = 3 \times 7$$
$$= 21$$

So 70% of 30 = 21

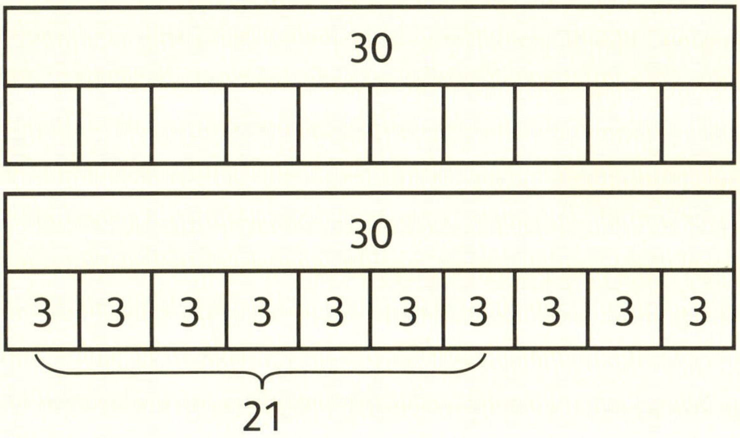

You can also use 10% to find **multiples of 10%**, such as 20%, 30%, 40%, 50%, 60%, 70% …

Chapter 5 Percentages

Example

10% of 30 = $\frac{1}{10}$ of 30

= 30 ÷ 10

= 3

70% = 10% × 7

so 70% of 30 = 3 × 7

= 21

You can also use 10% to find 5% and 1%.
For example:

5% = 10% ÷ 2

so 5% of 30 = 3 ÷ 2

= 1.5

1% = 10% ÷ 10

so 1% of 30 = 3 ÷ 10

= 0.3

Exercise 2

1) Copy and complete:

a) 10% of 40 = $\frac{1}{\Box}$ of 40

= 40 ÷ ☐

= ☐

b) 20% = 10% × 2

20% of 40 = ☐ × 2

= ☐

c) 30% = 10% × 3

30% of 40 = ☐ × 3

= ☐

d) 5% of 40 = 10% ÷ 2

5% of 40 = ☐ ÷ 2

= ☐

Finding percentages of quantities

2) Work out:
   a) 10% of 60
   b) 20% of 60
   c) 30% of 60
   d) 40% of 60
   e) 50% of 60
   f) 60% of 60
   g) 70% of 60
   h) 80% of 60
   i) 90% of 60

3) Work out:
   a) 10% of 90
   b) 90% of 90
   c) 10% of 20
   d) 5% of 20
   e) 10% of 700
   f) 1% of 700

4) a) In your jotter, write 75% as a fraction in its **simplest form**.
   b) Work out 75% of 24.

5) a) Work out 25% of 40.
   b) Copy and complete:
      75% = 25% × ☐
   c) Use your answer to part **b** to work out 75% of 40.

6) Work out:
   a) 75% of 20
   b) 75% of 8
   c) 75% of 12

7) A school has 420 pupils.
   10% of pupils go on a school trip.
   How many pupils go on the school trip?

8) A recipe requires 680 g of flour.
   25% of the flour is self-raising.
   How much flour is self-raising?

Chapter 5 Percentages

9) a) In your jotter, write £9 in pence.
   b) Use your answer to part **a** to work out 1% of £9.
      Give your answer in pence.

10) 240 people attend a pantomime.
    75% of them are children.
    20% of the children are from a youth club.
    How many children from the youth club are at the pantomime?

Percentage word problems

💡 I will learn to solve percentage problems that involve finding a percentage and then adding or subtracting.

Sometimes, finding a percentage is only one step towards solving a problem.

You may have to find a **discount**, **decrease** or **money off**.

Then you must **find the percentage and subtract**.

Example

A coat is £85.
In a sale it is discounted by 10%.
What is the sale price?

10% of £85 = $\frac{1}{10}$ of £85
         = £85 ÷ 10
         = £8.50

Sale price = £85 − £8.50
          = £76.50

Finding percentages of quantities

You may have to find a **rise**, **increase** or **extra amount**.
Then you must **find the percentage and add**.

Example

Abi got a score of 15 in a spelling test.
In the next test, her score increased by 20%.
What was her score in the next test?

10% of 15 = $\frac{1}{10}$ of 15 or 20% = $\frac{20 \div 20}{100 \div 20}$ = $\frac{1}{5}$

$\quad\quad$ = 15 ÷ 10 $\quad\quad\quad\quad\quad\quad\quad$ $\frac{1}{5}$ of 15 = 15 ÷ 5

$\quad\quad$ = 1.5 $\quad\quad\quad\quad\quad\quad\quad\quad\quad\quad\quad$ = 3

so 20% of 15 = 2 × 1.5
$\quad\quad\quad\quad\quad$ = 3

Score in next test = 15 + 3
$\quad\quad\quad\quad\quad\quad$ = 18

Exercise 3

1) A shop is selling a TV for £340.
   The shop offers a 10% discount for people living in Glasgow.
   a) What is 10% of £340?
   b) What is the price of the TV for people living in Glasgow?

2) An engagement ring is £780.
   Before Valentine's Day the ring's price rises by 10%.
   a) What is 10% of £780?
   b) What is the new price of the ring after the rise?

Chapter 5 Percentages

3) In the summer, 90 people are members of a cycling club.
   In the winter, the number of members decreases by 50%.
   How many members are there in the winter?

4) Ravi does 40 press ups each day for a week.
   The next week, he increases the number of press ups by 20%.
   How many press ups does he do each day the next week?

5) A sports shop offers 25% off in their sale.
   Some trainers cost £60 before the sale.
   How much are the trainers in the sale?

6) Yesterday, the wind speed was 20 miles per hour.
   Today it is expected to increase by 30%.
   What is the expected wind speed today?

7) A train ticket costs £8.
   The price increases by 5%.
   What is the new price?

8) 400 tickets are for sale for a sports event.
   Already, 90% of the tickets have sold.
   a) How many tickets have sold?
   The tickets are £8 each.
   b) How much money has been taken for tickets so far?

Finding percentages of quantities

Now try this!

Copy this grid:

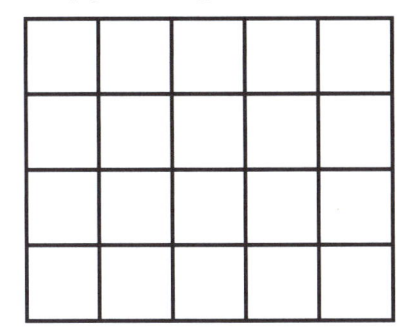

1) Use different colours to shade:
   a) 20% of the grid
   b) 35% of the grid
   c) 45% of the grid.

Copy the grid again.

2) Use different colours to shade:
   a) 25% of the grid
   b) 15% of the grid
   c) 60% of the grid.

Copy the grid again.

3) Use different colours to shade:
   a) 5% of the grid
   b) 50% of the grid
   c) 45% of the grid.

Add the percentages in question **1a**, **b** and **c**; then add those in question **2a**, **b** and **c**; and finally add the percentages in question **3a**, **b** and **c**.

What is the **total** percentage of the grid you have shaded each time?

Chapter 5 Percentages

Revisit, review, revise

1) Work out:
   - a) 10% of £20
   - b) 50% of 28 km
   - c) 25% of 160 m
   - d) 20% of 500 litres
   - e) 60% of 50p
   - f) 5% of 80 g
   - g) 75% of 64 cm
   - h) 1% of £7

2) There are 32 children in a class.
   25% learn Gaelic.
   How many children learn Gaelic?

3) Ben earns £500 each week.
   He spends 30% on rent.
   How much does he spend on rent?

4) A gift is £20.
   Wrapping costs 5% extra.
   How much are the gift and the wrapping **altogether**?

5) There are 40 actors in a play.
   20% of them sing in the play.
   How many do **not** sing in the play?

6) A puppy training lesson costs £32.
   The first lesson is discounted by 50%.
   How much is the first lesson?

7) Bella earns £15.50 an hour.
   Her pay rises by 10%.
   How much is her hourly pay now?

6 Perimeter and area
Rectangles and triangles

Perimeter and area of rectangles

💡 I will investigate the perimeter and area of rectangles.

Remember, remember

The **perimeter** of a shape is the total distance around the outside.

It is measured in units of length (mm, cm, m and so on).

The **area** of a shape is the **space** it takes up.

It is measured in **units squared** (mm², cm², m² and so on).

Area of a rectangle = length × height

Example

Perimeter = 7 + 4 + 7 + 4 = 22 cm

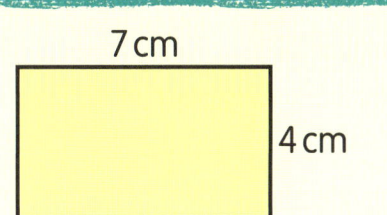

Area = 7 × 4 = 28 cm²

7 cm
4 cm

Rectangles with the **same perimeter** can have **different areas**.

9 cm
A
1 cm

4 cm
B
6 cm

71

Chapter 6 Perimeter and area

Rectangle A
Perimeter = 9 + 1 + 9 + 1
= 20 cm
Area = 9 × 1
= 9 cm²

Rectangle B
Perimeter = 4 + 6 + 4 + 6
= 20 cm
Area = 4 × 6
= 24 cm²

Similarly, rectangles with the **same area** can have **different perimeters**.

Exercise 1

1) a) Calculate the:
   i) area
   ii) perimeter
   of the rectangle and square.
   b) What do you notice?

   A: 6 cm × 2 cm
   B: 4 cm × 4 cm

2) a) Calculate the:
   i) area
   ii) perimeter
   of the rectangles.
   b) What do you notice?

   C: 3 cm × 4 cm
   D: 12 cm × 1 cm

Rectangles and triangles

3) Here is a square.
   a) What is the area of the square?
   b) In your jotter, draw a rectangle with the same perimeter.
   c) Work out the area of the rectangle.
   d) Draw two more different rectangles with the same perimeter and work out the areas of each.
   e) Are the areas of the rectangles smaller or larger than the area of the square?

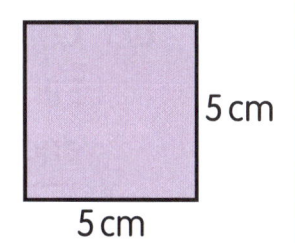

   5 cm
   5 cm

4) a) In your jotter, draw and label three different rectangles with an area of 100 cm².
      (They do not have to be to scale.)
   b) Write the perimeter of each rectangle underneath your diagrams.

5) a) In your jotter, draw and label the dimensions of three different rectangles with perimeter 30 cm.
   b) Work out the area of each of the rectangles you have drawn.

6) A farmer has 150 m of fence.
   Each fence panel is 1 m wide.
   The farmer makes a rectangular enclosure.
   a) In your jotter, draw and label four different rectangular enclosures she could make.
   b) Work out the area of each of the enclosures.

Chapter 6 Perimeter and area

c) Copy the table.

Fill in the table to show **ten** possible dimensions of the enclosure and the areas.

Length of enclosure (m)	Width of enclosure (m)	Area enclosed (m^2)

Now try this!

Use a spreadsheet or draw up a table to show all the possible **whole number** dimensions of a rectangle with a perimeter 100 m. Then use your spreadsheet to calculate the area of each rectangle.

	A	B	C	D
1	Perimeter (m)	Length (m)	Width (m)	Area (= length x width) (m^2)
2	100	1	49	49
3	100	2	48	96
4	100	3	47	141
5	100	4	46	184
6	100			
7	100			
8	100			
9				
10				

You can use a spreadsheet for calculations. To work out the area in this cell (box), type **=B2*C2** (*means multiply).

- What shape will enclose the largest area?

Look back at question 6.

- What is the largest area the farmer could have enclosed?

    (You may wish to use a spreadsheet to help.)

Rectangles and triangles

Area of a triangle

💡 I will learn how to calculate the area of a triangle.

A triangle has base 8 cm and height 5 cm.
Draw a rectangle as shown by the dashed lines.
You can see that the triangle has half the area of the rectangle.

Area of triangle = $\frac{1}{2}$ × area of a rectangle

$= \frac{1}{2} \times 8 \times 5$

$= 20 \text{ cm}^2$

Area of a triangle = $\frac{1}{2}$ × base × height

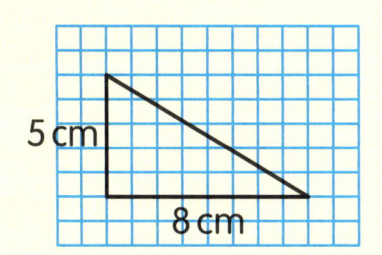

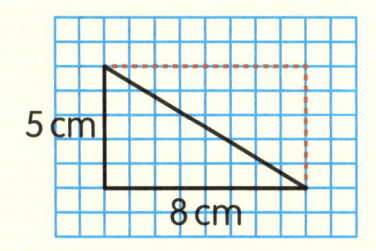

Remember, remember

Area is measured in **units squared**: mm², cm², m² and so on.

Exercise 2

The grids in this exercise are made of 1 cm × 1 cm squares.

1) a) Copy the right-angled triangle.
   b) Draw a rectangle around the triangle.
   c) Calculate the area of the rectangle.
   d) Calculate the area of the triangle.

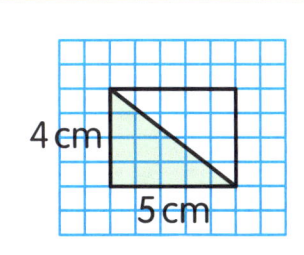

Chapter 6 Perimeter and area

2) **a)** Copy the right-angled triangle.
b) Draw a rectangle around the triangle.
c) Calculate the area of the rectangle.
d) Calculate the area of the triangle.

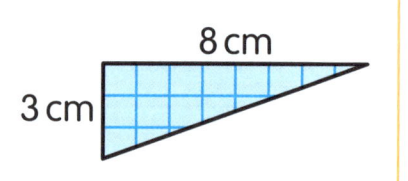

8 cm
3 cm

3) Calculate the area of each triangle.
Show each stage of your working like in part **a**.

a)
5 cm
10 cm

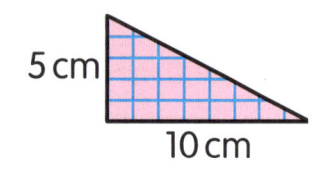

Area of triangle = $\frac{1}{2} \times 10 \times 5$
= _____ cm²

b)
12 cm
4 cm

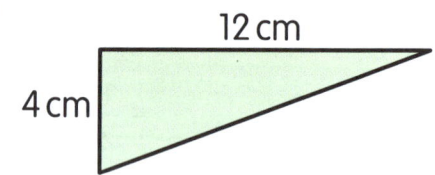

c)
10 cm
9 cm

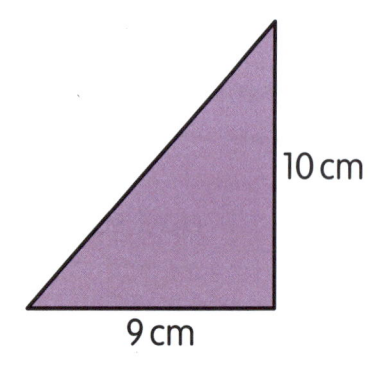

d)
11 cm
6 cm

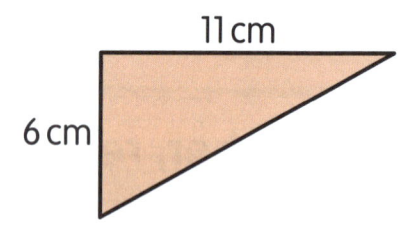

e) 2 cm
14 cm

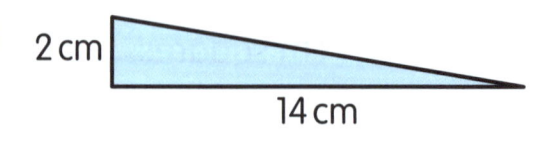

f) 8 cm
11.5 cm

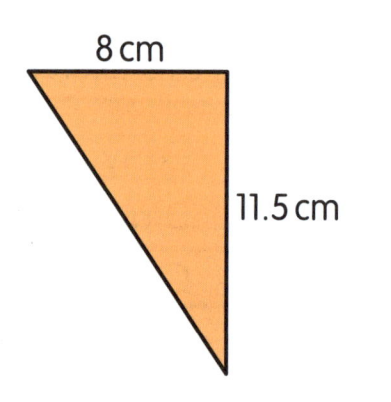

Rectangles and triangles

4) The area of a triangle is 30 cm².
The triangle has height 10 cm.
What is the length of the base?

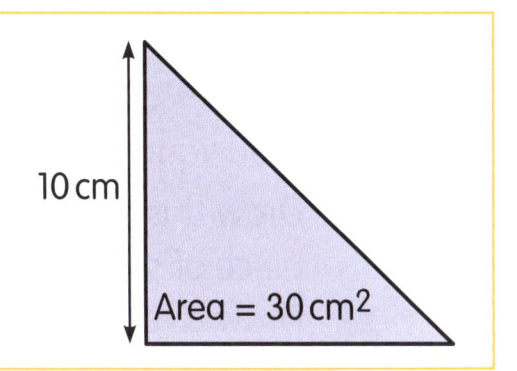

10 cm

Area = 30 cm²

5) A gardener plants bulbs in a triangular flower bed.
She plants 15 bulbs per m².
How many does she plant **altogether**?

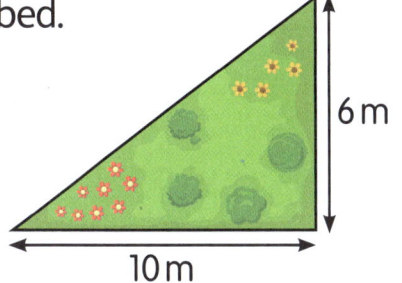

6 m

10 m

6) These shapes all have the same area:

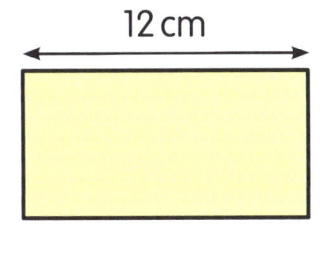

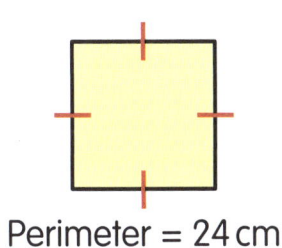

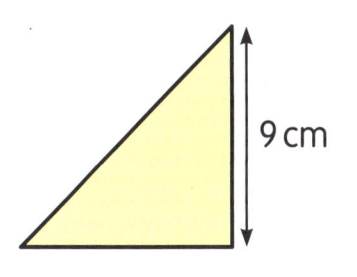

12 cm

Perimeter = 24 cm

9 cm

a) What is the area of the square?

b) What is the height of the rectangle?

c) How long is the base of the triangle?

Chapter 6 Perimeter and area

Now try this!

You will need squared paper and a pair of scissors.

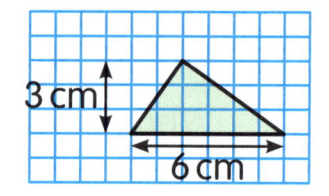

1) a) Draw this green triangle accurately on a piece of squared paper.

   b) Draw a rectangle around the triangle.

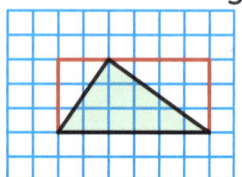

   c) Cut out the rectangle.

   d) Cut out the green triangle giving you three triangles.

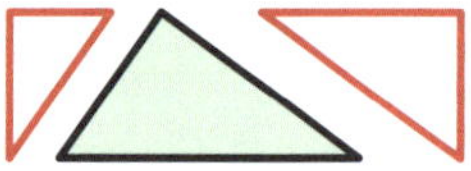

   e) Place the two red triangles on top of the green triangle. What do you notice?

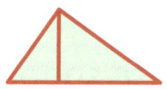

2) Try this starting with a different triangle. Does it always work?

3) What does this tell you about how to calculate the area of a triangle?

Revisit, review, revise

1) a) Calculate the area of each of the rectangles.

   i)  A   6 cm × 2 cm

   ii) 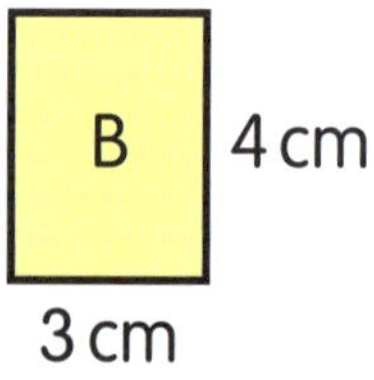 B   3 cm × 4 cm

   iii) 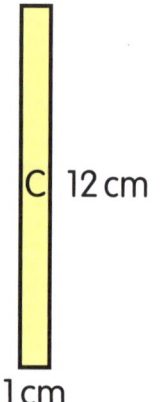 C   1 cm × 12 cm

   b) Calculate the perimeter of each of the rectangles.

Rectangles and triangles

2) a) In your jotter, draw **three** different rectangles with perimeter 14 cm.
   Label the width and height of each rectangle.
   b) Calculate the area of each rectangle.

3) a) Copy the right-angled triangle.
   b) Draw a rectangle around the triangle.
   c) Calculate the area of the rectangle.
   d) Calculate the area of the triangle.

   4 cm
   6 cm

4) Calculate the area of this triangle.

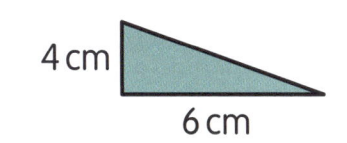

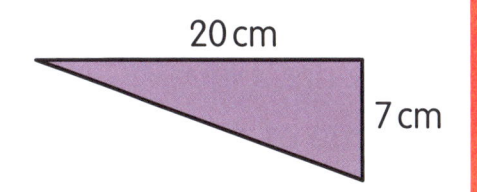

   20 cm
   7 cm

7 3D objects
Volumes and nets

Volume of a cuboid

💡 I will learn to calculate the volume of a cuboid using a formula.

Remember, remember

The top layer of this cuboid is made of 6 × 4 centimetre cubes.

There are 3 layers.

Volume of cuboid = 6 × 4 × 3 = 72 cm³

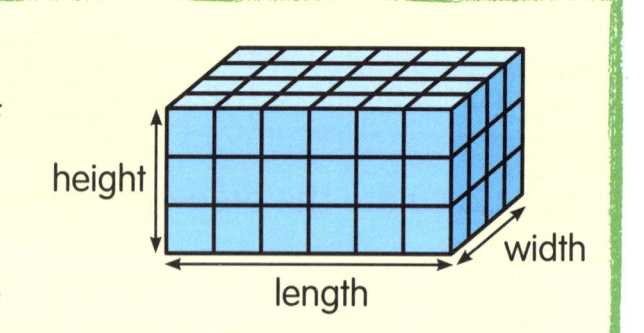

In mathematics, a **formula** is a rule written using mathematical symbols.

Volume of a cuboid = length × width × height

We can write this using letters to represent the words:

Volume of a cuboid = *l* × *w* × *h*

Volume is measured in **units cubed**, for example: mm³, cm³, m³.

Exercise 1

1) Copy the calculation below.

   Complete it to work out the volume of the cuboid.

   volume = *l* × *w* × *h*

   = 7 × ___ × ___

   = _____ cm³

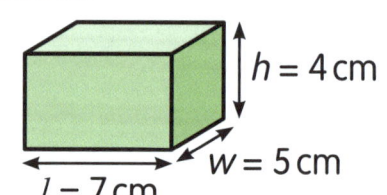

   $l = 7$ cm, $w = 5$ cm, $h = 4$ cm

Volumes and nets

2) Tim and Arvin are working out the volume of this cuboid:

Tim	Arvin
$V = l \times w \times h$	$V = l \times w \times h$
$= 10 \times 6 \times 5$	$= 10 \times 6 \times 5$
$= 60 \times 5$	$= 10 \times 30$
$= 300 \, cm^3$	$= 300 \, cm^3$

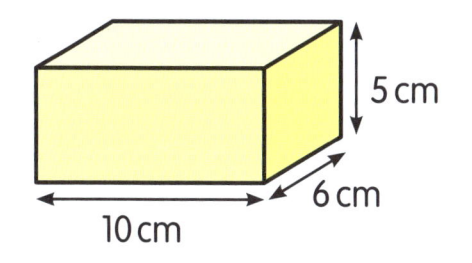

They are both correct.

Explain what is different in their calculations.

3) Calculate the volume of these cuboids.
Show your workings.

a) 10 cm, 3 cm, 3 cm

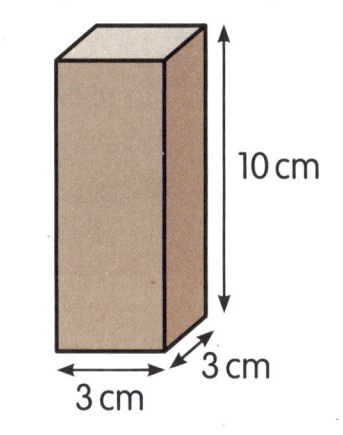

b) 6 cm, 4 cm, 2 cm

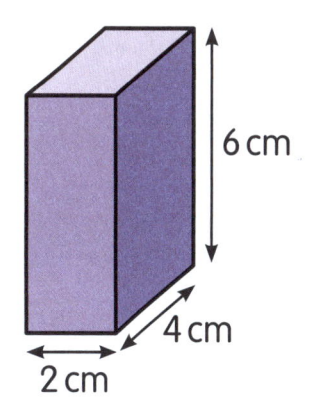

c) 8 cm, 6 cm, 7 cm

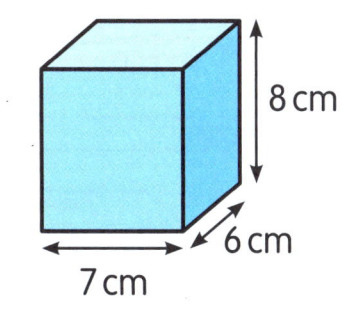

d) 4 mm, 5 mm, 6 mm

81

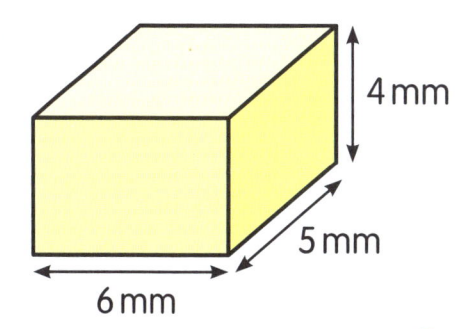

Chapter 7 3D objects

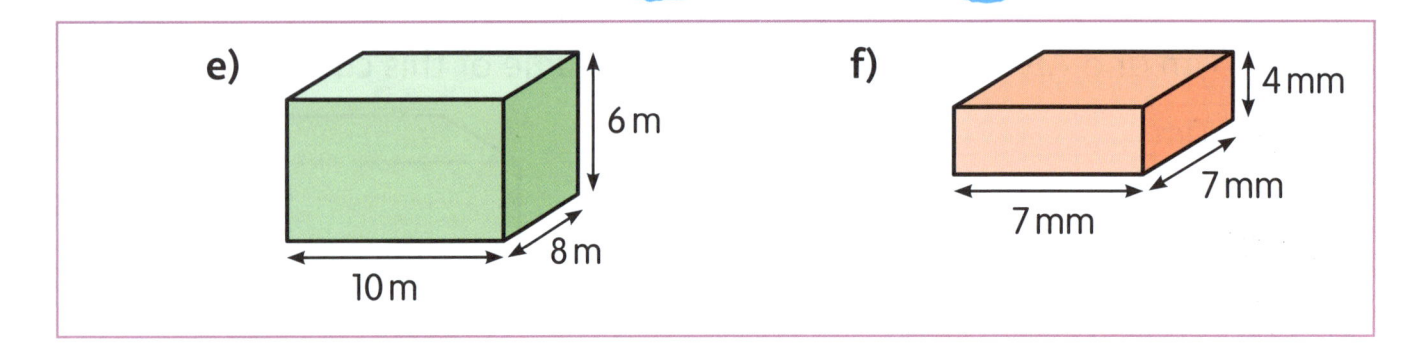

e) 6 m, 8 m, 10 m

f) 4 mm, 7 mm, 7 mm

4) Calculate the volume of each box.
You may use a calculator but show all your working.

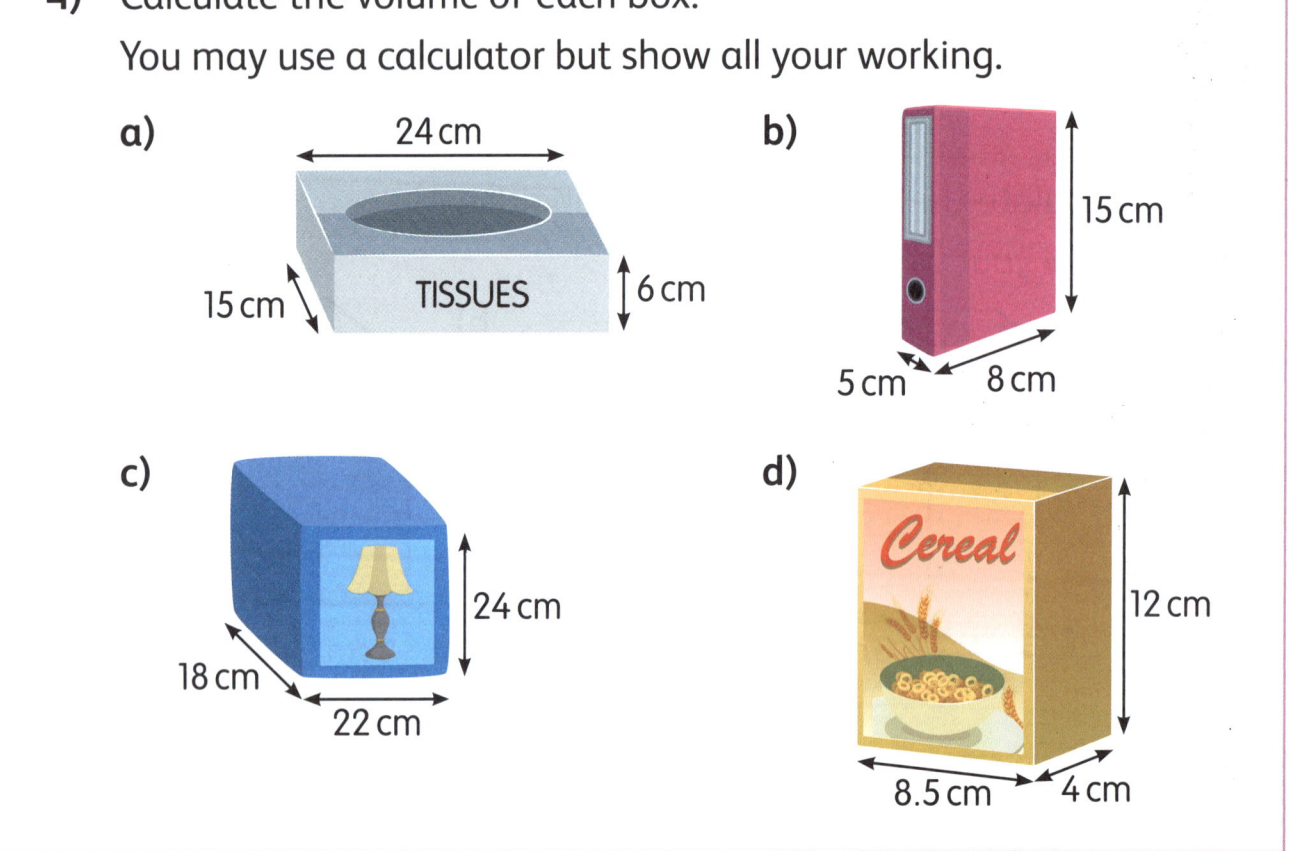

a) 24 cm, 15 cm, 6 cm (TISSUES)

b) 15 cm, 5 cm, 8 cm

c) 24 cm, 18 cm, 22 cm

d) 12 cm, 8.5 cm, 4 cm (Cereal)

5) The volume of this cuboid is 120 cm³.
Calculate its height (h).

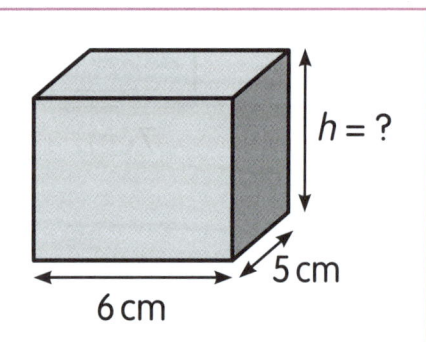

h = ?, 6 cm, 5 cm

82

Volumes and nets

6) Calculate the **missing** dimension of each cuboid.

   a) Volume = 160 cm³   **b)** Volume = 45 cm³

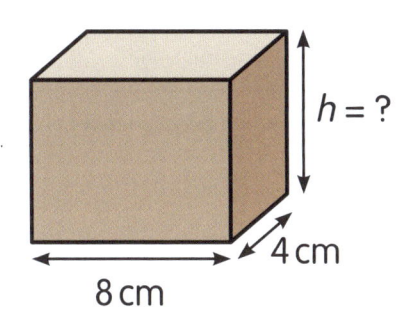

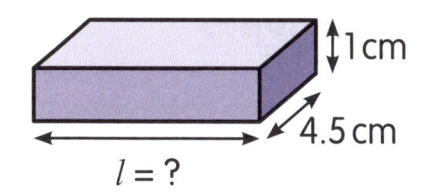

        $h = ?$ 8 cm   4 cm   1 cm   4.5 cm $l = ?$

7) A cube has volume 64 m³.

   a) What are the dimensions of the cube?

   b) What is the area of one of the faces of the cube?

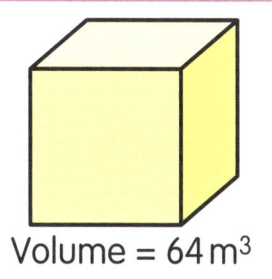

Volume = 64 m³

Now try this!

A storage container has volume 144 m³.

The container has a square base.

The dimensions of the container are whole metres.

Work out all the possible dimensions (lengths, widths and heights) of the container.

Volume = 144 m³

Chapter 7 3D objects

Nets

💡 I will learn to draw the nets of triangular prisms and other 3D shapes.

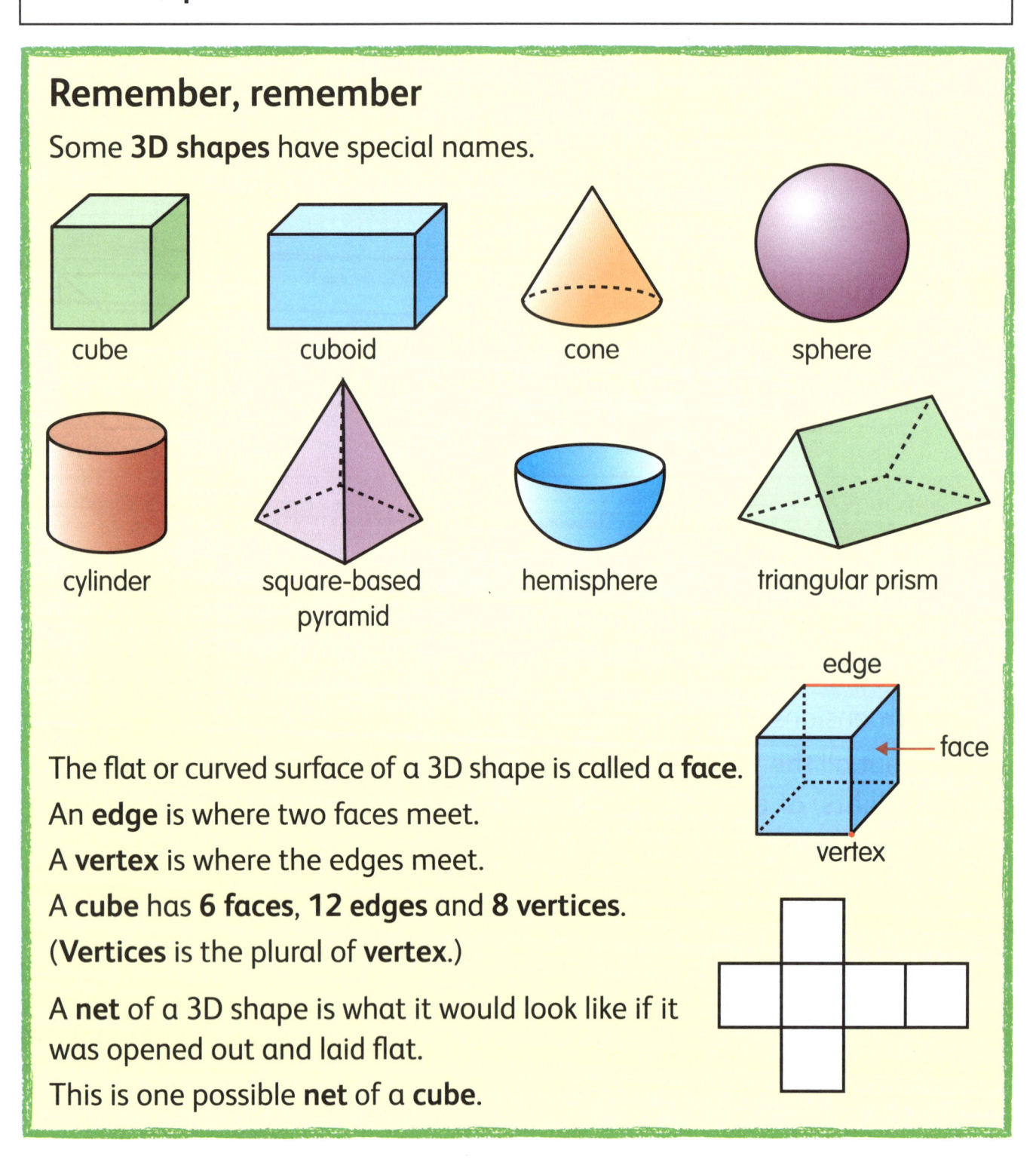

Remember, remember

Some **3D shapes** have special names.

cube   cuboid   cone   sphere

cylinder   square-based pyramid   hemisphere   triangular prism

The flat or curved surface of a 3D shape is called a **face**.

An **edge** is where two faces meet.

A **vertex** is where the edges meet.

A **cube** has **6 faces**, **12 edges** and **8 vertices**.

(**Vertices** is the plural of **vertex**.)

A **net** of a 3D shape is what it would look like if it was opened out and laid flat.

This is one possible **net** of a **cube**.

Volumes and nets

A **triangular prism** has 5 faces.
2 are **triangles** – these are the same shape.
The other 3 are rectangles – they are not all the same shape.

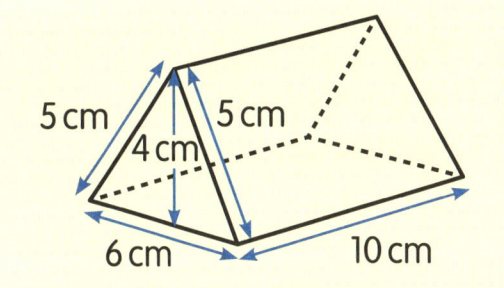

To draw an accurate net, use a ruler and squared paper.

Step 1: Draw the base.
Use a ruler to make the dimensions 10 cm by 6 cm.

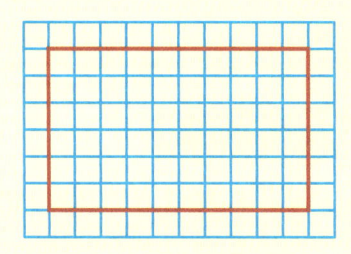

Step 2: Draw the two rectangular sides.
Use a ruler to make the dimensions 10 cm by 5 cm.

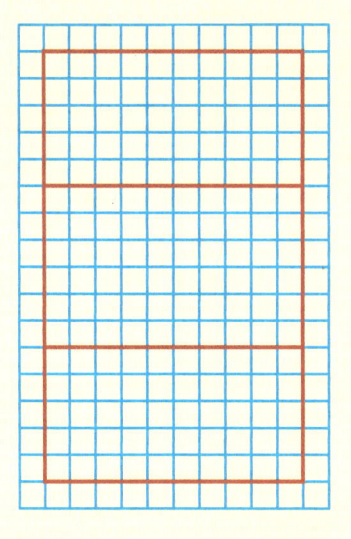

Chapter 7 3D objects

Step 3: Draw the triangles at each end. The base of the triangle is 6 cm, the height is 4 cm.

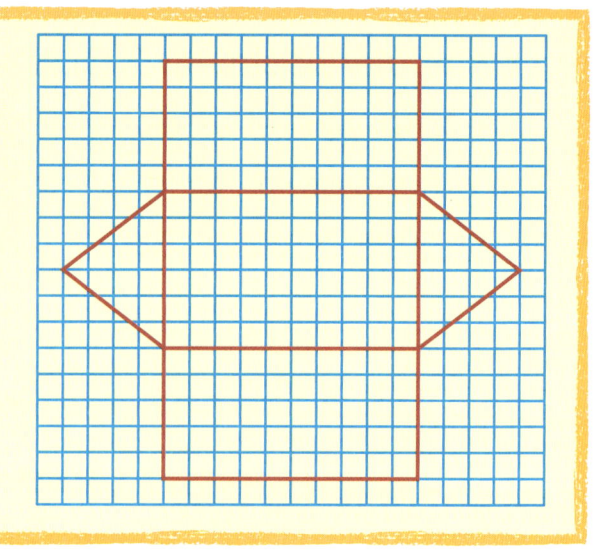

Exercise 2

You will need a ruler and a pair of scissors.

1) a) In your jotter, draw an **accurate** net of the triangular prism in the information box.
   b) Cut it out and fold it to check it works.

2) In your jotter, draw the net of this triangular prism.

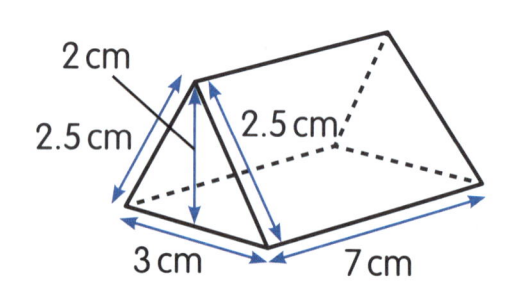

   2 cm, 2.5 cm, 2.5 cm, 3 cm, 7 cm

3) This is a **right-angled** triangular prism.

   Make an **accurate** drawing of the net in your jotter.

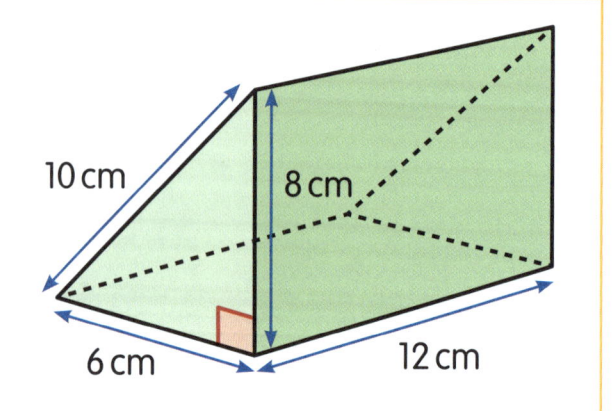

   10 cm, 8 cm, 6 cm, 12 cm

Volumes and nets

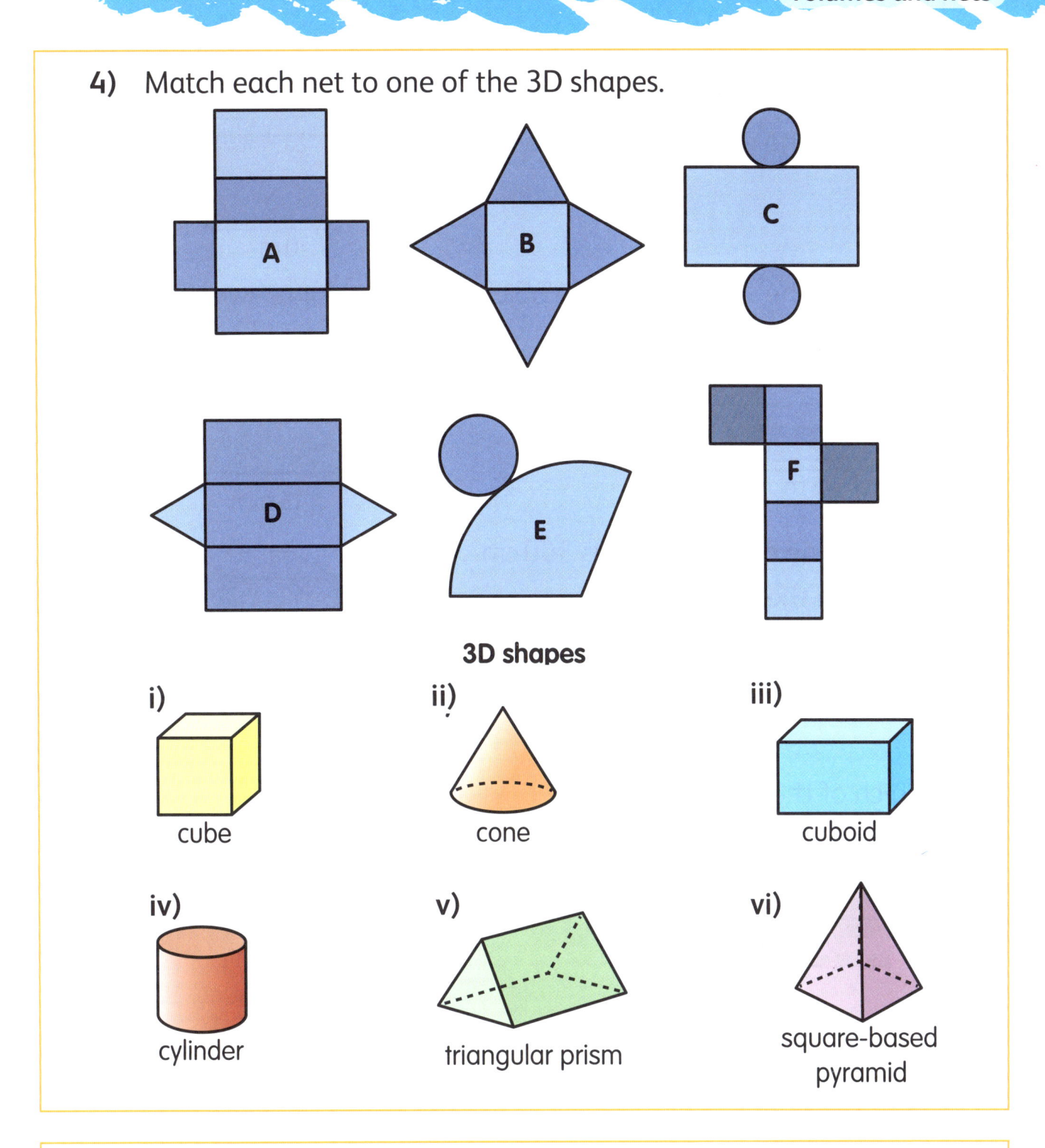

4) Match each net to one of the 3D shapes.

3D shapes

i) cube

ii) cone

iii) cuboid

iv) cylinder

v) triangular prism

vi) square-based pyramid

☀ 5) The **surface area** of a 3D shape is found by adding up the area of all the faces.

Calculate the **total** surface area (3 rectangles + 2 triangles) of the triangular prism in question 3.

Chapter 7 3D objects

Revisit, review, revise

1) Calculate the volume of this cuboid:

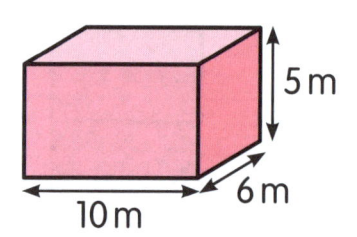

2) Calculate the volume of these objects, giving your answer in mm³, cm³ or m³:
   a) 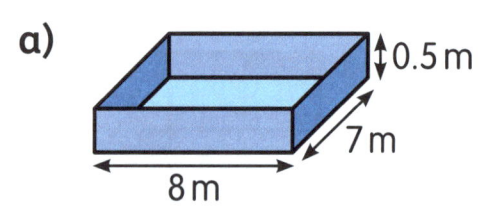
   b)

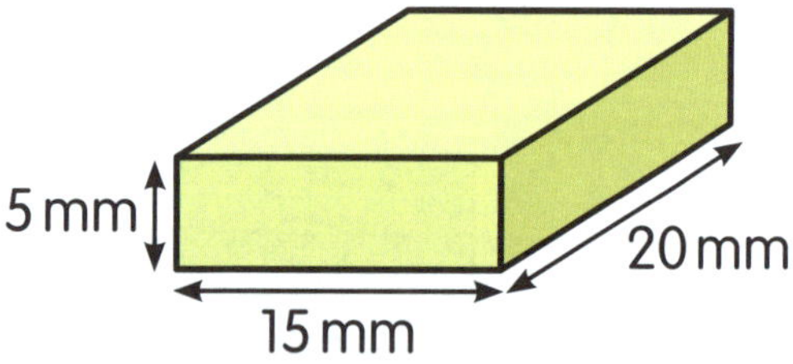

3) The volume of this cuboid is 360 cm³. Calculate the height (h).

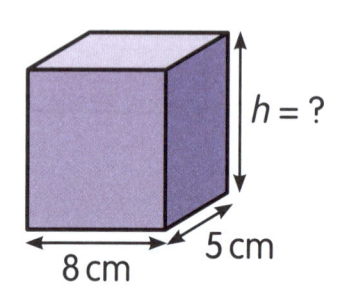

4) Which of these nets will **not** make a triangular prism?

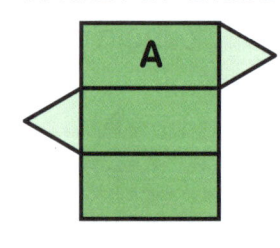

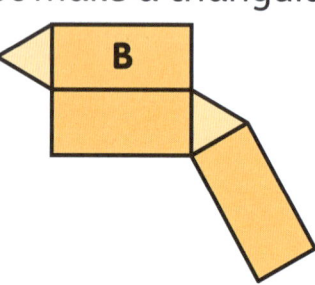

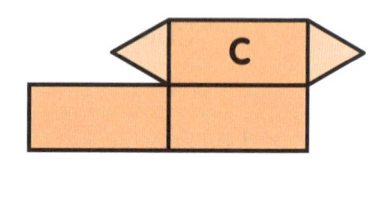

   A   B   C

5) What 3D shapes will these nets make?
   a)   b) 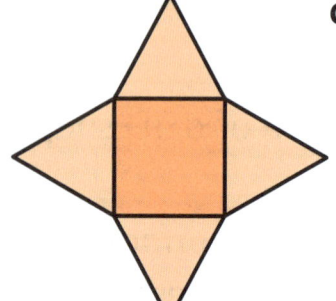   c)

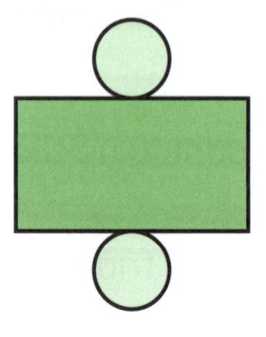

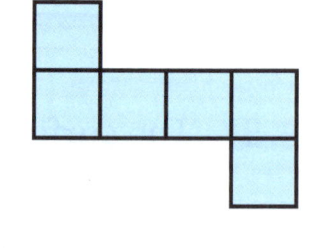

8 Whole numbers 1
Multiplying and dividing by multiples of 10, 100 and 1000

Multiplying whole numbers by multiples of 10, 100 and 1000

💡 I will learn to multiply whole numbers by multiples of 10, 100 and 1000.

Remember, remember

When you **multiply by 10**:
- digits move **1 place left**
- the space is filled with a zero.

Thousands	Hundreds	Tens	Ones
	3	7	2
3	7	2	0

372 × 10 =

When you **multiply by 100**:
- digits move **2 places left**
- spaces are filled with a zero.

When you **multiply by 1000**:
- digits move **3 places left**
- spaces are filled with a zero.

You can do multiplication in any order.
For example:
372 × 10 = 10 × 372 = 3720

Chapter 8 Whole numbers 1

Multiples of 10 are 10, 20, 30, 40, 50 …
Multiples of 100 are 100, 200, 300, 400, 500 …
Multiples of 1000 are 1000, 2000, 3000, 4000, 5000 …
Sometimes you may have to multiply by a multiple of 10, 100 or 1000.

Example

Work out 8 × 4000.

8 × 4000 = 8 × 1000 × 4   ← First, multiply by 1000
        = 8000 × 4   ← Then multiply by 4
        = 8 thousand × 4
        = 32 thousand
        = 32 000

Sometimes you may need to use a mix of a **mental method** and a **written method**.

Example

Work out 382 × 30.

382 × 30 = 382 × 10 × 3   ← First, multiply by 10
        = 3820 × 3

```
    3820      ← Then multiply by 3
×      3
    ² 
  11 460
```

382 × 30 = 11 460

Multiplying and dividing by multiples of 10, 100 and 1000

Exercise 1

1) Copy and complete:

a) $5 \times 30 = 5 \times 10 \times 3$
   $= \underline{} \times 3$
   $= \underline{}$

b) $7 \times 200 = 7 \times \underline{} \times 2$
   $= \underline{} \times 2$
   $= \underline{}$

c) $9 \times 6000 = 9 \times \underline{} \times 6$
   $= \underline{} \times 6$
   $= \underline{}$

2) Copy and complete to work out 437×20:

$437 \times 20 = 437 \times 10 \times 2$
$ = \underline{} \times 2$

```
    4 3 7 ☐
  ×       2
  ─────────
```

$437 \times 20 = \underline{}$

3) Work out **mentally**:

a) 3×20
b) 6×90
c) 2×400
d) 3×700
e) 4×2000
f) 6×3000
g) 6×5000
h) 200×8
i) 7000×7

4) Work out:

a) 41×20
b) 122×40
c) 617×30
d) 13×300
e) 200×37
f) 92×700

Chapter 8 Whole numbers 1

Sometimes you may have to multiply **more than one** multiple of 10, 100 or 1000.

Example

Work out 60 × 700.

60 × 700 = 10 × 6 × 100 × 7

= 6 × 7 × 10 × 100   Because you can do multiplication in any order

= 42 × 1000

= 42 000

5) Copy and complete:
   a) 30 = ____ × 3
   b) 800 = ____ × 8
   c) 30 × 800 = 3 × 8 × ____ × ____

   = ____ × ____

   = ____

6) Work out **mentally**:
   a) 20 × 30
   b) 40 × 90
   c) 600 × 80
   d) 30 × 400
   e) 80 × 700
   f) 300 × 2000

7) A box contains 20 pencils. How many pencils in 80 boxes?

Multiplying and dividing by multiples of 10, 100 and 1000

8) This year, there are 300 runners in a fun run.
Next year, the organisers want to **triple** the number of runners.
How many runners do they want for next year?

9) 12 people work in an office.
They are each paid a summer holiday bonus of £200.
How much is paid in bonuses?

10) There are 60 seconds in 1 minute.
There are 60 minutes in 1 hour.
How many seconds in 1 hour?

Dividing whole numbers by multiples of 10, 100 and 1000

> I will learn to divide whole numbers by multiples of 10, 100 and 1000.

Remember, remember

When you **divide by 10**:
- digits move **1 place right**.

Hundreds	Tens	Ones
4	8	0
	4	8

480 ÷ 10 =

When you **divide by 100**:
- digits move **2 places right**.

When you **divide by 1000**:
- digits move **3 places right**.

480 ÷ 10 = 48

Chapter 8 Whole numbers 1

Sometimes you may have to divide by a multiple of 10, 100 or 1000.

Example

Work out $6000 \div 30$.

$6000 \div 30 = 6000 \div 10 \div 3$ ← First, divide by 10
$= 600 \div 3$ ← Then divide by 3
$= 6 \text{ hundred} \div 3$
$= 2 \text{ hundred}$

$6000 \div 30 = 200$

Sometimes you may need to use a mix of a **mental method** and a **written method**.

Example

Work out $4300 \div 20$.

$4300 \div 20 = 4300 \div 10 \div 2$ ← First, divide by 10
$= 430 \div 2$

```
        2 1 5   ← Then divide by 2
    2 ) 4 3 ¹0
```

$4300 \div 20 = 215$

Multiplying and dividing by multiples of 10, 100 and 1000

Exercise 2

1) Copy and complete:

a) $80 \div 20 = 80 \div 10 \div 2$
$= \underline{} \div 2$
$= \underline{}$

b) $600 \div 20 = 600 \div 10 \div 2$
$= \underline{} \div 2$
$= \underline{}$

c) $9000 \div 30 = 9000 \div 10 \div 3$
$= \underline{} \div 3$
$= \underline{}$

2) Copy and complete to work out $2800 \div 40$:

$2800 \div 40 = 2800 \div 10 \div 4$
$= \underline{} \div 4$

$4 \overline{) 28 }$

$2800 \div 40 = \underline{}$

3) Work out **mentally**:

a) $60 \div 30$
b) $900 \div 30$
c) $8000 \div 400$
d) $60\,000 \div 2000$
e) $2100 \div 300$
f) $120\,000 \div 300$

4) What numbers are **missing**?

a) $40 \times \underline{} = 8000$
b) $\underline{} \times 200 = 1400$
c) $3000 \times \underline{} = 18\,000$
d) $\underline{} \times 70 = 630\,000$

5) Work out:

a) $510 \div 30$
b) $7100 \div 20$
c) $3040 \div 40$
d) $22\,800 \div 600$
e) $108\,500 \div 700$
f) $253\,200 \div 30$

Chapter 8 Whole numbers 1

6) 1200 pens are sent to a school.
   30 pens are given to each class.
   How many classes receive pens?

7) There are 320 gold stars in a pack.
   There are 40 gold stars on a sheet.
   How many sheets in the pack?

8) 45 000 people attend a football match.
   They sit in 600 rows.
   How many people sit in each row?

9) a) How many hours is 2880 minutes?
   b) How many days is this?

Now try this!

Which of these calculations has the answer 1 million?
a) 500 × 20
b) 2000 × 50
c) 200 × 5000
d) 500 × 2000
e) 50 × 20 000

In your jotter, write another multiplication using multiples of 10, 100 or 1000 that has an answer 1 million.

Which of these calculations has the answer 50?
a) 1500 ÷ 30
b) 150 000 ÷ 300
c) 15 000 ÷ 30
d) 150 000 ÷ 3000
e) 15 000 ÷ 300

Write another division using multiples of 10, 100 or 1000 that has an answer 50.

Multiplying and dividing by multiples of 10, 100 and 1000

Revisit, review, revise

1) Work out **mentally**:
   a) 5 × 20
   b) 4 × 60
   c) 9 × 200
   d) 6 × 7000
   e) 50 × 20
   f) 80 × 30
   g) 90 × 500
   h) 6000 × 40
   i) 80 ÷ 20
   j) 600 ÷ 30
   k) 2700 ÷ 900
   l) 10 000 ÷ 200

2) What numbers are **missing**?
   a) ___ × 600 = 120 000
   b) 81 000 ÷ ___ = 90

3) Work out:
   a) 31 × 30
   b) 191 × 60
   c) 27 × 400
   d) 500 × 28
   e) 2120 ÷ 40
   f) 3360 ÷ 70
   g) 32 800 ÷ 800
   h) 45 090 ÷ 90
   i) 909 000 ÷ 9000

For these problems, you must decide whether you need to **multiply** or **divide**.

4) A box contains 200 nails.
   How many nails in 7 boxes?

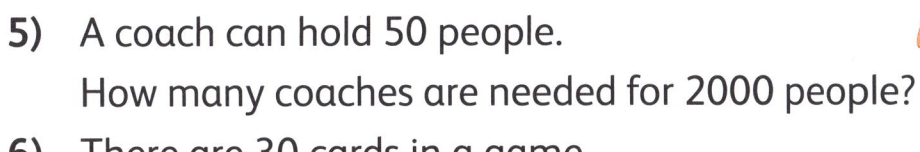

5) A coach can hold 50 people.
   How many coaches are needed for 2000 people?

6) There are 30 cards in a game.
   418 games are made.
   How many cards **altogether**?

7) A printer prints 38 800 leaflets.
   They are put into boxes of 400 leaflets.
   How many boxes?

9 Statistics
Representing data and interpreting graphs and charts

Pie charts

> 💡 I will learn to interpret a pie chart.

Remember, remember

To find a **fraction** of an amount, find the **unit fraction** and then **multiply**.

To find $\frac{3}{4}$ of 20:

$\frac{1}{4}$ of 20 = 20 ÷ 4
       = 5

$\frac{3}{4}$ of 20 = 3 × 5
       = 15

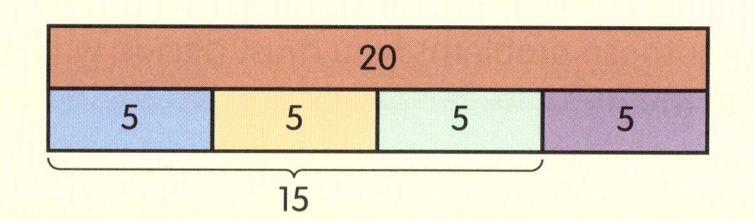

To find a **percentage** of an amount, work out the **equivalent fraction**.

50% = $\frac{1}{2}$ 25% = $\frac{1}{4}$ 10% = $\frac{1}{10}$

You can use these to find other percentages.

To find 30% of 20:

10% of 20 = $\frac{1}{10}$ of 20
          = 20 ÷ 10
          = 2

30% of 20 = 3 × 2
          = 6

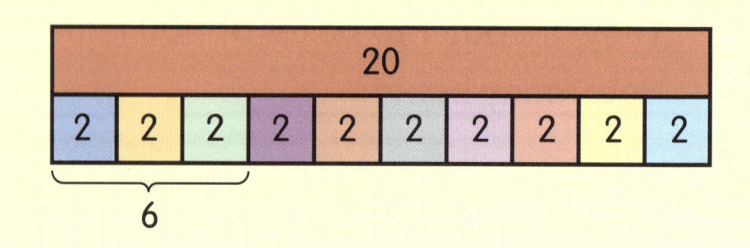

Representing data and interpreting graphs and charts

A **pie chart** is a way to display data.
It shows the **proportion** or **fraction** of the data that is in a category.
This pie chart shows the favourite pets of a group of 32 children.

Favourite pets

$\frac{1}{4}$ of the class chose cat

$\frac{1}{4}$ of 32 = 32 ÷ 4
      = 8

8 children chose cat

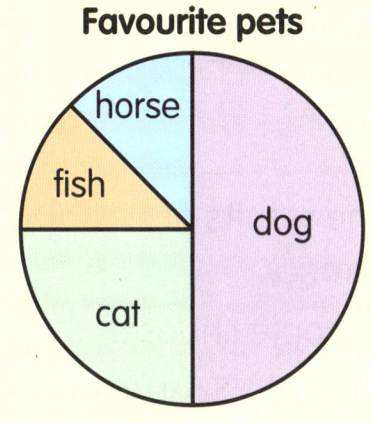

$\frac{1}{2}$ of the class chose dog

$\frac{1}{2}$ of 32 = 32 ÷ 2
      = 16

16 children chose dog

Each piece of a pie chart is called a **sector**.

Exercise 1

1) At a party, children choose a drink.
   The pie chart shows their choices.

   Drink choice

   a) What is the **most popular** drink?
   b) What fraction of the party choose:
      i) lemonade
      ii) fruit juice
      iii) water?

   There are 100 children at the party.

   c) How many choose:
      i) lemonade
      ii) fruit juice
      iii) water?

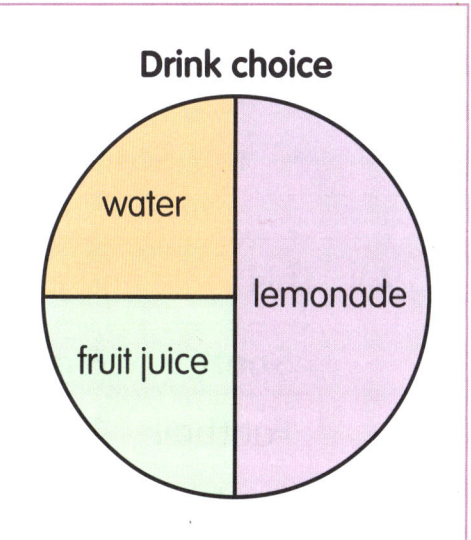

Chapter 9 Statistics

2) This pie chart has been divided into 10 equal sectors.

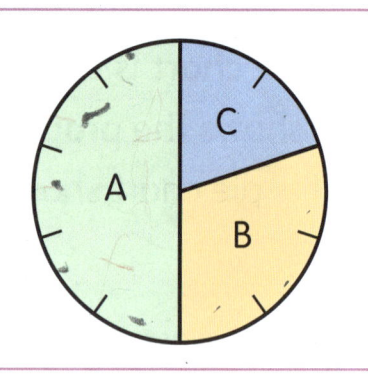

    a) How many tenths are green (A)?
    b) How many tenths are yellow (B)?
    c) How many tenths are blue (C)?

3) The pie chart shows the results of a survey about favourite restaurants.

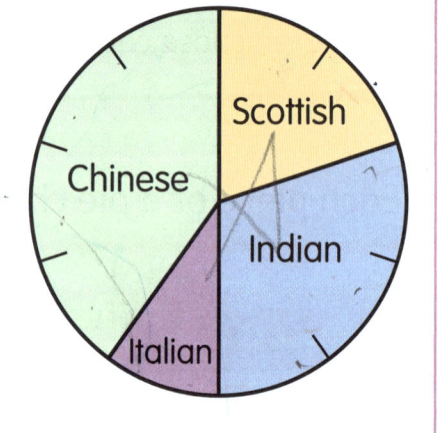

    a) What fraction of people choose:
        i) Chinese   ii) Scottish
        iii) Italian   iv) Indian?

    b) List the foods in order, from **most** popular to **least** popular.

    c) 50 people took part in this survey. How many of them prefer:
        i) Italian food   ii) Indian food
        iii) Scottish food   iv) Chinese food?

Favourite restaurant

4) This table and pie chart show the sports played by 40 adults:

Sport	Frequency
Football	10
Rugby	5
Golf	20
Tennis	5

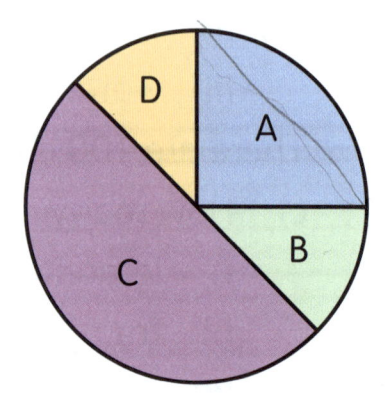

Which sector represents:

    a) football   b) golf?

Representing data and interpreting graphs and charts

5) 200 people are asked to name their favourite holiday destination.
The results are shown in the pie chart.
How many choose:
  a) USA
  b) Portugal
  c) Spain
  d) Greece?

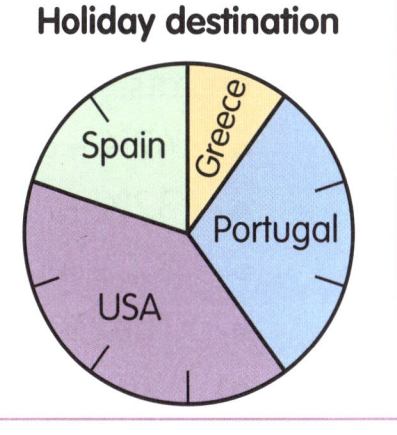

Holiday destination

6) This pie chart has been divided into 20 equal parts.
  a) What fraction does each part represent?
  b) What fraction represents:
    i) dinner
    ii) tea
    iii) lunch
    iv) breakfast?

400 people are surveyed.
  c) What is $\frac{1}{20}$ of 400?
  d) How many people choose:
    i) dinner
    ii) tea
    iii) lunch
    iv) breakfast?

Favourite meal

☀ 7) This pie chart shows how pupils travel to school.
  a) What **percentage** of pupils walk to school?
  b) What percentage take a bus?

800 children are surveyed.
  c) How many travel by:
    i) train
    ii) car?

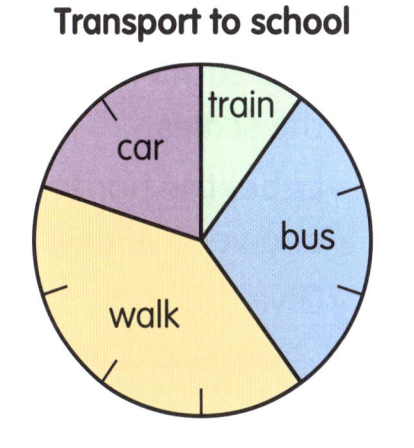

Transport to school

Chapter 9 Statistics

☀ **8)** A garage records the repairs they carry out on cars.
- 42% – change tyres
- 32% – fix lights
- 8% – replace exhaust
- The rest were minor repairs.

a) What percentage of repairs were minor repairs?

b) Which sector represents:

  i) change tyres   ii) fix lights   iii) replace exhaust?

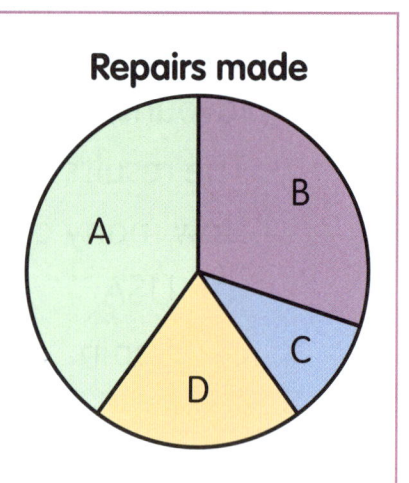

Representing data

💡 I will learn to draw bar charts, line graphs and pie charts.

When drawing statistical graphs like **bar charts**, **line graphs** or **pie charts**, it is important to **label** them correctly and label **scales** accurately.

Bar chart
- Use **equal intervals** on the scales.
- **Label** the horizontal and vertical axes clearly.
- Give the chart a **title**.

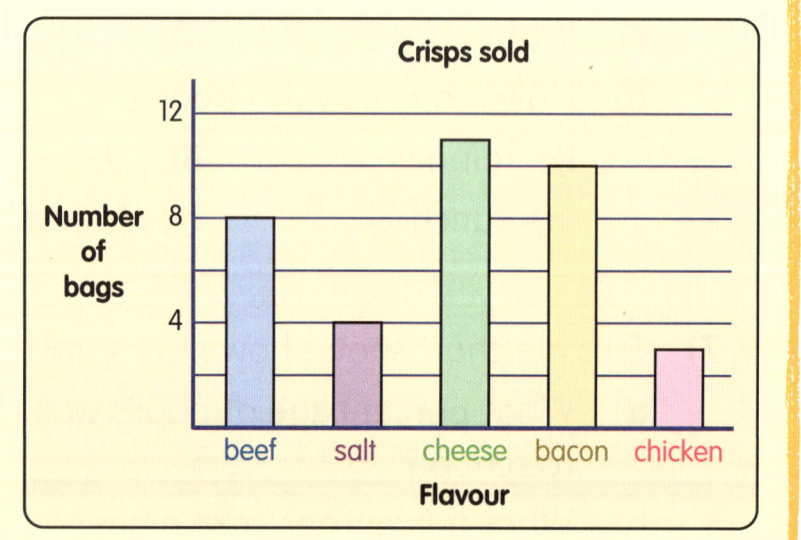

Representing data and interpreting graphs and charts

Line graph

- Use **equal intervals** on the scales.
- If the scale **does not start at 0**, show this using ⌇.
- **Label** the horizontal and vertical axes clearly.
- Give the graph a **title**.
- **Plot points** with a ×.

Newspaper deliveries

Pie chart

- Decide **how many** sectors the chart has to be split into.
- Decide **what** each sector represents.
- Colour and label each sector.
- Give the chart a **title**.

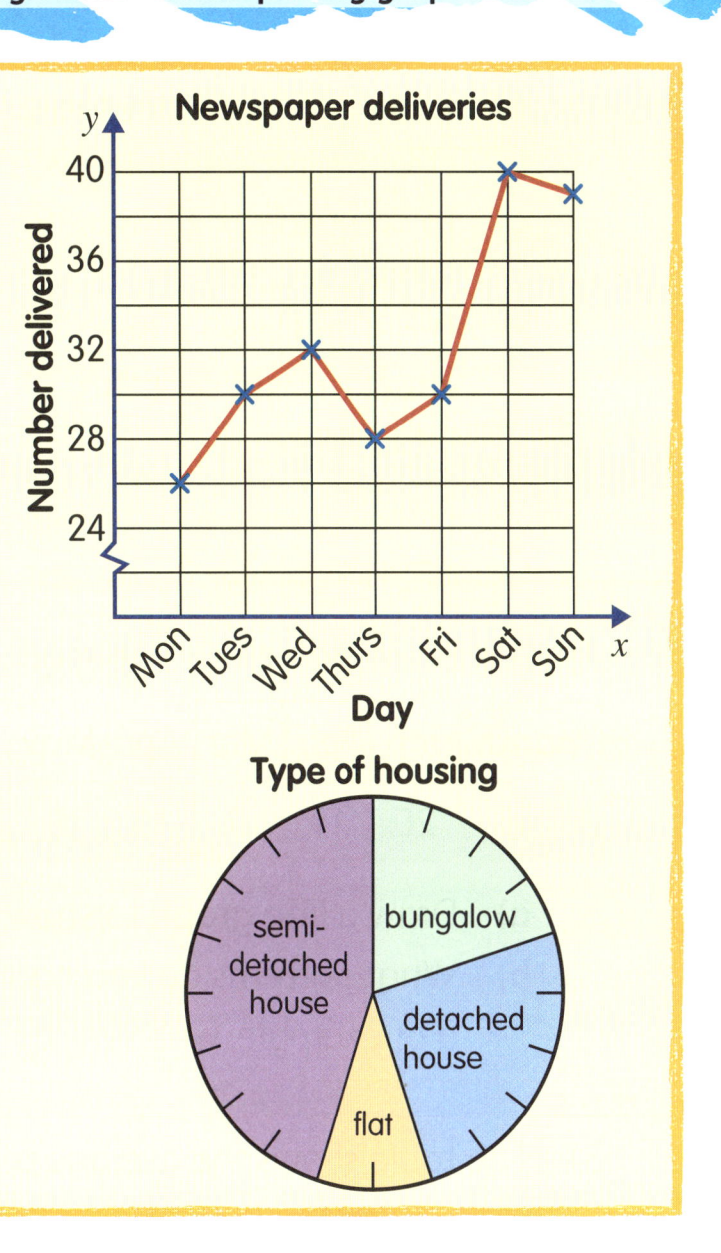

Type of housing
(semi-detached house, bungalow, detached house, flat)

Exercise 2

1) A shop records the fruit customers buy:

pear	apple	banana	grapes	apple	banana	apple	grapes
orange	banana	apple	banana	orange	apple	banana	apple
apple	banana	grapes	grapes	apple	grapes	orange	grapes
banana	apple	pear	grapes	banana	apple	apple	banana

Chapter 9 Statistics

1) a) Copy this frequency table.
   b) Use the information given to complete the frequency table.
   c) Draw and label a **bar chart** to represent this information.

Fruit	Tally	Frequency
apple		
banana		
orange		
pear		
grapes		

2) A shop records the number of umbrellas it sells each month.

Month	Jan	Feb	Mar	Apr	May	Jun	Jul	Aug	Sep	Oct	Nov	Dec
Sales	20	17	6	19	6	1	0	5	11	14	19	17

   a) Draw a **line graph** to show the sales figures.
   b) What patterns do you notice in the data?
      (For example, when were most umbrellas sold?)

3) The table shows the average temperature (°C) in two different cities in the UK:

Month	Jan	Feb	Mar	Apr	May	Jun	Jul
Edinburgh	3	4	6	7	10	13	15
London	5	7	9	11	14	16	19

Representing data and interpreting graphs and charts

a) Copy the axes shown onto squared paper.

Draw two line graphs on the **same axes** to show the temperatures in each city.

Use one colour for Edinburgh and a different colour for London.

Give your graph a title.

b) In which month is the **difference** between the temperatures **smallest**?

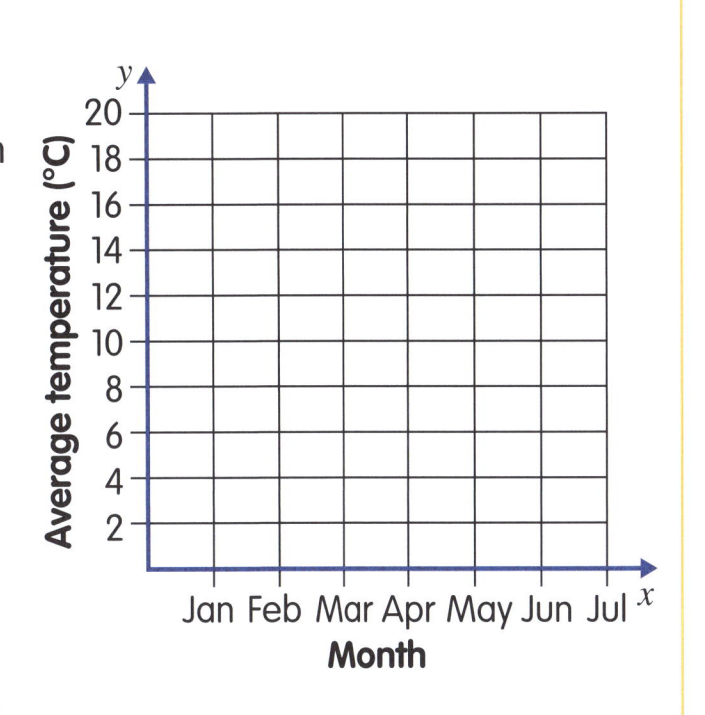

4) The table shows the type of houses people in a town live in:

semi-detached house	40%
bungalow	20%
detached house	30%
flat	10%

a) Trace the blank pie chart.

b) Complete the pie chart to show the information in the table.

c) Label the pie chart and give it a title.

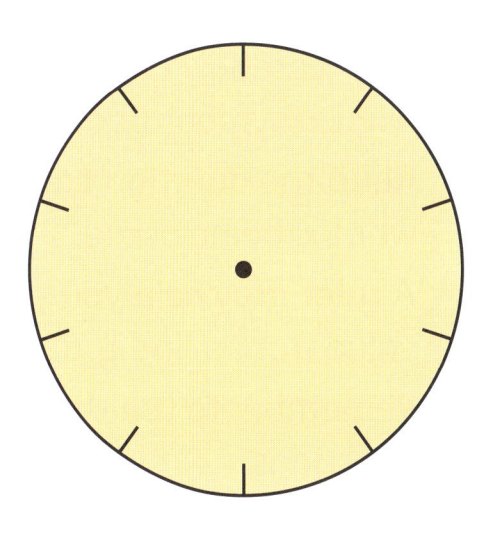

Chapter 9 Statistics

5) On a school trip:
   - 35% of travellers were juniors
   - 40% were seniors
   - 15% were teachers
   - the remaining travellers were parents.

   a) What percentage were parents?
   b) Trace the blank pie chart.
      Complete the pie chart to show this information.

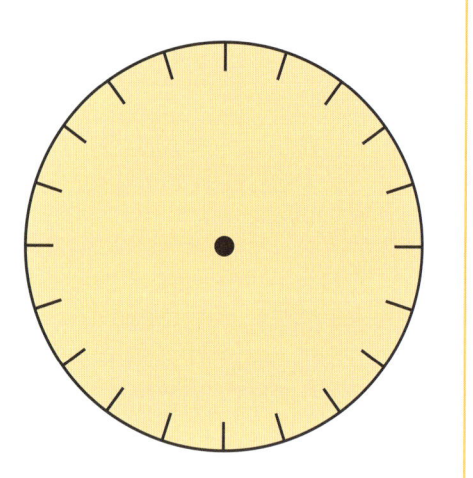

Interpreting data

💡 I will learn to interpret data from pictographs, bar charts, pie charts and line graphs.

When interpreting data from graphs and charts:
- Look carefully at any **scales** or **keys** so you know exactly what a symbol, bar or cross indicates.
- **Read** the question **carefully** to make sure you answer what is being asked.
- A **ruler** may help you to make sure you read the correct value from a **line graph**.
- Remember to use the correct **units** when answering questions.
- If you are asked to give a **reason** for trends in the data, think about what you know about real life.

Representing data and interpreting graphs and charts

Exercise 3

1) The pictograph shows the number of people waiting at a station.

   Key: ★ stands for 25 people.

7:00 a.m.	★★
7:30 a.m.	★★★★★ (with partial)
8:00 a.m.	★★★★★
8:30 a.m.	★★★ (with partial)
9:00 a.m.	★ (with partial)

   a) How many people are at the station at:
      i) 7:00 a.m.
      ii) 7:30 a.m.
      iii) 8:30 a.m.
      iv) 9:00 a.m.?
   b) How many **more** people were there at 8:00 a.m. than 7:00 a.m.?
   c) Suggest a reason why 8:00 a.m. was the busiest time at the station.
   d) Why do you think the station was quietest at 9:00 a.m.?

2) A restaurant records the chicken dishes ordered by customers in a week. The results are shown in the bar graph.
   a) How many chose:
      i) salsa   ii) tikka
      iii) jalfrezi   iv) jaipuri?
   b) Which dish was **least** popular?
   c) 100 people chose chicken korma. Why would this be difficult to show on the bar chart?

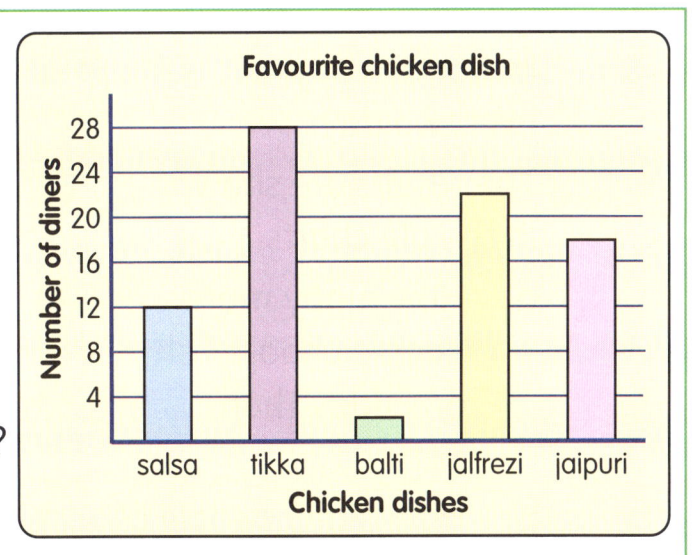

Chapter 9 Statistics

3) This line graph shows the number of downloads of a song in a week.

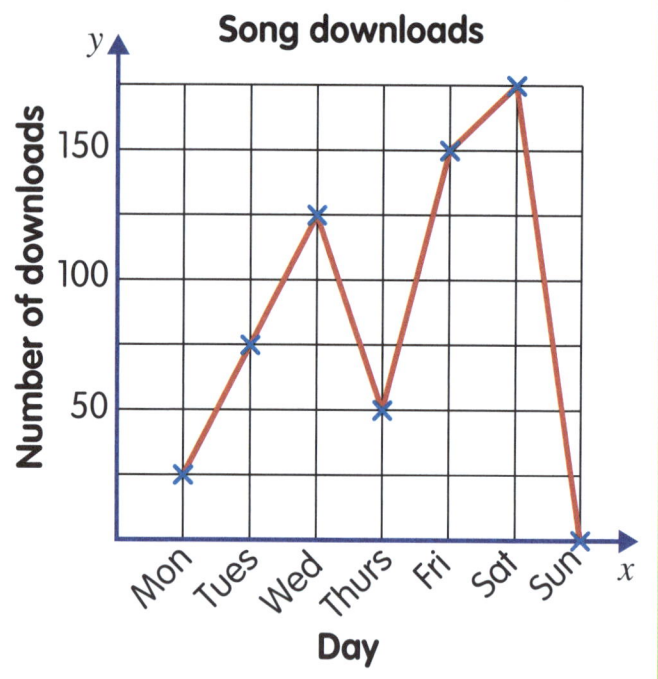

   a) How many times is it downloaded on:
      i) Wednesday
      ii) Friday?
   b) On which day is it downloaded **most**?
   c) How many **more** times is it downloaded on Friday than on Tuesday?
   d) Between which two days was there the **largest rise** in number of downloads?

4) The owner of a fish and chip van records what 400 customers buy over two days.

   The results are shown in the pie charts.

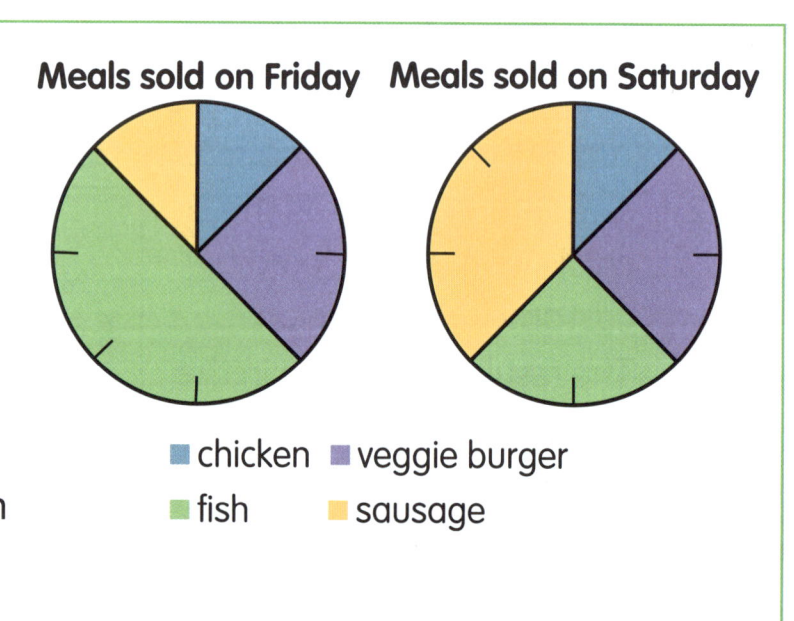

   a) How many **more** people choose fish on Friday than Saturday?
   b) How many people choose sausage **altogether** on the two evenings?
   c) What is the **least** popular meal over the two nights?
   d) What is the **most** popular meal over the two nights?

Representing data and interpreting graphs and charts

5) Lodl (a supermarket) produces this bar chart to show how their prices compare with other supermarkets.

State **three** things that are wrong with this bar chart.

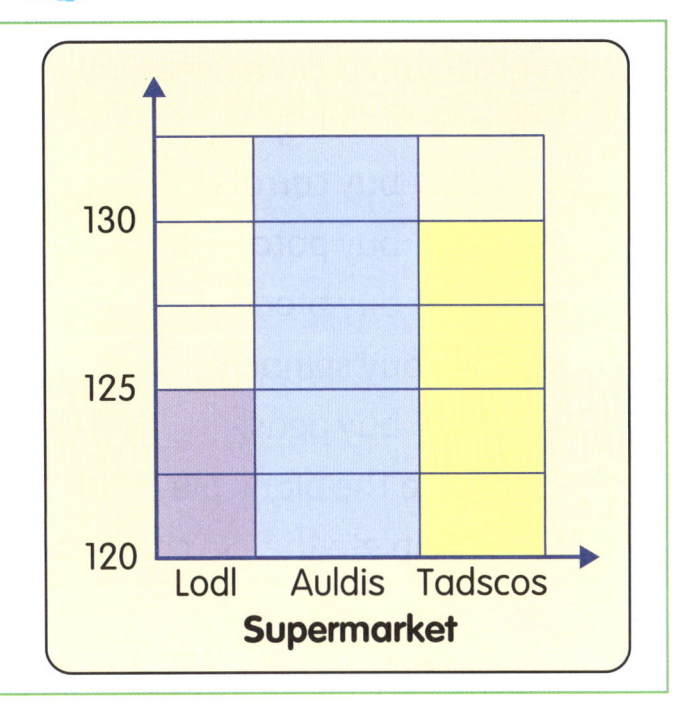

Now try this!

Where have you seen graphs and charts representing data in real life?

Look in books and on the internet.

Discuss with a partner whether you think the graphs and charts have been drawn accurately and how you might improve them.

Revisit, review, revise

1) 80 people are asked where they like to go on holiday.

   a) What fraction choose the mountains?
   b) How many choose:
      i) the beach
      ii) the countryside
      iii) the mountains
      iv) the city?

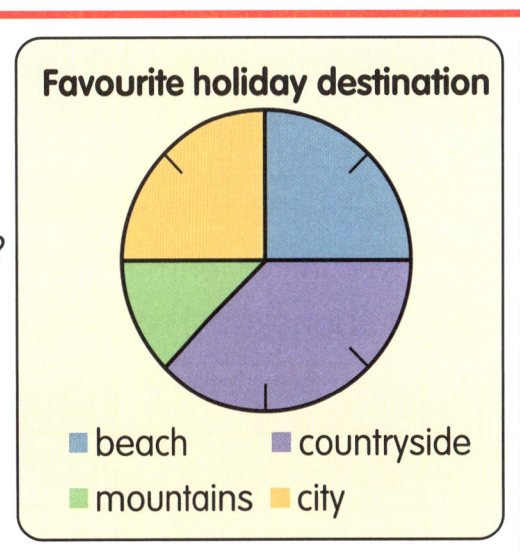

Chapter 9 Statistics

2) A grocer records the vegetables customers buy one morning:
   - 20% buy carrots
   - 50% buy potatoes
   - 10% buy broccoli
   - 5% buy spinach
   - 15% buy peas.

   a) Trace the blank pie chart.

   b) Complete the pie chart to show the information.

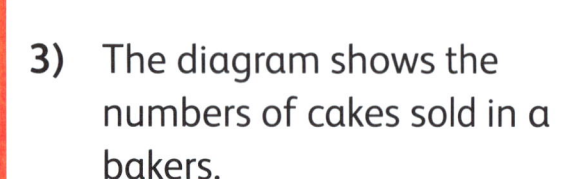

3) The diagram shows the numbers of cakes sold in a bakers.

   Key: ● represents 6 cakes

   a) How many cakes were sold on Tuesday?

   b) On which two days were the **same** number of cakes sold?

   c) How many **more** cakes were sold on Friday than on Wednesday?

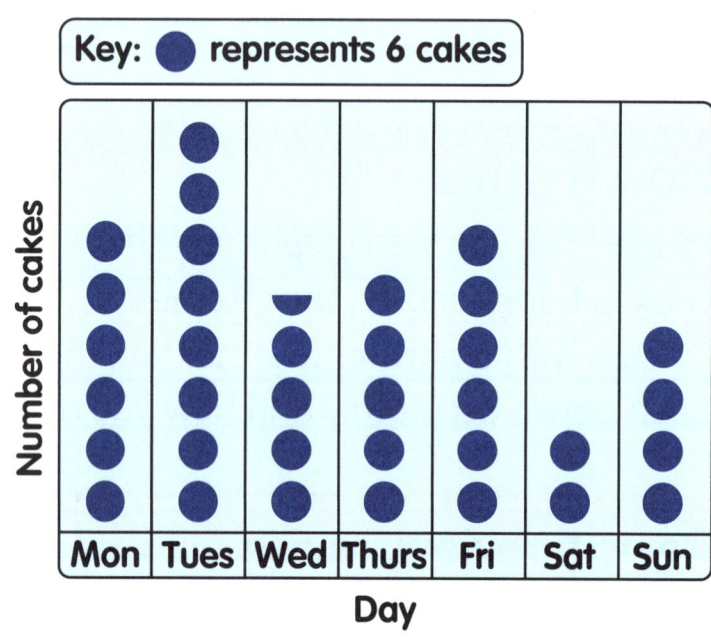

4) Two online learning companies record the number of visits (in thousands) to their websites over a 5-year period.

	Year 1	Year 2	Year 3	Year 4	Year 5
Easy Learn	19	21	22	24	25
Online Lessons	10	14	19	23	27

Representing data and interpreting graphs and charts

a) Copy the axes onto squared paper.
Draw two line graphs on the **same axes** to show how many thousands of pupils visit each website each year.
Use a different colour for each company.
Give your graph a title.

b) Between which two years do the visits to Online Lessons **increase** the most?

c) Which year is the **difference** in the number of visits between the two companies **greatest**?

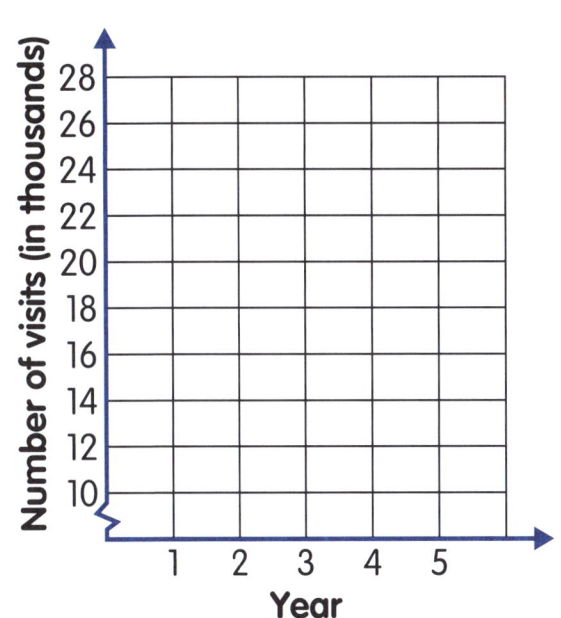

5) The line graph shows the average monthly temperature in Glasgow and Sydney.

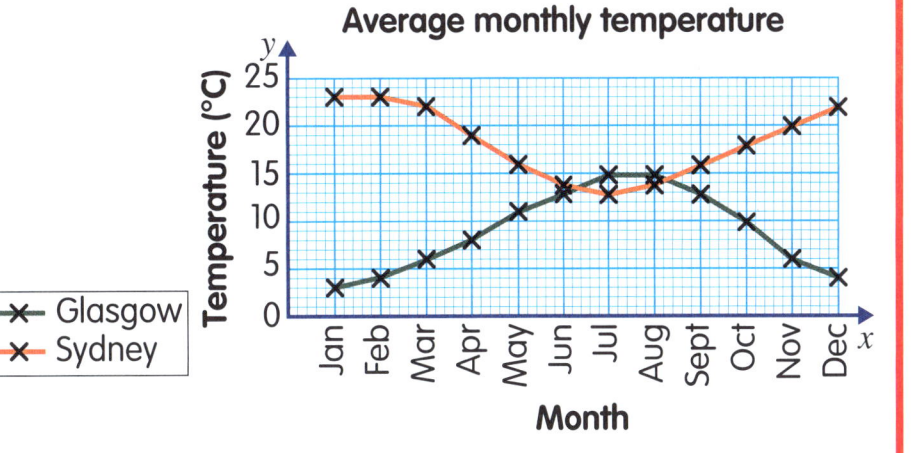

a) What was the temperature in May in:
   i) Glasgow
   ii) Sydney?

b) In which months was the temperature **higher** in Glasgow than Sydney?

c) Which month was the temperature **lowest** in:
   i) Glasgow
   ii) Sydney?

10 Whole numbers 2
Order of operations

Working out calculations using the order of operations

💡 I will learn to add, subtract, multiply and divide in the correct order.

Remember, remember

In mathematics, there are four **operations**:

add	subtract	multiply	divide
+	−	×	÷

Work out $6 + 4 \times 7$.

Zara says: *The answer is 70*

because $6 + 4 = 10$
and $10 \times 7 = 70$

Ash says: *The answer is 34*

because $4 \times 7 = 28$
and $6 + 28 = 34$

Who is correct?

Mathematicians follow an **order of operations**:

> **Multiply and divide first.
> Then add and subtract.**

To work out $6 + 4 \times 7$, you must multiply first, then add.
34 is the correct answer.

Order of operations

Exercise 1

1) Copy and complete:
   a) 5 + 10 × 2 = 5 + ___
       = ___
   b) 20 − 8 ÷ 2 = 20 − ___
       = ___
   c) 8 × 6 − 5 = ___ − 5
       = ___
   d) 12 ÷ 3 + 9 = ___ + 9
       = ___

2) Write in your jotter which part of each calculation you should work out first:
   a) 7 + 8 × 4   7 + 8   or   8 × 4
   b) 3 × 6 + 1   3 × 6   or   6 + 1
   c) 11 − 2 × 5   11 − 2   or   2 × 5
   d) 9 ÷ 3 + 6   9 ÷ 3   or   3 + 6
   e) 8 + 6 ÷ 2   8 + 6   or   6 ÷ 2
   f) 20 − 8 ÷ 4   20 − 8   or   8 ÷ 4

3) Use the order of operations to work out each calculation in question 2.

4) Work out:
   a) 12 − 6 ÷ 2   b) 6 ÷ 2 + 12   c) 12 − 6 × 2
   d) 12 ÷ 6 − 2   e) 6 × 2 + 12   f) 6 + 12 ÷ 2

When a calculation has only × and ÷ or + and −, then work from left to right.

5) Work out:
   a) 8 − 5 + 1   b) 4 × 10 ÷ 5   c) 10 ÷ 2 × 5

Chapter 10 Whole numbers 2

6) What are the **missing** operations (+, –, ×, ÷) in these calculations?
   a) 20 ___ 10 ___ 5 = 7
   b) 20 ___ 5 ___ 2 = 10

7) Copy and complete:
   a) 3 × 2 + 4 × 5 = ___ + 4 × 5
              = ___ + ___
              = ___
   b) 4 × 9 ÷ 6 + 3 = ___ ÷ 6 + 3
              = ___ + ___
              = ___

8) Work out these calculations:
   a) 9 – 2 × 4 + 5
   b) 4 × 3 + 12 ÷ 6
   c) 15 ÷ 3 + 2 ÷ 2

Using order of operations to solve problems

💡 I will learn to use the order of operations to solve problems.

Sometimes you must write a calculation to solve a problem before using the order of operations to work out the answer.

Exercise 2

1) Saf is paid £10 per hour.
   He works 4 hours.
   He receives £25 in tips.
   a) To work out how much Saf earns, you can use a calculation like this:
      10 × ___ + ___
      Copy and complete the calculation.
   b) How much does Saf earn?

Order of operations

2) A pack of batteries costs £5.

   Single batteries cost £2.

   Harry buys 6 packs of batteries and a single battery.

   a) In your jotter, write the calculation you would use to work out how much Harry pays.

   b) How much does Harry pay?

3) Sasha is 14 years old.

   Her brother is half her age add a year.

   a) In your jotter, write the calculation you would use to work out how old Sasha's brother is.

   b) How old is Sasha's brother?

4) A bookcase has 8 shelves.

   There are 10 books on each shelf.

   Evie borrows 2 books.

   a) In your jotter, write the calculation you would use to work out how many books are left in the bookcase.

   b) How many books are left in the bookcase?

5) A cinema ticket costs £7.

   Sami goes to the cinema 5 times in one month.

   If you go to the cinema 5 times in a month, then you get £3 back.

   How much does Sami spend on cinema tickets in the month?

Chapter 10 Whole numbers 2

6) Jas has 5 pots of penny coins.

Each pot contains 20p.

Jas also has 6 additional pennies.

How much does Jas have **altogether**?

Write your answer as £ ____ . ____

7) In your jotter, write a calculation using 3, 6 and 12 once each.

Your calculation must have the answer 10.

Now try this!

Use a calculator to work out these calculations:

$6 + 3 \times 10 - 2$

$3 \times 10 - 6 \div 2$

Does your calculator use the order of operations?

> **Multiply and divide first.**
> **Then add and subtract.**

Explain to a partner how you know.

Order of operations

Revisit, review, revise

1) Work out:
   a) 7 + 12 − 5
   b) 2 × 6 ÷ 3
   c) 9 + 3 × 2
   d) 24 ÷ 3 − 5
   e) 11 − 5 × 2
   f) 63 ÷ 9 − 2

2) There are 6 mugs in a box.
   Tina buys 5 boxes.
   She gives 10 mugs to a friend.
   a) In your jotter, write the calculation you would use to work out how many mugs Tina keeps.
   b) How many mugs does Tina keep?

3) A tree is 12 m tall.
   A bush is half this height subtract 4 m.
   How tall is the bush?

4) Work out:
   45 − 36 ÷ 9 + 3

11 More symmetry
Symmetry and coordinates

Symmetry

💡 I will learn to identify the lines of symmetry on a shape and complete a symmetrical pattern.

Remember, remember

A shape has a **line of symmetry** if, when you fold the shape over the line, the 2 halves **exactly** match.

A shape can have **any number** of lines of symmetry.

This hexagon has 2 lines of symmetry:

This pentagon has 0 lines of symmetry:

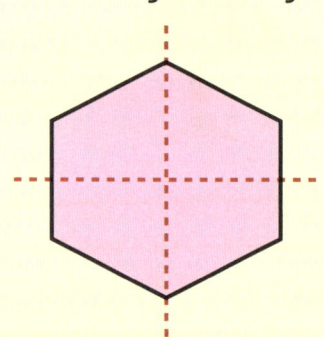

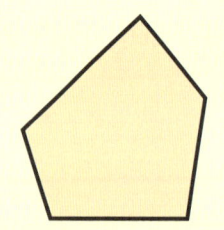

To complete a symmetrical pattern or shape, reflect colours and shapes in the lines of symmetry given.

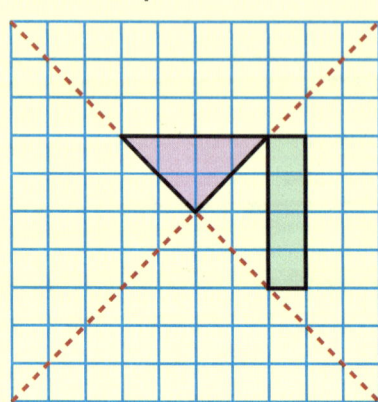

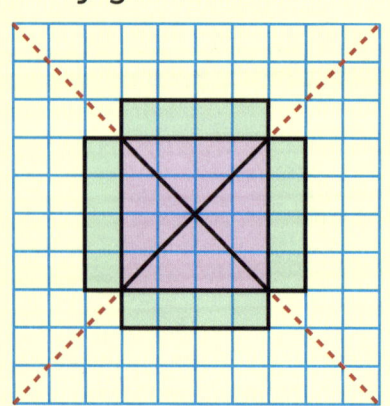

Symmetry and coordinates

Exercise 1

1) Copy these shapes onto squared paper.
   Complete the shapes so that the dashed lines are **lines of symmetry**.

   a)

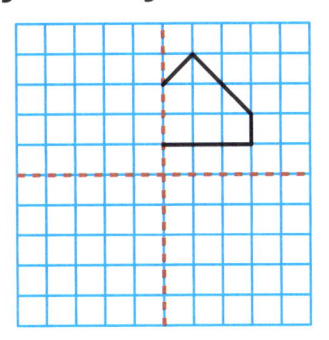

   b)

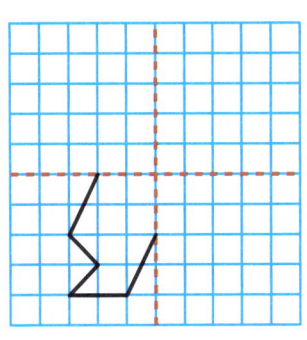

   c)

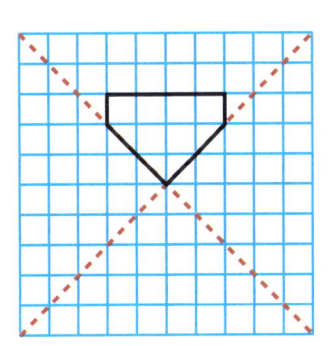

   d)

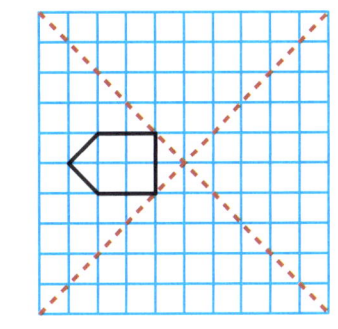

2) Copy each shape onto squared paper.
   Draw on any lines of symmetry.
   Write down the number of lines of symmetry each shape has.

   a)

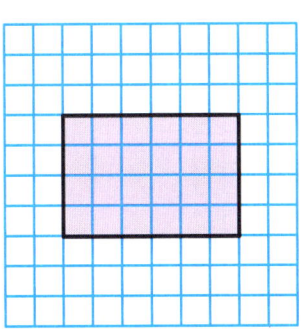

   b)

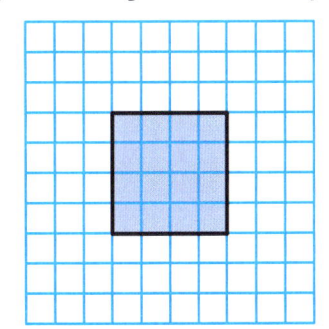

Chapter 11 More symmetry

c)

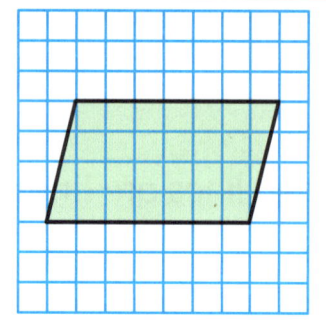

d)

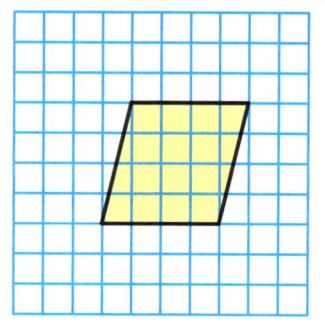

e)

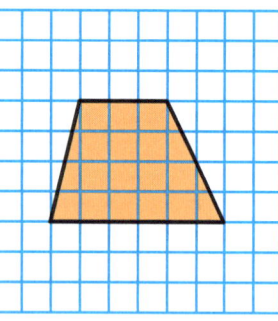

f)

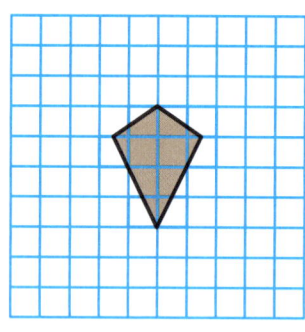

3) How many lines of symmetry has:

a) an isosceles triangle

b) an equilateral triangle

c) a scalene triangle?

4) Copy these shapes onto squared paper.

Complete and colour the shapes so that the dashed lines are lines of symmetry.

a)

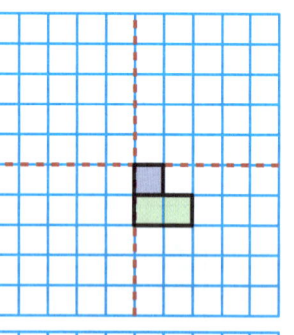

b)

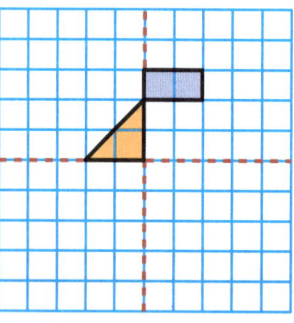

c)

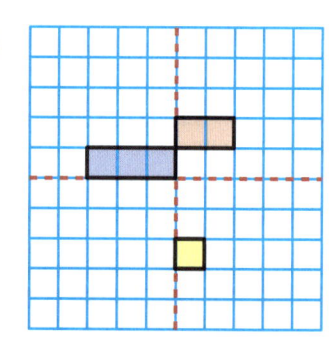

d)

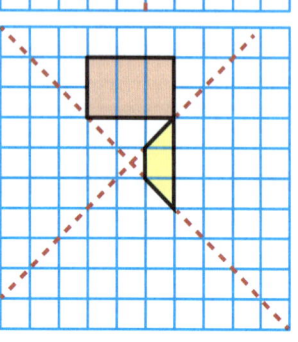

e)

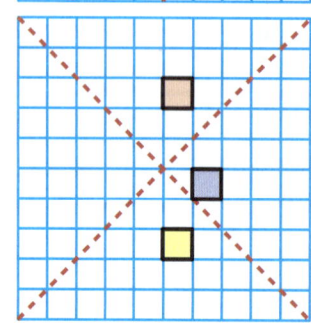

Symmetry and coordinates

5) How many lines of symmetry has a **regular** pentagon?

6) The dashed lines are lines of symmetry.
   a) Copy and complete the shape.
   b) What is the name of the shape?

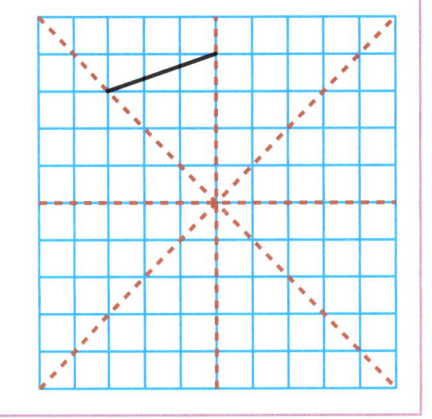

7) In your jotter, write down the name of a shape with **six** lines of symmetry.

Now try this!

Logos for companies and products often have symmetry.
Look around you or on the internet for logos for different companies.
Find logos which have different numbers of lines of symmetry.

Coordinates

💡 I will learn to plot coordinates.

Remember, remember

The x-axis is the horizontal axis.
The y-axis is the vertical axis.
The point (0, 0) is the origin.

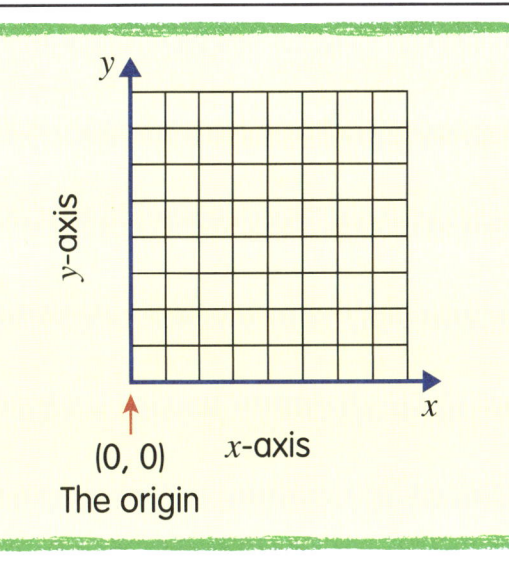

Chapter 11 More symmetry

Coordinates are given in the form (*x*, *y*).

The point **M** has *x*-coordinate 5 and *y*-coordinate 4.

This is written (5, 4).

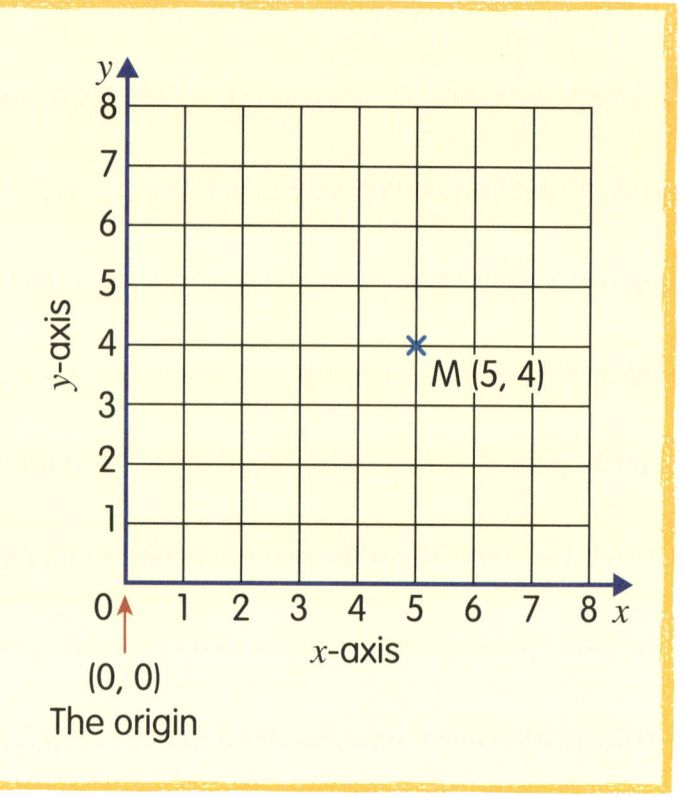

(0, 0) The origin

Example

Points **C** and **D** and a line are shown on a coordinate grid.

Mark on the points **C′** and **D′** to make the dashed line a line of symmetry.

Join the points to make a shape.

Write down the coordinates of all the corners of the shape.

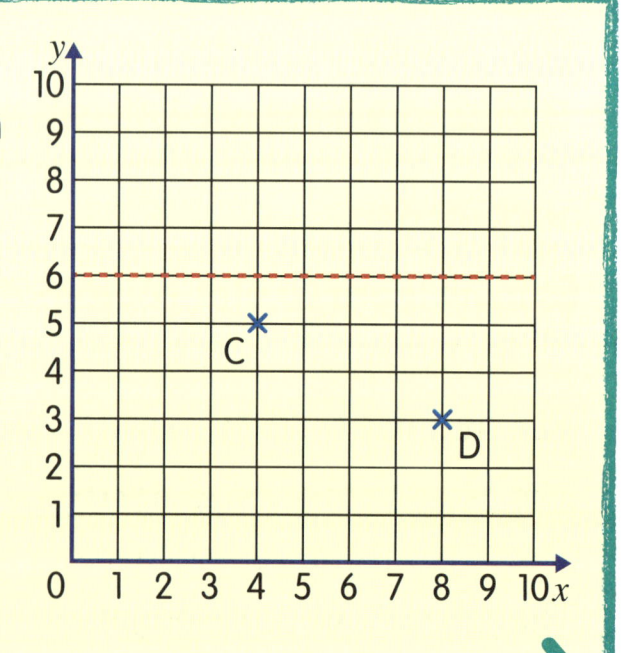

Symmetry and coordinates

Answer

The coordinates of **C** are (4, 5) and those of **C′** are (4, 7).

The coordinates of **D** are (8, 3) and those of **D′** are (8, 9).

The points must be the same distance from the line on both sides.

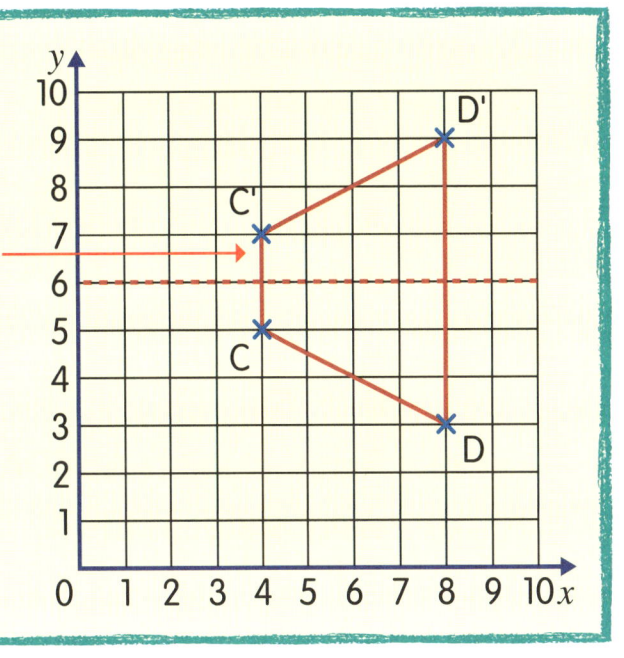

Exercise 2

1) Write down the coordinates of the points:
   a) A
   b) B
   c) C
   d) D
   e) E
   f) F.

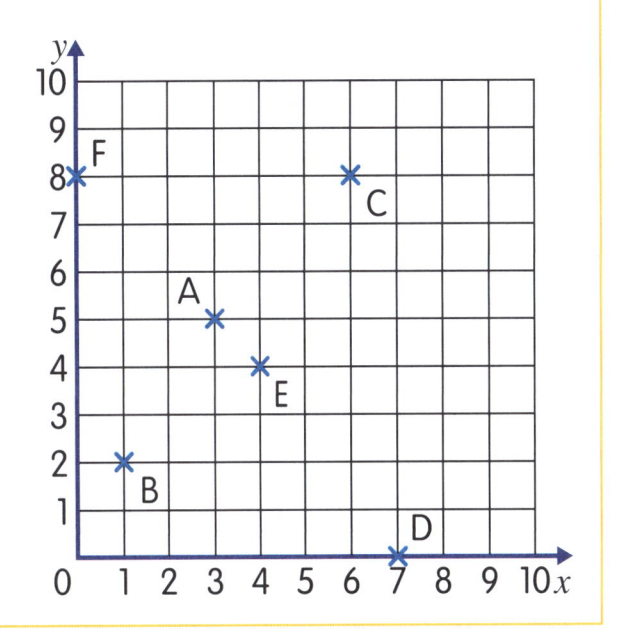

Chapter 11 More symmetry

2) a) Copy the coordinate grid onto squared paper.
   b) Mark on the points:
      A (3, 4)
      B (6, 2)
      C (9, 4)
      D (6, 6).
   c) Join the points **ABCDA**.
   d) What shape is this?

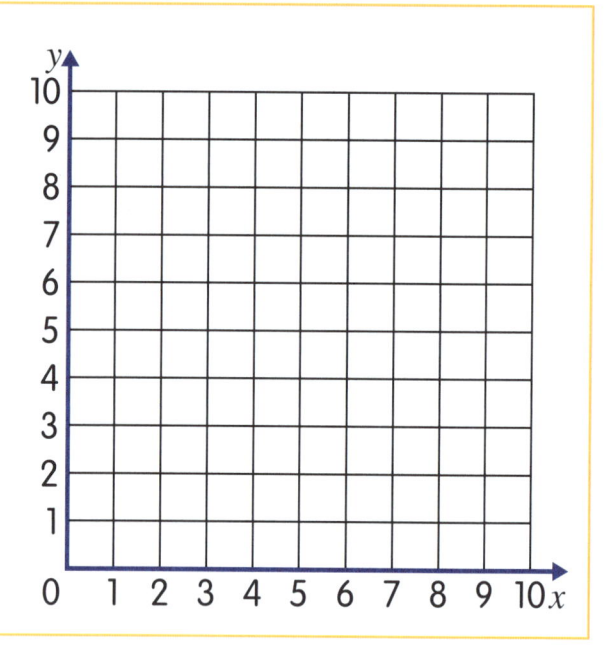

3) a) In your jotter, write down the coordinates of the points:
      i) A
      ii) B
      iii) C.

   ABCD is a trapezium.
   ABCD has one line of symmetry.

   b) Write down the coordinates of the point **D**.

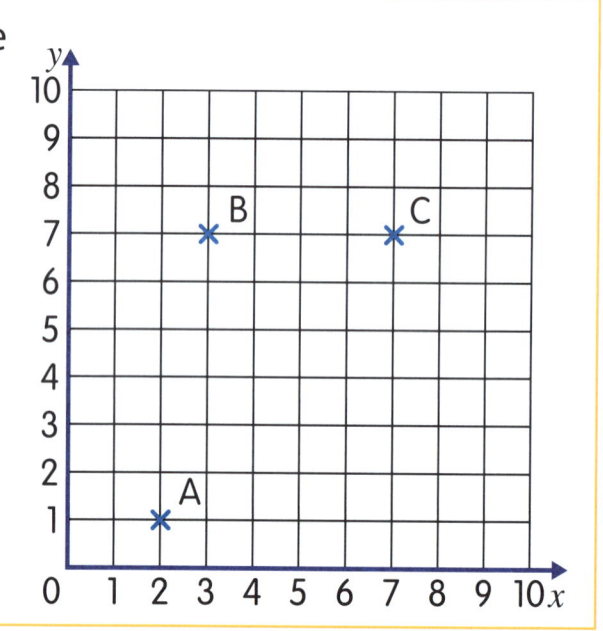

Symmetry and coordinates

4) **EFGH** is a parallelogram.

   a) In your jotter, write down the coordinates of **H**.

   b) How many lines of symmetry does the shape **EFGH** have?

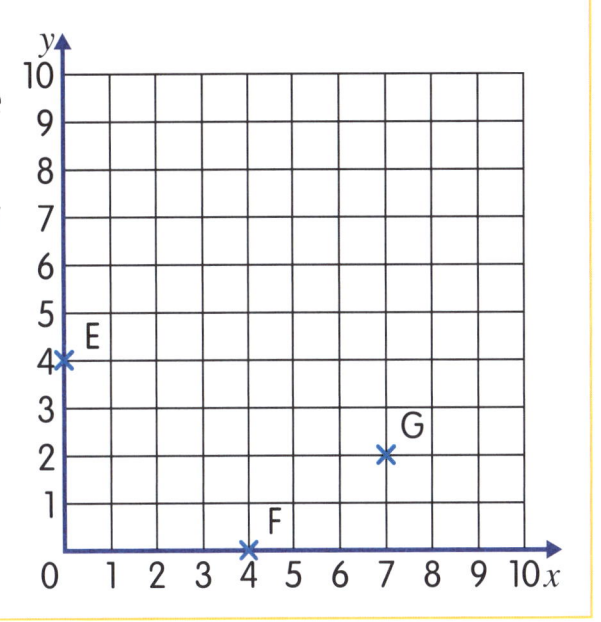

5) a) Copy the coordinate grid onto squared paper. Mark on the points **A**, **B**, **C** and the line shown.

   b) Write the coordinates of the points **A**, **B** and **C** on the grid, next to the points.

   c) Mark on points **A′**, **B′** and **C′** to make the dashed line a line of symmetry.

   d) Write down the coordinates of the points **A′**, **B′** and **C′**.

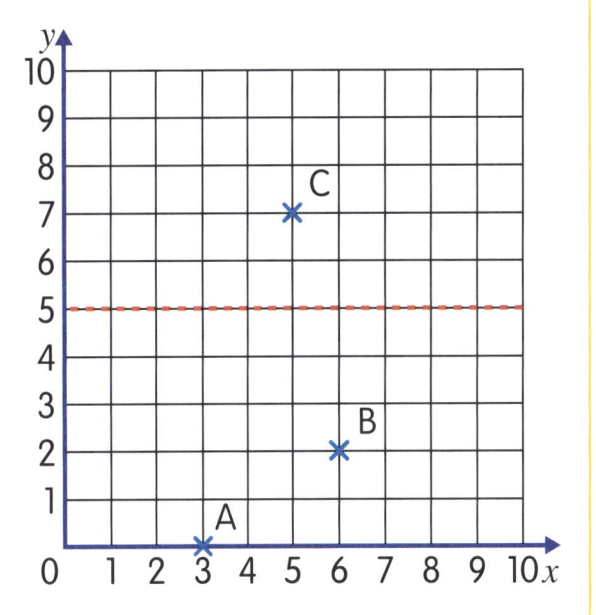

   e) What do you notice about the relationship between the coordinates of the points **A** and **A′**, **B** and **B′**, and **C** and **C′**?

Chapter 11 More symmetry

6)
a) Copy the coordinate grid onto squared paper.
Mark on the points E, F, G and the dashed line shown.

b) Write down the coordinates of the points E, F, G on the grid, next to the points.

c) Mark on points E′, F′ and G′ to make the dashed line a line of symmetry.

d) Write down the coordinates of the points E′, F′ and G′.

e) What do you notice about the relationship between the coordinates of the points E and E′, F and F′, and G and G′?

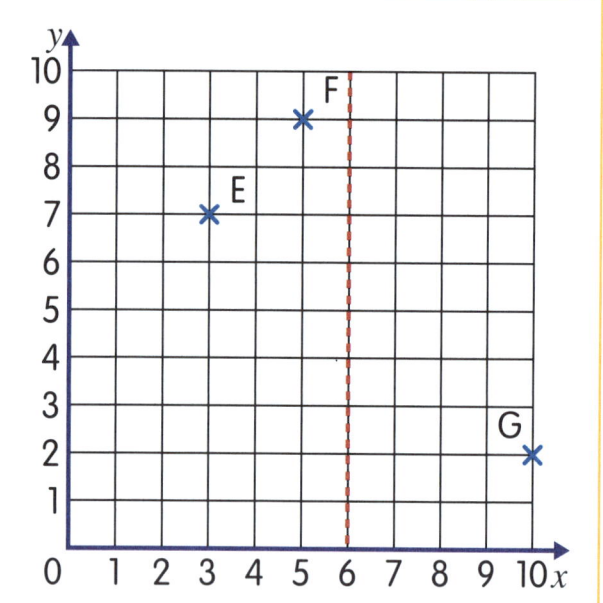

7)
a) Copy the coordinate grid onto squared paper.
Mark on the points and the line.

b) Write down the coordinates of the points C, D, E, F on the grid, next to the points.

c) Mark on points C′, D′, E′ and F′ to make the dashed line a line of symmetry.

d) Write down the coordinates of the points C′, D′, E′, and F′.

e) What do you notice about the relationship between the coordinates of the points C and C′, D and D′, E and E′, and F and F′?

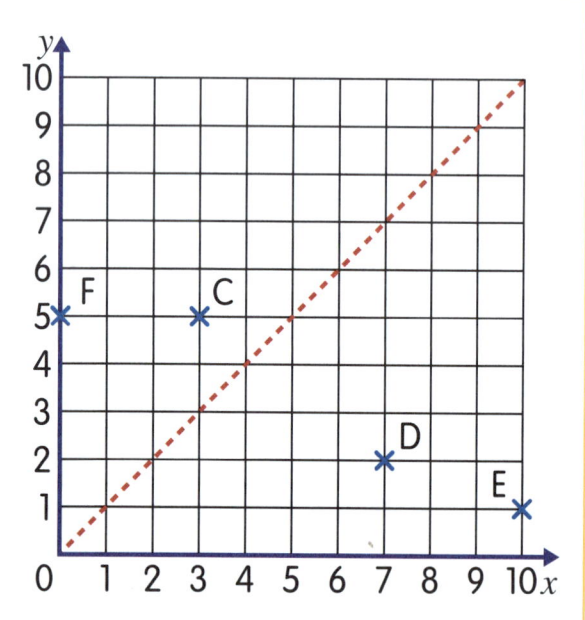

Symmetry and coordinates

Now try this!

a) Copy the coordinate grid onto squared paper.

Draw the trapezium **ABCD** on the grid.

Draw a line of symmetry on the shape.

Write down the coordinates of **three** points on the line of symmetry.

b) What do you notice about the coordinates?

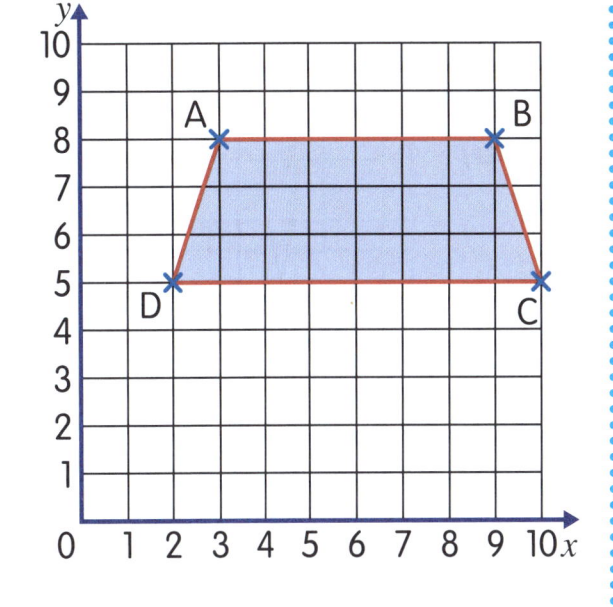

Try drawing other quadrilaterals on a coordinate grid. Draw on any lines of symmetry and write down coordinates of the points on these lines.

Describe any patterns you notice.

Revisit, review, revise

1) Copy these shapes onto squared paper.
   Complete the shapes so that the dashed lines are lines of symmetry.

   a)

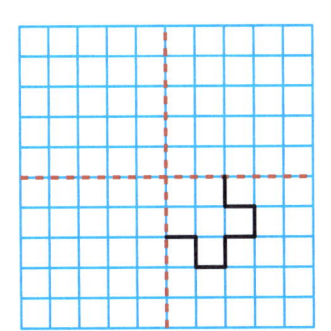

   b)

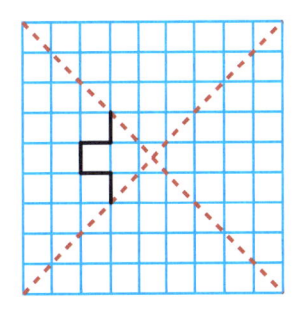

Chapter 11 More symmetry

2) How many lines of symmetry does a parallelogram have?

3) How many lines of symmetry does a regular decagon have?

4) Copy these shapes onto squared paper.

   Complete and colour the shapes so that the dashed lines are lines of symmetry.

   a)

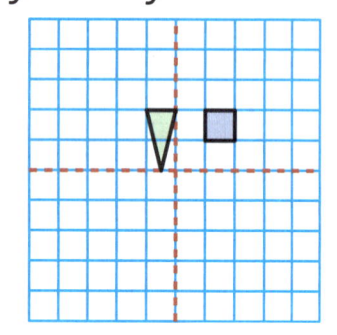

   b)

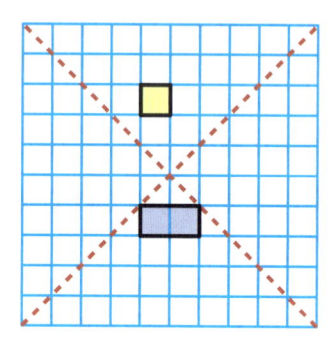

5)

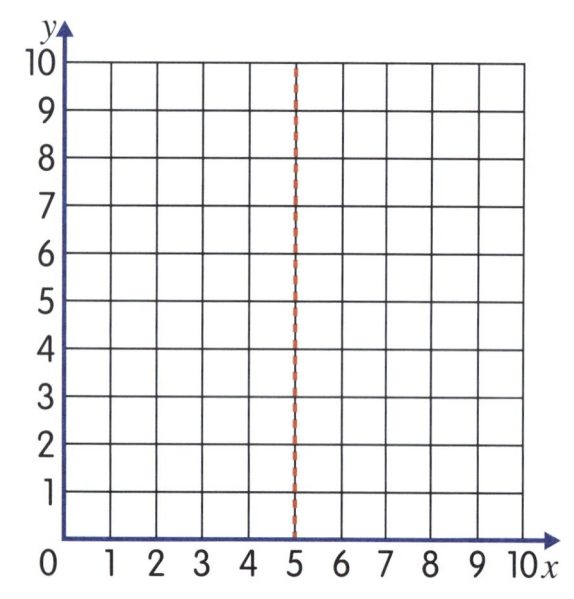

   a) Copy the coordinate grid onto squared paper. Include the dashed line.
   b) Mark on the points:
      A (2, 8)   B (8, 6).
   c) Mark on points A′ and B′ to make the dashed line a line of symmetry.
   d) Join the points to make a quadrilateral.
   e) What is the name of the quadrilateral?

12 Time
Measuring time and calculating distances travelled

Measuring time

💡 I will learn to read stopwatches and convert between units of time.

Remember, remember

There are **12 months** in **1 year**.

There are **365 days** in **1 year** (or 366 days in a leap year).

There are **24 hours** in **1 day**.

There are **60 minutes** in **1 hour**.

There are **60 seconds** in **1 minute**.

For accuracy, especially in sport, time can be measured in **tenths** or **hundredths** of a second.

This **stopwatch** shows the time in minutes and seconds.

The time is: 4 minutes 13.07 seconds.

This is 4 minutes, 13 seconds and 7 hundredths of a second.

The time can be rounded to:

- 4 minutes (to the nearest minute)
- 4 minutes 13 seconds (to the nearest second)
- 4 minutes 13.1 seconds (to the nearest tenth of a second).

To convert between units of time, make sure you know the facts in the Remember, remember box above.

Chapter 12 Time

Example

How many minutes in 1.5 hours?
1 hour = 60 minutes
0.5 hours = 0.5 × 60 = 30 minutes
1.5 hours = 60 + 30 = 90 minutes

Example

How many hours in $1\frac{1}{4}$ days?
1 day = 24 hours
$\frac{1}{4}$ day = $\frac{1}{4}$ × 24 = 6 hours
$1\frac{1}{4}$ days = 24 + 6 = 30 hours

Exercise 1

1) What times are shown on these stopwatches?

   a)  1:23:02
   b)  4:16:25
   c)  3:00:04
   d)  0:58:93

2) Round these times to the nearest second:
   a) 32.9 seconds
   b) 14.09 seconds
   c) 3 minutes 15.3 seconds
   d) 8 minutes 7.62 seconds

3) Round your answers from question 1 to the nearest:
   i) minute
   ii) second.

4) How many seconds in:
   a) 10 minutes
   b) 1.5 minutes
   c) $2\frac{1}{2}$ minutes
   d) 45 minutes?

5) How many minutes in:
   a) 5 hours
   b) 4.5 hours
   c) $1\frac{3}{4}$ hours
   d) $8\frac{1}{2}$ hours?

Measuring time and calculating distances travelled

6) How many hours in:
  a) June
  b) August
  c) a fortnight?

7) A tachograph is used to regulate how long lorry and bus drivers drive without a break.

The tachograph on a minibus shows how long a driver has been driving.

The times are in hours, minutes and seconds.

What times are shown on these tachographs?

a) hrs min secs: 4 13 25 03 1/100

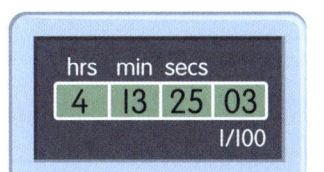

b) hrs min secs: 08 49 10 34 1/100

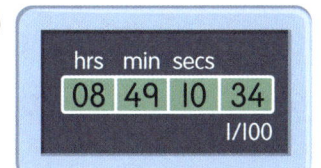

c) hrs min secs: 03 26 54 70 1/100

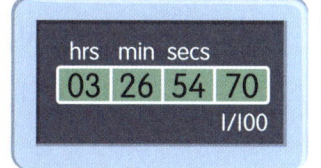

8) Round the times in question 7 to:
  i) the nearest hour
  ii) the nearest minute
  iii) the nearest second.

9) Here are the lap times in minutes and seconds for 4 motocross bikers:

Ash: 2:57:96
Ali: 3:01:02
Mason: 3:42:16
Selleck: 3:39:44

a) Who was fastest?
b) Who was slowest?
c) How much faster was the fastest rider than the slowest rider?

Chapter 12 Time

Now try this!

You should brush your teeth for 2 minutes **twice** every day.

Assuming you start brushing your teeth when you are 1 year old and live until you are 80, work out how many minutes you spend brushing your teeth in your lifetime.

Convert this time into days.

Round your answer to the nearest whole number of days.

(You may use a calculator to help you.)

Now carry out a similar calculation to work out how long you spend at primary school in your lifetime.

(Be careful, you only have school for approximately 38 weeks a year.)

Distance and time

💡 I will learn to calculate distances travelled or time taken for journeys.

You can work out how far you have travelled if you know how long you have been travelling.

For example, if you walk 4 km each hour you will walk:

4 km in 1 hour

4 + 4 = 8 km in 2 hours

4 + 4 + 4 = 12 km in 3 hours … and so on.

In 10 hours you will walk:

10 × 4 km = 40 km.

Measuring time and calculating distances travelled

The length of time a journey takes depends upon how fast you travel.

For example, if you cycle 12 km per hour and want to travel 24 km, it will take you:
24 ÷ 12 = 2 hours.

Example
A car travelled at 45 km per hour for 3 hours.
What distance did it cover?
The car travels 3 × 45 km = 135 km.

Example
A plane flies at 180 miles per hour (mph).
How long will it take to travel 720 miles?
It will take: 720 ÷ 180 = 4 hours.

Exercise 2

1) Work out the distance travelled if you:
   a) walk for 2 hours at 5 km per hour
   b) walk for 4 hours at 3 miles per hour
   c) drive for 4 hours at 50 mph
   d) row for 6 hours at 1 mph
   e) cycle for 5 hours at 9 km per hour.

Chapter 12 Time

2) Calculate the distance travelled by a:
   a) lorry, driving at 30 mph for 7 hours
   b) train, travelling at 100 mph for 5 hours
   c) plane, flying at 380 mph for 4 hours
   d) hot-air balloon, floating at 2 mph for 15 hours
   e) coach, moving at 55 mph for 6 hours
   f) fire engine, doing 80 mph for $\frac{1}{2}$ hour.

3) How long will it take to travel:
   a) 10 miles when walking at 2 miles per hour
   b) 100 miles when driving at 50 mph
   c) 2000 km when flying at 400 km per hour
   d) 12 km when skating at 4 km per hour
   e) 700 miles when driving at 70 mph
   f) 3 miles when walking at 6 miles per hour?

4) A plane leaves Benidorm at 13:25 and arrives in Glasgow at 16:25. The plane flies 420 miles each hour.
   a) How long does the flight take?
   b) How many miles does the plane fly?

5) A tug boat leaves Kincardine at 2:50 p.m. and sails at 15 miles per hour along the River Forth.
   How far is the tug boat from Kincardine at 6:50 p.m.?

Measuring time and calculating distances travelled

6) A steam train leaves Gretna at 6:45 a.m.
   It travels to Aberdeen at 82 miles per hour.
   The journey is 287 miles.
   a) How long does the journey take?
   b) When does the train arrive in Aberdeen?

7) A plane leaves London's Heathrow Airport at 21:30 on Sunday to fly 5890 miles to Mexico.
   It travels at a steady 620 mph.
   a) How long does the journey take
   b) At what time (our time) and on what day does the plane reach Mexico?

8) Do you agree with James?
   Explain your answer.

   To answer all these questions, you must multiply the two numbers in the question together.

Revisit, review, revise

1) a) What time is shown on the stopwatch?
   b) Round the time to the nearest:
      i) minute
      ii) second.

   4:32:07 stopwatch

2) Round these times to the nearest second:
   a) 35.7 seconds
   b) 19.28 seconds
   c) 2 minutes 8.05 seconds

Chapter 12 Time

3) Put these times in order from **shortest** to **longest**:

1 minute 15.2 seconds	$\frac{3}{4}$ minute	3.5 minutes
178 seconds		

4) How many minutes in $5\frac{1}{4}$ hours?

5) How many seconds in 7.5 minutes?

6) How many hours in a week?

7) Erin drives 225 miles at 45 miles per hour. How long does it take her?

8) Sharif hikes at 5 km per hour for 7 hours. How far does he walk?

9) A train leaves Edinburgh at 09:45. It travels 40 km per hour and arrives at its destination at 11:15. How far has it travelled?

13 Decimal fractions 2
Decimal fraction answers

Dividing that gives a decimal answer

💡 I will learn to divide whole numbers that give a decimal answer.

Remember, remember
You already know how to divide a decimal by a single digit.

Example
Work out 27.88 ÷ 4.

Line up the decimal points

4 goes into 27 (ones) 6 times remainder 3 (ones)

4 goes into 38 (tenths) 9 times remainder 2 (tenths)

4 goes into 28 (hundredths) 7 times

```
      6 . 9  7
  4 ) 2 ²7 . ³8 ²8
```

27.88 ÷ 4 = 6.97

A zero on the end of a number, after the decimal point, does not change its value.

Example
  71 = 7 tens + 1 one
 71.0 = 7 tens + 1 one + 0 tenths
71.00 = 7 tens + 1 one + 0 tenths + 0 hundredths
71, 71.0 and 71.00 all have the same value.

Chapter 13 Decimal fractions 2

When dividing, remainders can be written as decimal fractions. First you must write the whole number you are dividing as a decimal, with 0 tenths or 0 hundredths.

Example

Work out 71 ÷ 5

5 goes into 21 (ones)
4 times
remainder 1 (one)

5 goes into 7 (tens)
1 time remainder 2 (tens)

$$5 \overline{)7\,^{2}1.^{1}0} = 14.2$$

Write 71 as 71.0
Line up the decimal points

Carry the remainder 1 (one)
5 goes into 10 (tenths) 2 times

71 ÷ 5 = 14.2

Example

Work out 7.4 ÷ 4

Line up the decimal points

4 goes into 34 (tenths)
8 times remainder 2 (tenths)

4 goes into 7 (ones)
1 time remainder 3 (ones)

$$4 \overline{)7.\,^{3}4\,^{2}0} = 1.85$$

Write 7.4 as 7.40
Carry the remainder 2 (tenths)
4 goes into 20 (hundredths) 5 times

7.4 ÷ 4 = 1.85

Decimal fraction answers

Sometimes, the whole number you are dividing as a decimal must be written with 0 tenths or 0 tenths and 0 hundredths.

Example

Work out $258 \div 8$

8 goes into 18 (ones) 2 times remainder 2 (ones)

8 goes into 25 (tens) 3 times remainder 1 (ten)

$$8 \overline{)2^25^18.^20^40} = 32.25$$

Write 258 as 258.0
Line up the decimal points
Carry the remainder 2 (ones)

8 goes into 20 (tenths) 2 times remainder 4 (tenths)

Write 258.0 as 258.00
Carry the remainder 4 (tenths)

8 goes into 40 (hundredths) 5 times

$258 \div 8 = 32.25$

Exercise 1

1) Copy and complete:

   a) $4 \overline{)5\,^18.^2\Box}$ = □□.□

   $58 \div 4 =$ _____

   b) $8 \overline{)1^14\,^66.^2\Box^4\Box}$ = □□.□□

   $146 \div 8 =$ _____

2) Work out by writing a decimal point then a zero at the end of each number you are dividing.

   a) $5 \overline{)32}$

   b) $2 \overline{)63}$

   c) $5 \overline{)147}$

Chapter 13 Decimal fractions 2

3) Work out by writing a decimal point then two zeroes at the end of each number you are dividing.

   a) 4 ⟌ 33   b) 8 ⟌ 90   c) 4 ⟌ 949

4) Work out:

   a) 2 ⟌ 75   b) 4 ⟌ 86   c) 5 ⟌ 213

   d) 8 ⟌ 106   e) 8 ⟌ 570   f) 4 ⟌ 398

5) In your jotter, write these divisions using ⟌. Then work out the answer.

   a) 43 ÷ 5   b) 97 ÷ 2   c) 31 ÷ 4
   d) 133 ÷ 2   e) 829 ÷ 5   f) 1674 ÷ 8

6) A pack of 4 light bulbs costs £6.
   How much is 1 light bulb?
   (Remember that money in pounds always has two digits after the decimal point.)

7) A piece of string is 364 cm long.
   It is cut into 8 equal lengths.
   How long is each length?

8) A carton contains 946 ml of juice.
   The juice is shared equally between 5 cups.
   How much in each cup?

Decimal fraction answers

9) Kim divides her luggage equally between two suitcases.
Together they weigh 39 kg.
How heavy is each suitcase?

10) 5 cans of beans are stacked on top of each other.
Each can is the same size.
The height of the stack is 54 cm.
How tall is one can?

11) Alice has £99.
She shares it equally between herself and her three sisters.
How much do they each get?

12) Work out an eighth of 18 594.

Now try this!

1) Work out:
   a) $1 \div 4$ b) $2 \div 4$ c) $3 \div 4$ d) $4 \div 4$
   e) $5 \div 4$ f) $6 \div 4$ g) $7 \div 4$

2) Use your answers to question 1 to **predict** the answers to:
   a) $9 \div 4$ b) $10 \div 4$ c) $11 \div 4$

Compare your predictions with others in your class.
Did you all make the same predictions?

Chapter 13 Decimal fractions 2

Revisit, review, revise

1) Work out:

   a) $2\overline{)59}$ b) $5\overline{)59}$ c) $4\overline{)59}$ d) $4\overline{)858}$

   e) $5\overline{)858}$ f) $8\overline{)858}$ g) $8\overline{)1092}$ h) $2\overline{)3677}$

   Give your answers as decimal fractions.

2) Divide 63 by:

   a) 2   b) 4   c) 5   d) 6

3) A bucket holds 9 litres of water.
   The water is shared equally between four watering cans.
   How much water in each watering can?

4) A pack of 8 burgers costs £6.
   How much is 1 burger?

5) Alistair works 5 days this week.
   He is paid £512.
   How much does he earn each day?

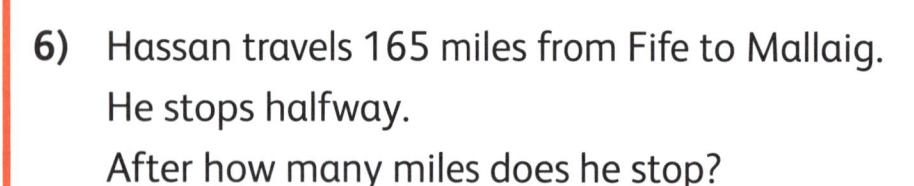

6) Hassan travels 165 miles from Fife to Mallaig.
   He stops halfway.
   After how many miles does he stop?

14 More angles
Angles and scale drawings

Finding missing angles

> 💡 I will learn about complementary and supplementary angles and how to use these to calculate missing angles.

Remember, remember

An angle is a measure of turn.

Angles are measured in **degrees** (°).

A complete turn is 360° 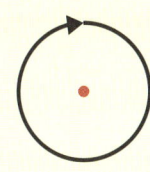   A half turn is 180° 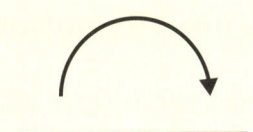   A quarter turn is 90° 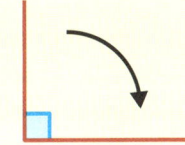   A three-quarters turn is 270°

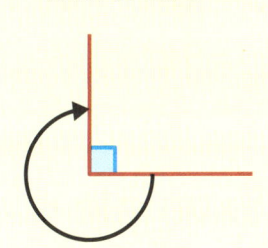

Two angles are **complementary** when they **sum to 90°** ('sum to' means 'add up to').

These angles are complementary:
40° + 50° = 90°

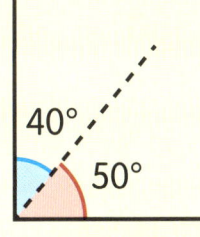

Two angles are **supplementary** when they **sum to 180°**.

These angles are supplementary:
110° + 70° = 180°

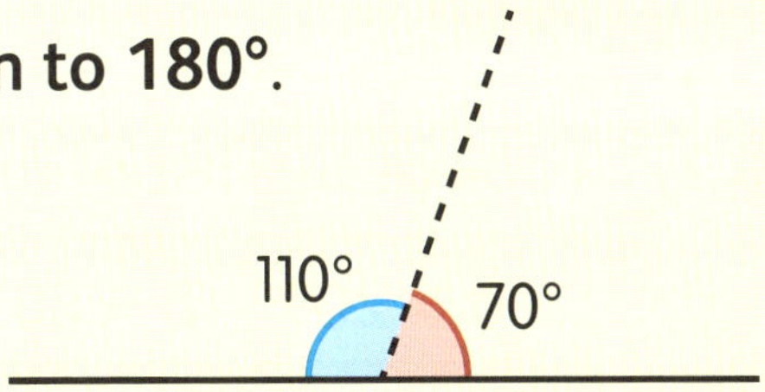

Chapter 14 More angles

You can calculate missing angles using the facts:
- Angles in a **right angle** sum to **90°**.
- Angles on a **straight line** sum to **180°**.
- Angles **round a point** sum to **360°**.

When you are asked to **calculate**, **find** or **work out** a missing angle in a diagram, **do not measure** it as the diagram may not be drawn accurately.

Example

Calculate the size of angle a.
Angles on a straight line sum to 180°, therefore:
$a = 180° − 88°$
   $= 92°$

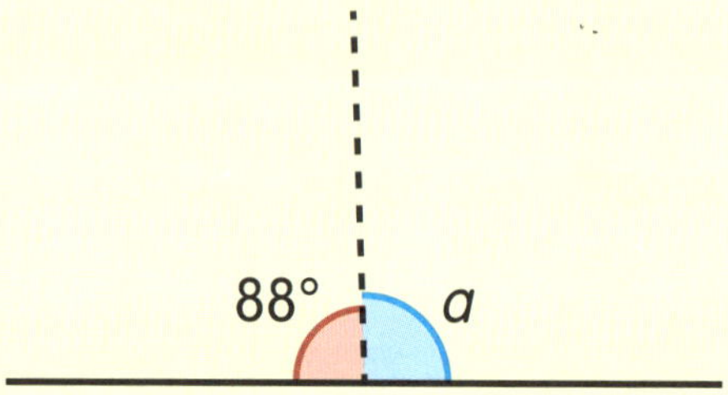

Example

Calculate the size of angle b.
Angles round a point sum to 360°, therefore:
$b = 360° − 140° − 95°$
   $= 125°$

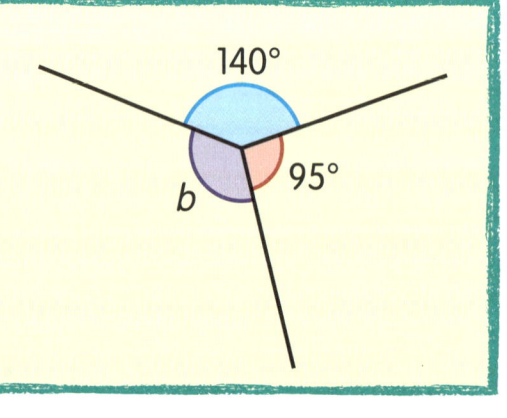

Exercise 1

1) Look at this list of angles:

   | $a = 20°$ | $b = 40°$ | $c = 70°$ | $d = 90°$ | $e = 100°$ | $f = 110°$ |

   Which **pair** of angles in the list is:
   a) complementary
   b) supplementary?

Angles and scale drawings

2) Angles *m* and *n* are supplementary.

$n = 65°$

What is the size of angle *m*?

3) Angles *x* and *y* are complementary.

$x = 15°$

What is the size of angle *y*?

4) Calculate the sizes of the angles marked with letters.
Show your calculations.

a) 30°, a

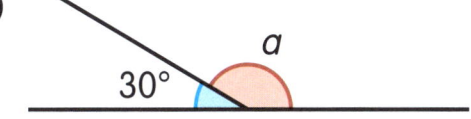

b) b, 72°

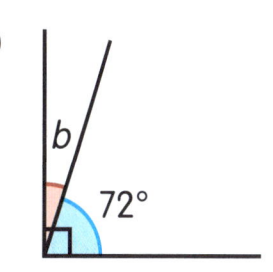

c) c

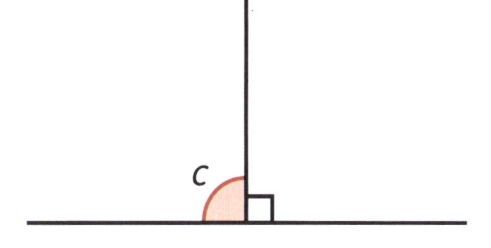

d) 225°, d

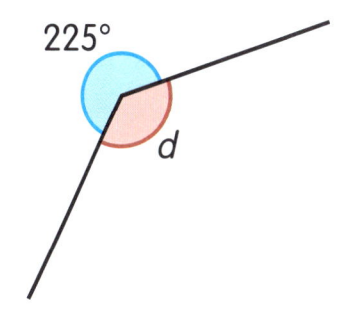

e) e, 112°, 188°

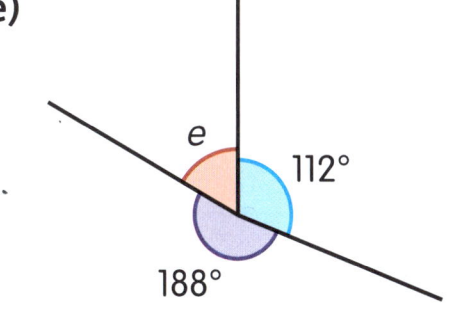

f) f

145

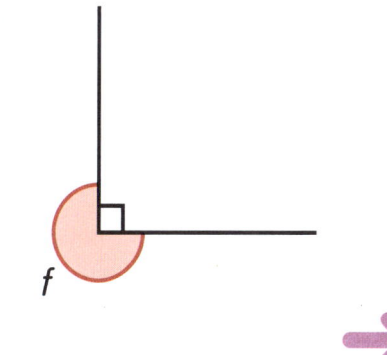

Chapter 14 More angles

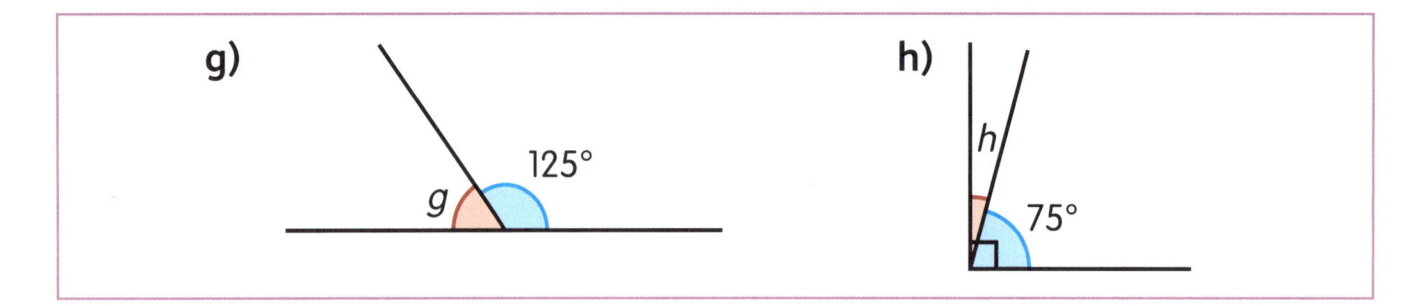

g) 125°, g

h) h, 75°

5) Work out the sizes of the angles marked with letters. Show your calculations.

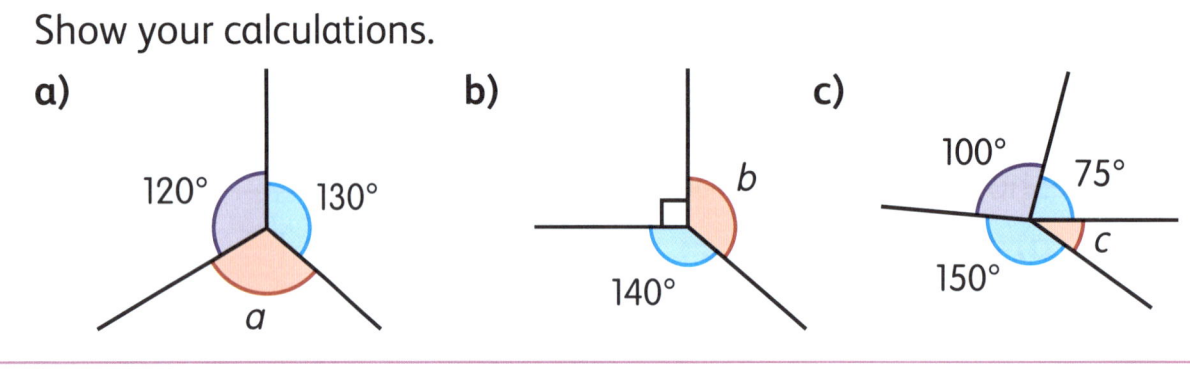

a) 120°, 130°, a

b) b, 140°

c) 100°, 75°, 150°, c

6) Angles *a* and *b* are the same size.
What is the size of angle *b*?

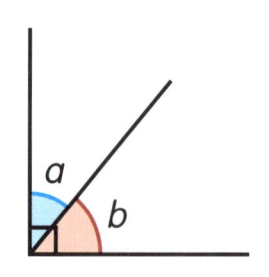

7) Angles *x*, *y* and *z* are all the same size.
What is the size of angle *x*?

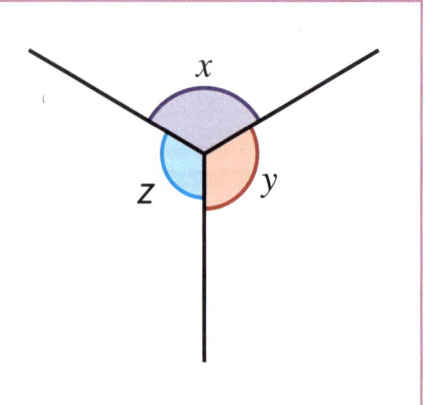

Angles and scale drawings

8) a) Which angles are supplementary to the 30° angle?
   b) Copy the diagram.
      Write on the sizes of the two angles that are supplementary to 30°. 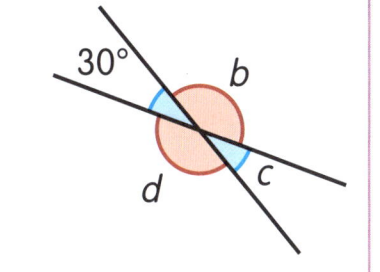
   c) Calculate the size of the other angle in the diagram.
   d) What do you notice?
   e) Will this always be true?
      Explain your answer.

Now try this!

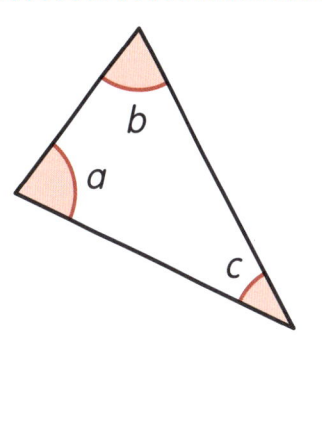

You will need a ruler and a protractor.
Draw any triangle (use a ruler).
Measure the angles in the triangle.
Find the sum of the angles in the triangle:
a + b + c = _____
Repeat for other triangles.
Compare your answers with other people in the class.
What do you notice?

Compass points

I will learn how to use angles to describe directions.

Remember, remember

An **acute** angle is between 0° and 90°.

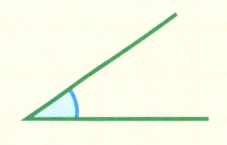

Chapter 14 More angles

An **obtuse** angle is between 90° and 180°.

A **reflex** angle is between 180° and 360°.

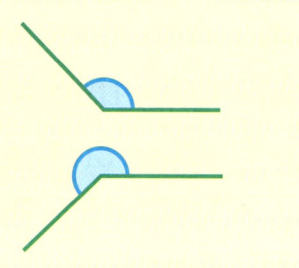

The four main compass points are **North (N)**, **East (E)**, **South (S)** and **West (W)**.

The ones between are **North-East (NE)**, **South-East (SE)**, **South-West (SW)** and **North-West (NW)**.

(North and South are always written first.)

The compass points are at **regular intervals** around a point.

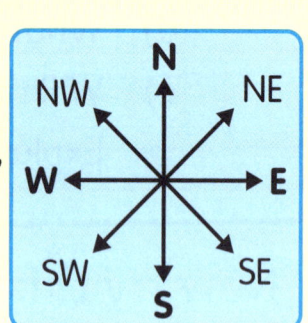

Exercise 2

1) What angle would you turn through if you turn **clockwise** from:
   a) North to South
   b) E to N
   c) South-West to West
   d) NE to SE?

2) What angle would you turn through if you turn **anticlockwise** from:
   a) North to South
   b) E to N
   c) South-West to West
   d) NE to SE?

3) Look at your answers to question 1 and question 2. What do you notice?

Angles and scale drawings

4) Are these angles acute, obtuse or reflex?
   a) A turn anticlockwise from North to South-West.
   b) A turn clockwise from NE to E.
   c) A turn clockwise from NW to S.

5) a) Chi faces East.
      She turns 45° clockwise.
      Which direction is she now facing?
   b) Mohammed cycles NE.
      At a roundabout, he turns his bike 45° anticlockwise.
      In which direction is he now travelling?
   c) A yacht sails South-West.
      It turns 90° anticlockwise.
      In which direction is the yacht now sailing?

6) A jet is flying SE.
   The pilot turns it to face West.
   What angle and in which direction could she turn?
   Give **both** possible answers.

Now try this!

Here is a compass showing further points. They are named NNE, ENE, ESE, SSE and so on.

Explain to a partner how these extra directions have been named.

Work out the angle between the 16 points on this compass.

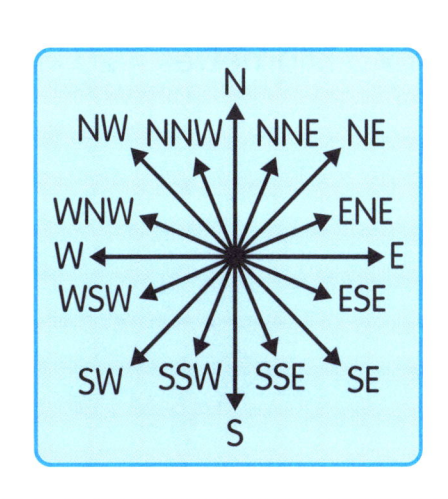

Chapter 14 More angles

Using scales

💡 **I will learn to interpret and use a scale on a diagram.**

Remember, remember

1 kilometre = 1000 metres

1 metre = 100 centimetres

1 centimetre = 10 millimetres

The map shows Jareed Island. It is drawn with a scale of **1 cm = 5 km**.

This means **1 centimetre** on the diagram represents **5 kilometres** in real life.

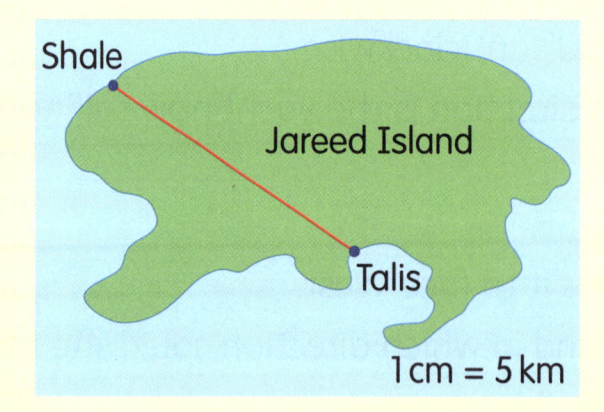

1 cm = 5 km

The distance from Shale to Talis on the map is 4 cm.

The actual distance between the two towns is:

4 × 5 kilometres = 20 kilometres.

Angles and scale drawings

Exercise 3

You will need a ruler.

1) These lines are drawn using a scale of **1 cm = 2 m**.
   Measure each line and calculate its actual length.
   a) _____
   b) _____
   c) __
   d) _____

2) This scale drawing of the floor of a gym is drawn to a scale of **1 cm = 6 m**.
   a) Measure the length and width of the hall.
   b) Work out the dimensions of the hall in real life.

3) This bus has been drawn using a scale of **1 cm = 1.5 m**.

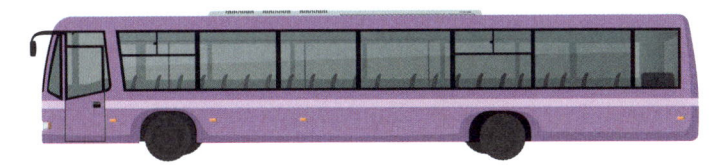

   a) Calculate the **real** height of the bus.
   b) Calculate the **real** length of the bus.

4) This flag is drawn to a scale of **1 cm = 40 cm**.
   a) Calculate the **real** height of the flag.
   b) Calculate the **real** width of the flag.

Chapter 14 More angles

5) A rectangular field is used for grazing sheep.
The scale is **1 cm = 40 m**. 
   a) Measure the diagram and calculate the **real** length and width of the field.
   b) Calculate the **real perimeter** of the field.
   c) Calculate the **real area** of the field.

6) This table top has been drawn to scale: **1 cm = 30 cm**.
   a) Measure the length of the table top.
   b) Calculate the real length of the table top. Give your answer in metres (as a decimal). 
   c) Calculate the real width of the table top in metres.

7) A helicopter delivers mail to a group of islands.
   The dots show where the helicopter lands. 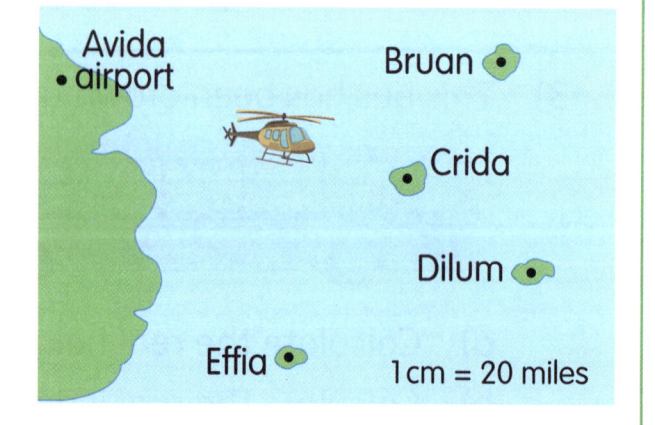
   a) Measure the distance from Avida to Bruan.
   b) Use the scale to calculate the **real** distance from Avida to Bruan.
   c) Calculate the **real** distances from Avida to:
      i) Crida ii) Dilum iii) Effia.
   d) The pilot flies from Avida to Bruan, then to Crida, on to Dilum and finally to Effia before returning to Avida.
   How far does she fly **altogether**?

Angles and scale drawings

Scale drawings

💡 I will learn to draw scale diagrams.

Scale drawings are useful in many jobs.

Maps are scale drawings of places.

This is a scale drawing of Kelvingrove Park in Glasgow.

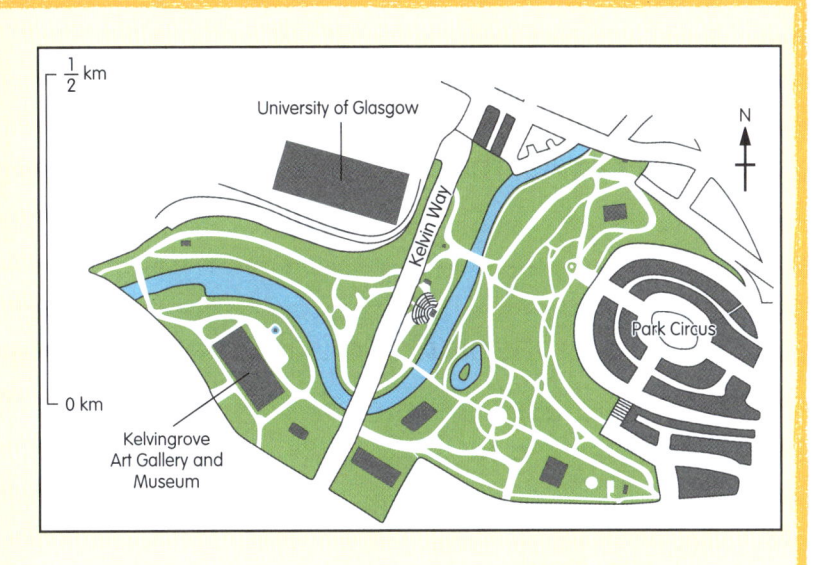

Example

A rectangular garden measures 12 metres by 9 metres.

Use a scale of **1 cm = 2 metres** to make a scale drawing: **1 cm** on the drawing represents **2 metres** in real life.

To work out how many cm long and wide to draw the garden, divide the distances by 2 and change the units:

length = 12 ÷ 2 = 6 cm
width = 9 ÷ 2 = 4.5 cm

Chapter 14 More angles

Exercise 4

1) A rectangular living room measures 6 metres by 4 metres.

   Draw an accurate scale diagram of the room using a scale of **1 cm = 1 metre**.

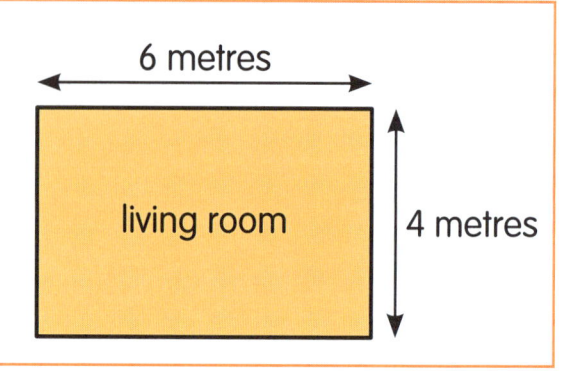

2) A rectangular field is 35 metres wide and 60 metres long.

   Ama uses a scale of **1 cm = 5 metres** to make an accurate scale diagram of the field.

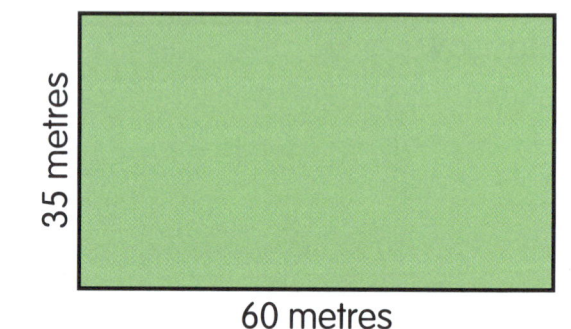

   a) Copy and complete Ama's calculations to work out the dimensions of the drawing:
   width = 35 ÷ 5 = ____ cm
   length = 60 ÷ 5 = ____ cm

   b) Draw an accurate scale diagram of the field.

3) The rectangular door of a garden shed is 160 centimetres by 60 centimetres.

   Draw an accurate scale diagram of the door using a scale **1 cm = 20 cm**.

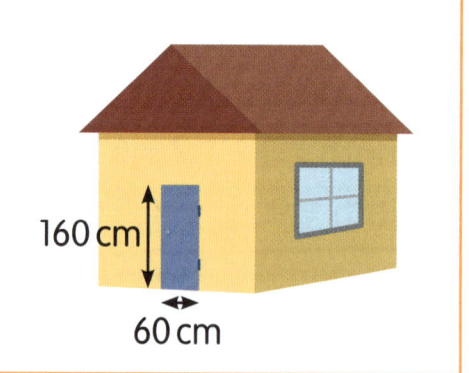

Angles and scale drawings

4) A rectangular plot of land measures 360 metres by 150 metres.

Draw an accurate scale diagram of the land using a scale of **1 cm = 30 m**.

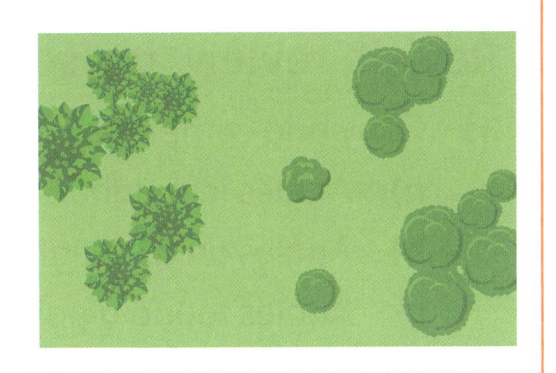

5) The diagram shows the floor of a warehouse.

Draw an accurate scale diagram of the floor using a scale of **1 cm = 2 metres**.

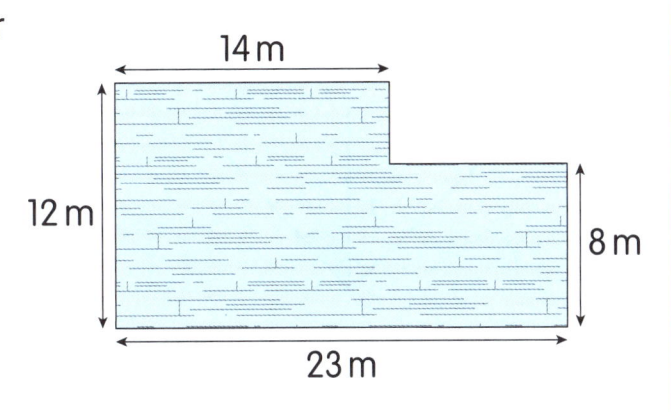

14 m
12 m
8 m
23 m

6) An orienteering course is in the shape of a right-angled triangle.

a) Make an accurate scale diagram of the course using a scale of **1 cm = 200 metres**.

b) Measure the length of the third part of the course on your drawing.

c) Use the scale to work out the length of the third part of the course in real life.

d) How far is the course altogether in real life? Give your answer in kilometres.

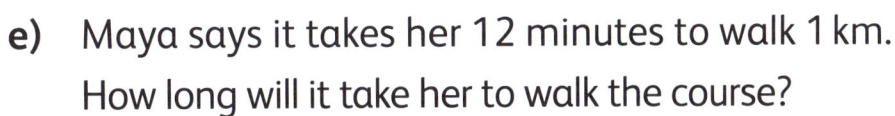

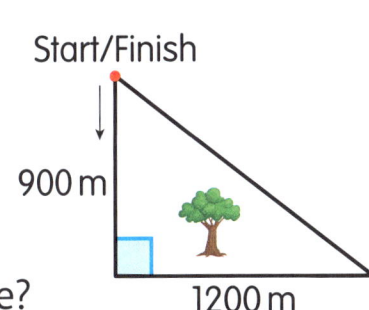

e) Maya says it takes her 12 minutes to walk 1 km. How long will it take her to walk the course?

Start/Finish
900 m
1200 m

155

Chapter 14 More angles

Revisit, review, revise

1) Copy and complete:
   a) Angles in a right angle sum to ____°
   b) Angles on a straight line sum to ____°
   c) Angles round a point sum to ____°
   d) Supplementary angles sum to ____°
   e) Complementary angles sum to ____°

2) Calculate the sizes of the angles marked with letters.

   a) a, 43°

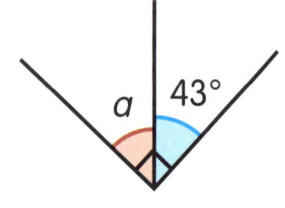

   b) 50°, b

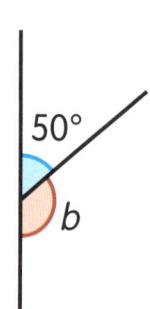

   c) 85°, 120°, c

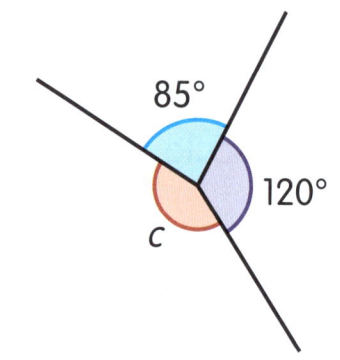

   d) d, 30°

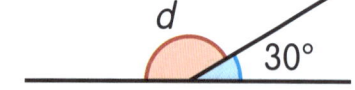

   e) e, 22°

3) What angle would you turn through if you turn:
   a) clockwise from N to SE
   b) anticlockwise from SW to NE?

4) The wind is blowing from the NW.
   It turns through 135° clockwise.
   Where is it blowing from now?

Angles and scale drawings

5) This football pitch has been drawn to a scale of **1 cm = 10 metres**.

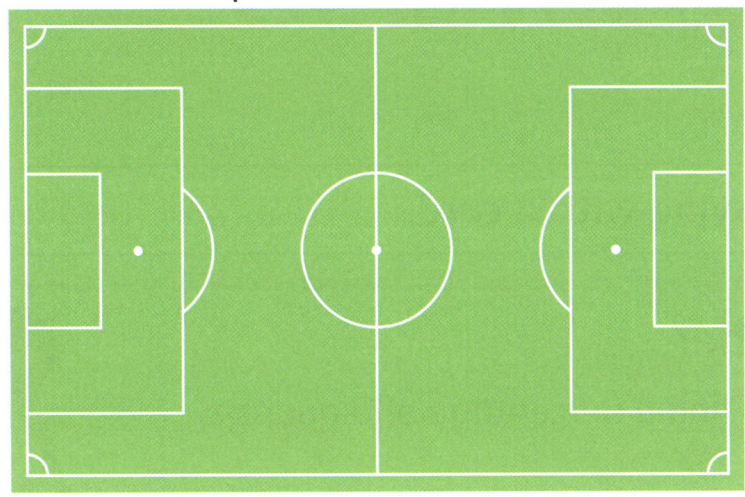

   a) What are the real dimensions of the pitch?
   b) What is the real area of the pitch?

6) This sketch shows the side view of a house.
   a) Make an accurate scale diagram of it using a scale of **1 cm = 100 cm**.
   b) Measure the length of the sloping roof in your diagram in centimetres.
   c) Calculate the real length of the sloping roof.

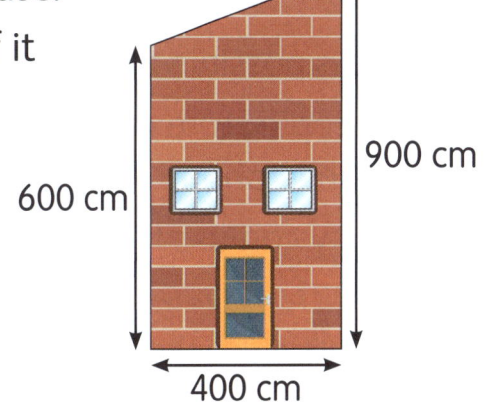

600 cm
900 cm
400 cm

15 Money 2
Cards and credit

Cards

💡 I will learn about paying with a card.

Remember, remember

You already know how to find a percentage of a quantity using fractions.

You also already know how to add and subtract money, either mentally or using the column method.

Often it is possible to pay using a card.

Some people store card information in their mobile phone.

Then they can use their phone to make a payment.

A **debit card** is linked to a bank account.

When you pay with a debit card, the money comes from the account.

If there is not enough money in the account, then the card may not work or you may be fined.

A **prepaid card** is not linked to a bank account.

You put money onto the card in advance.

If there is not enough money on the card, then the card will not work.

Cards and credit

A **credit card** does not have money stored in an account or on the card.
When you pay with a credit card, you are borrowing money.
After a month, you can pay back the money for no extra charge.
If you only pay back some of the money, then you pay **interest**.
The interest is a percentage of the money owed.
If you do not pay back any money, or you are late with a payment, then you may be fined.

Example

Mr McBride uses his **credit card** to pay for a new TV that costs £500.
He does not pay back the £500 at the end of the month.
Mr McBride is charged 24% **interest** on his credit card each year.
How much does he owe for the TV after 1 month?

Answer

24% interest **each year**

So 24% ÷ 12 = 2% interest **each month**

$2\% = \dfrac{2 \div 2}{100 \div 2} = \dfrac{1}{50}$

2% of £500 = $\dfrac{1}{50}$ of £500

$\dfrac{1}{50}$ of £500 = £500 ÷ 50
        = £10

After 1 month, Mr McBride owes £500 + £10 = £510.

If the money is on credit, then the amount owing grows over time.
In the example above, Mr McBride would owe:

£510 after 1 month   £520.20 after 2 months   £530.60 after 3 months
£541.22 after 4 months   £552.04 after 5 months   £563.08 after 6 months.

After 12 months, Mr McBride would owe over £600 for the TV.

Chapter 15 Money 2

There are advantages to using a credit card.

A credit card can be a better way to pay online.

That's because credit card companies usually help if a website takes your money and does not deliver your goods.

When you use credit cards, you build up a **credit score**.

This score is used to decide how likely you are to pay back a loan or a mortgage (money borrowed to buy a house).

The higher your credit score, the more likely you are to be a reliable person to lend money to.

Exercise 1

1) Here is a debit card:

   In your jotter, write down:
   a) the name on the card
   b) the 16-digit number
   c) the date the card is valid from
   d) the date the card will stop working
   e) the 3 digits on the back of the card, next to the signature.

2) Iain has £50 on a prepaid card.

   He buys a T-shirt for £12.50.

   How much is left on his prepaid card?

Cards and credit

3) In your jotter, write **credit card** or **debit card** for each statement.
   Gary goes to a concert.
   a) He pays £45 for his ticket.
      If he pays this back, it will help his credit score.
   b) He pays £20 for a concert T-shirt.
      £20 comes out of his bank account.
   c) He pays £10 for a drink and a snack.
      As long as he pays this back at the end of the month, he will not pay interest.

4) Freya has £986 in her bank account.
   She uses her debit card to pay for her shopping.
   The bill for the shopping is £77.95.
   How much is left in Freya's bank account?

5) Mr Campbell buys a cooker online.
   The price of the cooker is £875.
   He can pay with his debit card or a credit card.
   a) How soon will he pay if he uses his debit card?
   b) In your jotter, write down **two** advantages of Mr Campbell using his credit card.

6) Dev eats in a restaurant and orders:
   - soup £5.35
   - risotto £12.95
   - apple pie £7.50.
   a) What is his bill?
   b) Dev adds 10% for a tip.
      What is the bill after the tip is added?
   c) Dev has £260.53 in his bank account.
      He uses his debit card to pay for the meal.
      After paying, he checks his bank account on his mobile phone.
      How much is left in his bank account?

Chapter 15 Money 2

7) Layla uses her credit card to pay for a holiday.
She is charged 3% interest on her credit card **each month**.
The holiday costs £900.
She does not pay back the £900 at the end of the month.
How much does she owe for the holiday after 1 month?

8) Paul says, 'I only use a debit card because …'
Nish says, 'I only use a credit card because …'
Who do you think finished their sentence with each of these statements? (Paul or Nish?)
   a) I can only spend the money in my bank account and no more.
   b) I may want to get a mortgage to buy a house in the future.
   c) I do a lot of shopping online, and this card gives me more protection.
   d) I don't know if my wages have been paid into my bank account yet.

Now try this!

Use the internet to search the following:
1) 'Credit card example'
   In your jotter, write the names of three credit cards.
2) 'Banks in Scotland'
   In your jotter, write the names of three banks in Scotland.

Which banks are close to where you live?

Next time you pass one of them, go in and see what information you can find out about their debit cards.

Cards and credit

Revisit, review, revise

1) In your jotter, write **debit card**, **prepaid card** or **credit card** for each description.
   a) This card allows you to borrow money.
   b) Money is stored on this card.
   c) This card is linked to a bank account.

2) Beth has £97 left on a prepaid card.
   She buys a train ticket for £15.75 and then a bus ticket for £2.80.
   How much is left on Beth's prepaid card after buying these tickets?

3) Discuss with a partner one **advantage** of using a:
   a) debit card   b) prepaid card   c) credit card.

   In your jotter, write a paragraph describing the advantages of each of these cards.

4) Discuss with a partner one **disadvantage** of using a:
   a) debit card   b) prepaid card   c) credit card.

   In your jotter, write a paragraph describing the disadvantages of each of these cards.

5) Anand uses his credit card to pay for a sofa that is £850.
   He is charged 2% interest on his credit card each month.
   He does not pay back the £850 at the end of the month.
   How much does Anand owe for the sofa after 1 month?

16 Negative numbers
In temperatures and on number lines

Negative temperatures

> 💡 I will learn about negative temperatures.

Temperature measures hot and cold.

One unit for temperature is **degrees Celsius** (°C) (or Centigrade).

Temperature can be measured on a **thermometer**.

The lowest temperature on this thermometer is 0°C.

The highest temperature on this thermometer is 50°C.

There is liquid inside a thermometer.

The liquid expands (gets bigger) as it gets hotter.

The mark on the scale where the liquid stops tells you the temperature.

The temperature on this thermometer is 20°C.

The **lower** the temperature, the **colder** it is.

The **higher** the temperature, the **warmer** it is.

20°C is the temperature of a warm summer's day in Scotland.

Sometimes the temperature is colder than 0°C.

Then the temperature is **negative**.

Negative temperatures are written with −

The temperature on this thermometer is −10°C (negative 10 degrees Celsius).

−10°C was the temperature in Drumnadrochit on 19 January 2023.

It was very cold!

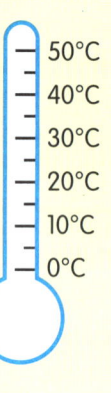

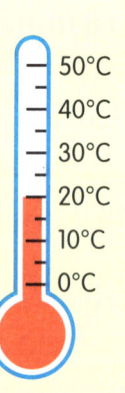

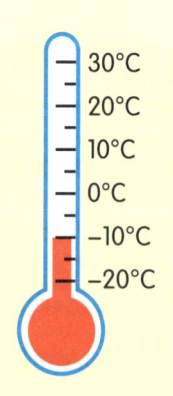

In temperatures and on number lines

Thermometers can have different scales. They also may be shown this way round.

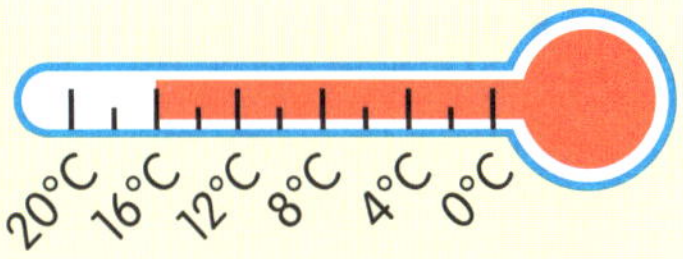

Sometimes, thermometers are digital.

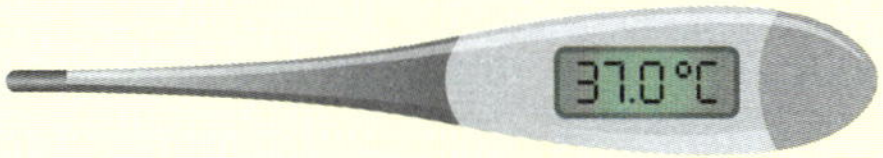

Exercise 1

1) What are the temperatures on these thermometers?

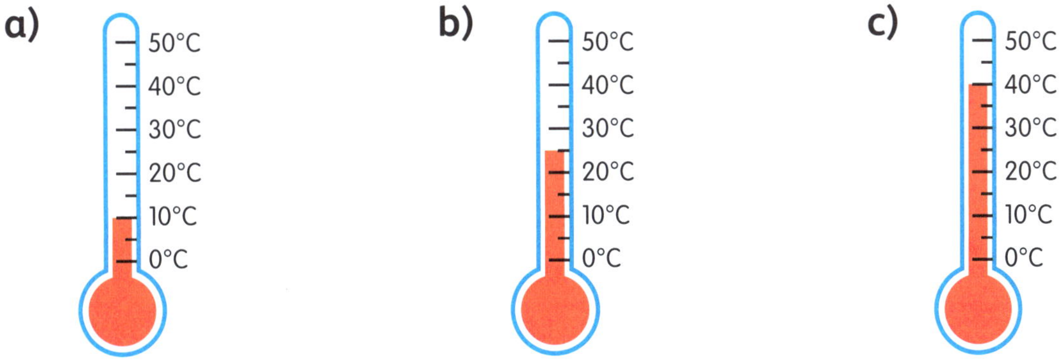

   a) b) c)

2) Which thermometer in question 1 shows the **coldest** temperature? (**a**, **b** or **c**)

3) What are the **missing** numbers **A** and **B** on this thermometer?

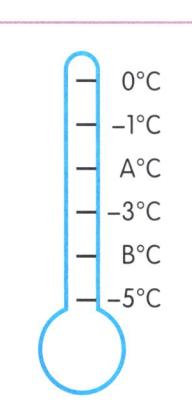

   0°C
   −1°C
   A°C
   −3°C
   B°C
   −5°C

165

Chapter 16 Negative numbers

4) What are the temperatures on these thermometers?

   a) [thermometer showing -3°C]

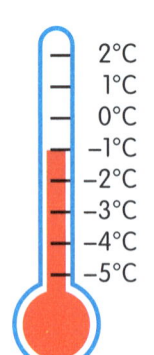

   b) [thermometer showing -2°C]

   c) [thermometer showing -4°C]

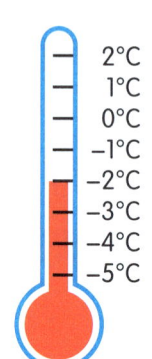

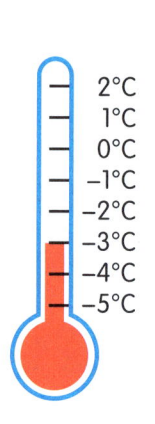

5) Which thermometer in question 4 shows the **lowest** temperature? (**a**, **b** or **c**)

6) What are the temperatures on these thermometers?

   a) [thermometer showing -8°C]

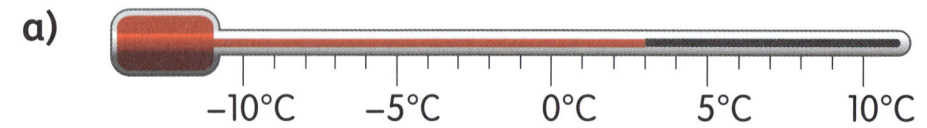

   b) [thermometer showing -4°C]

   c) [thermometer showing -9°C]

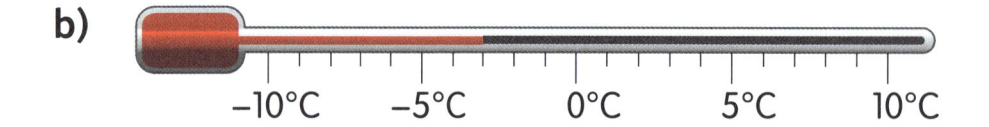

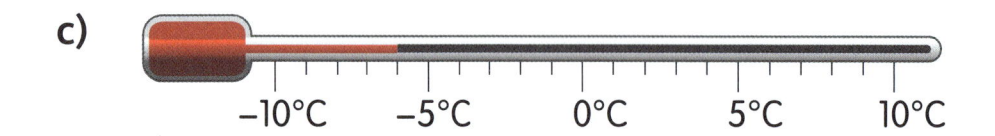

7) This thermometer counts up in steps of 2°C.
   What is the temperature on this thermometer?

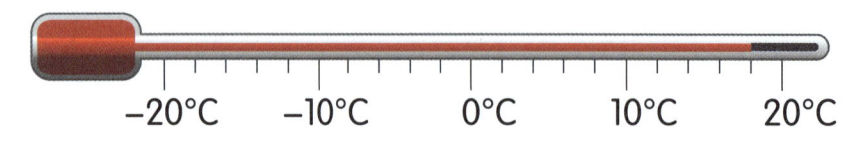

   [thermometer with scale -20°C, -10°C, 0°C, 10°C, 20°C]

In temperatures and on number lines

8) What are the temperatures on these thermometers?

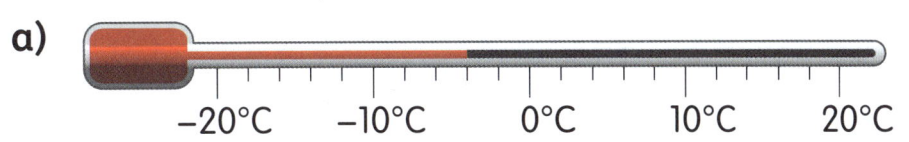

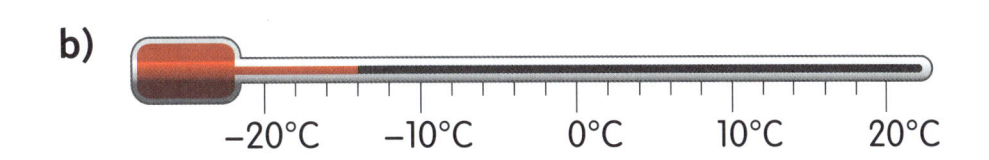

a) −20°C −10°C 0°C 10°C 20°C

b) −20°C −10°C 0°C 10°C 20°C

9) Which thermometer in question 8 shows the **warmer** temperature? (**a** or **b**)

10) a) Copy and complete:
This thermometer counts up in steps of ___ .
b) What is the temperature on this thermometer?

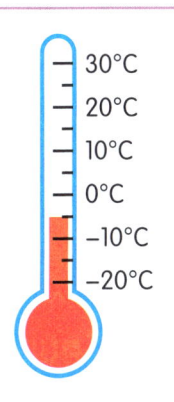

30°C
20°C
10°C
0°C
−10°C
−20°C

11) One winter's day, the temperature was:
−2°C in Perth
−5°C in Aviemore.
Was it **colder** in Perth or in Aviemore?

12) In your jotter, write each set of temperatures in order, from **coldest to hottest**.
a) 0°C, −7°C, 7°C
b) 2°C, −4°C, −1°C, −8°C, 1°C

Chapter 16 Negative numbers

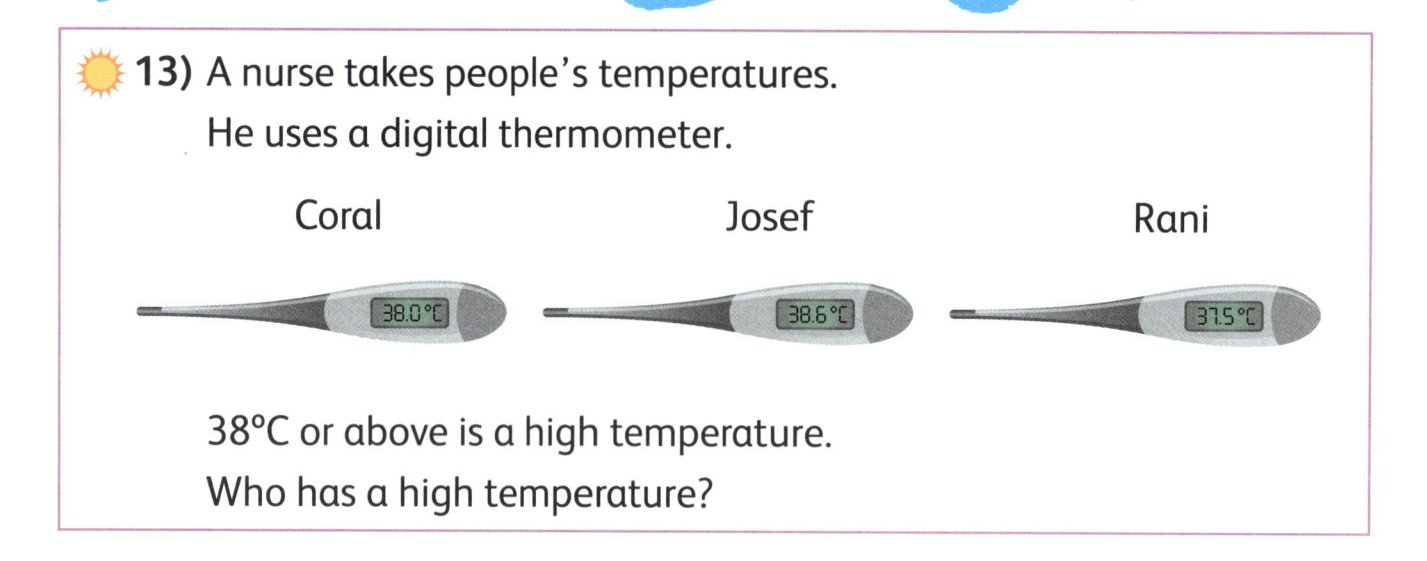

☀ **13)** A nurse takes people's temperatures.
He uses a digital thermometer.

Coral — 38.0°C
Josef — 38.6°C
Rani — 37.5°C

38°C or above is a high temperature.
Who has a high temperature?

Negative numbers on a number line

💡 I will learn about negative numbers on a number line.

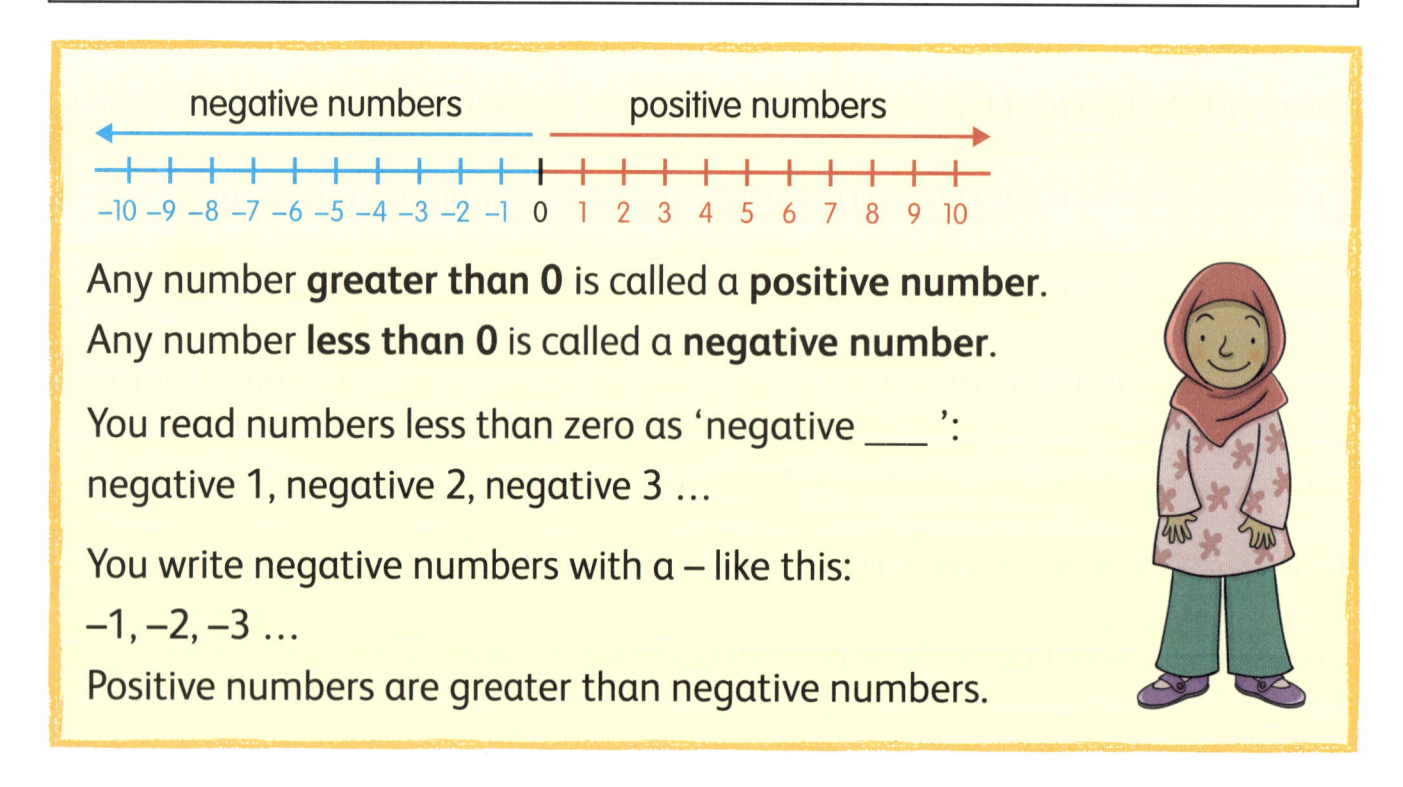

negative numbers ← | → positive numbers
–10 –9 –8 –7 –6 –5 –4 –3 –2 –1 0 1 2 3 4 5 6 7 8 9 10

Any number **greater than 0** is called a **positive number**.
Any number **less than 0** is called a **negative number**.

You read numbers less than zero as 'negative ___':
negative 1, negative 2, negative 3 …

You write negative numbers with a – like this:
–1, –2, –3 …

Positive numbers are greater than negative numbers.

In temperatures and on number lines

Exercise 2

1) Copy this number line:

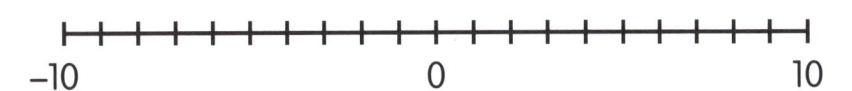

   ```
   |—+—+—+—+—+—+—+—+—+—+—+—+—+—+—+—+—+—+—+—|
   -10              0                    10
   ```

   a) Mark the rest of the numbers on the number line.
   b) On your number line, circle 6 and negative 6.
   c) Which is **bigger**: negative 6 or 6?

2) Danny says:

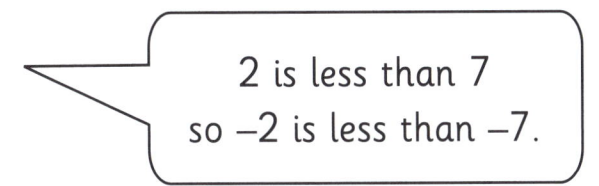

   > 2 is less than 7 so −2 is less than −7.

   Is Danny correct? (Yes or no)
   Use your number line to help you.

3) Use the number line you drew for question **1a** to work out the following:
   a) Is −1 **less** than or **greater** than 1?
   b) Is −3 **less** than or **greater** than −1?
   c) Is 2 **less** than or **greater** than −1?

4) Copy and complete with < or > between each pair of numbers. Use the number line you drew for question **1a** to help.
   a) 4 ___ −5   b) −4 ___ 5   c) −5 ___ −4

Chapter 16 Negative numbers

5) What are the **missing** numbers on these number lines?

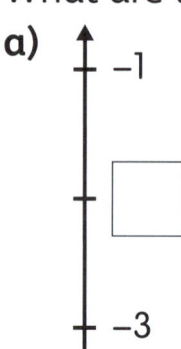

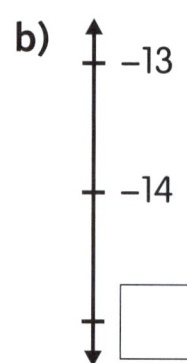

  a) −1, ☐, −3

  b) −13, −14, ☐

6) An office block has a ground floor, floor 0.

   There are 3 floors above floor 0.

   There are 2 floors below, in the basement.

   Copy and complete the diagram showing the floor buttons in the lift.

2
0

7) What are the **missing** numbers on these number lines?

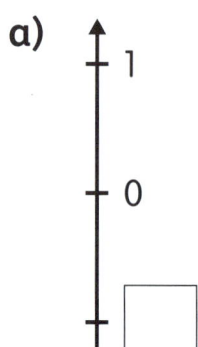

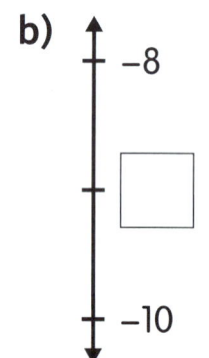

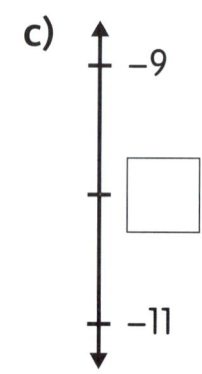

  a) 1, 0, ☐

  b) −8, ☐, −10

  c) −9, ☐, −11

8) In your jotter, write each group of numbers in order. Start with the **smallest**.

  a) 5, −2, 3, −9

  b) −4, −14, 4, 0

9) Here is a list of negative numbers:

   −43, −340, −430, −403, −304

  a) Which is **smallest**?

  b) Which is **biggest**?

In temperatures and on number lines

Now try this!

Make a set of 14 cards:
- 2 cards with an = symbol
- 2 cards with a > symbol
- 2 cards with a < symbol
- 8 number cards, each showing any number from −12 to 1 (You may only use a number once.)

Use the cards to play this game with a partner.

To start

Put all 12 symbol cards (yours and your partner's) face down in a pile.

Spread out the 16 number cards, face down, and shuffle them about.

Take turns to randomly choose a number card until you have 8 each.

Hold your cards in your hand – make sure the other player cannot see them.

To play

1) Player 1 puts down a number card, face up.

2) Turn over the symbol card from the top of the pile and put it next to the number card.

   For example: | −4 | < |

3) Player 2 must put down a card to make the statement true.

   For example: | −4 | < | −1 |

   - If Player 2 makes a true statement, put the two number cards to one side.
   - If Player 2 does not have a number card that can make a true statement, they pick up Player 1's number card.

Chapter 16 Negative numbers

4) Return the symbol card, face down, to the bottom of the pile of symbol cards.

5) Repeat, taking it in turns to put down a card and a symbol for the other player to make a true statement.

The first player to get rid of all their number cards is the winner.

Revisit, review, revise

1) What temperatures do these thermometers show?

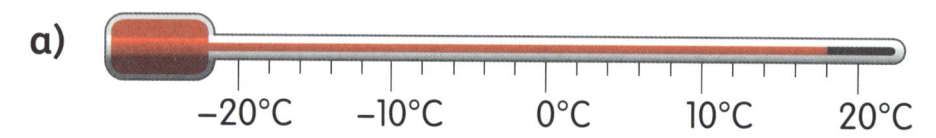

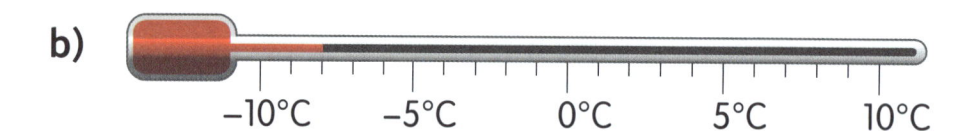

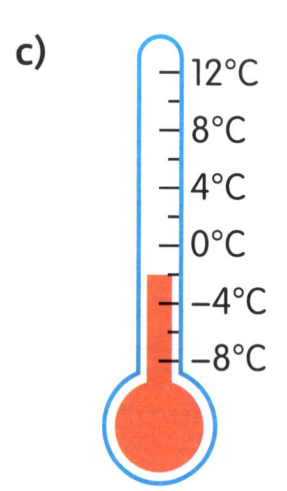

   a) −20°C −10°C 0°C 10°C 20°C

   b) −10°C −5°C 0°C 5°C 10°C

   c) 12°C, 8°C, 4°C, 0°C, −4°C, −8°C

2) Which thermometer in question 1 shows the **coldest** temperature? (a, b or c)

In temperatures and on number lines

3) In your jotter, write these temperatures in order, from **coldest to hottest**.
   a) 9°C, –9°C, –19°C
   b) 3°C, –6°C, –3°C, –4°C, 0°C

4) These two temperatures were recorded at Glencoe mountain resort:

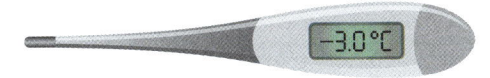

   –3.0°C   1.0°C

   Which temperature is the **coldest**?

5) Copy and complete this number line:

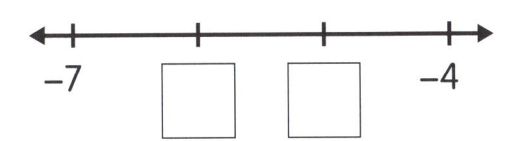

   –7 ☐ ☐ –4

6) Which is **bigger**: negative 8 or 4?

7) Copy and complete with < or > between each pair of numbers:
   a) 3 ___ –13
   b) –3 ___ 13
   c) –13 ___ –3

8) In your jotter, write each set of numbers in order. Start with the **smallest**.
   a) 2, –1, –2, 0
   b) –9, 5, 11, –10, –5, 9

17 Algebra
Forming and solving one-step equations

Function machines

> 💡 I will learn to use a function machine to solve equations.

Add (+), subtract (−), multiply (×) and divide (÷) are all **mathematical operations**.

An **inverse operation** in mathematics is the opposite operation; it undoes the operation.

- The inverse of + 3 is − 3
- The inverse of × 2 is ÷ 2
- The inverse of −7 is + 7
- The inverse of ÷ 5 is × 5

A **function machine** is a machine that takes an **input**, applies **operations** and gives an **output**.

This function machine adds 7 (+ 7):

Input → + 7 → Output

When the **input** is 5:

5 → + 7 → 12

the **output** is 12.

Forming and solving one-step equations

A function machine can have more than one operation.

Input → × 2 → + 3 → Output

For this machine, when the **input** is 11:

11 → × 2 → + 3 → 25

the **output** is 25.

You can find the **input** of a function machine if you know the **output**.

Input → × 2 → + 3 → 37

Work backwards through the function machine using **inverse operations**.

Input ← ÷ 2 ← − 3 ← 37

17   34 ÷ 2 = 17   37 − 3 = 34

In this example, the **input** is 17.

Exercise 1

1) In your jotter, write down the inverse of the operations:
   a) × 9   b) + 12   c) − 11   d) ÷ 4
   e) − 11.5   f) + $\frac{1}{2}$ g) × 0.2   h) ÷ 1000

Chapter 17 Algebra

2) In your jotter, write down the **output** of each function machine:

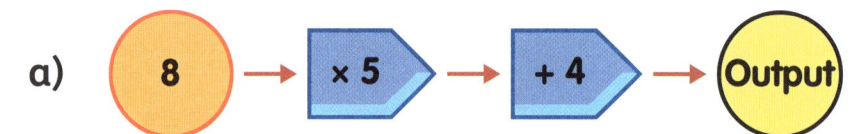

a) 8 → × 5 → + 4 → Output

b) 7 → + 2 → × 3 → Output

c) 9 → − 6 → × 10 → Output

d) 19 → + 5 → ÷ 3 → Output

e) 80 → ÷ 2 → + 1 → Output

f) 10 → × 6 → ÷ 5 → Output

3) Here is a function machine.

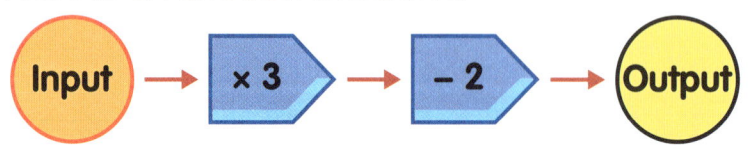

Input → × 3 → − 2 → Output

What is the output when the input is:
a) i) 9   ii) 12   iii) 8.5   iv) 0.8?

b) Copy and complete the function machine that will find the input using inverse operations.

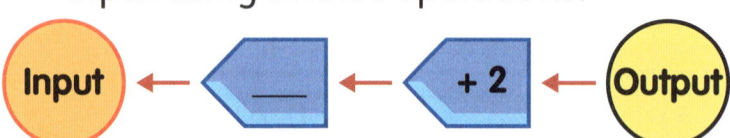

Input ← ___ ← + 2 ← Output

c) What is the input when the output is:
   i) 16   ii) 43   iii) 2.5   iv) 298?

Forming and solving one-step equations

4) Work out the input of these function machines:

a) Input → − 2 → ÷ 7 → 4

b) Input → × 3 → + 5 → 29

c) Input → ÷ 2 → + 1 → 7

d) Input → − 3 → × 13 → 0

Solving equations

💡 I will learn to solve a basic equation.

Remember, remember

An **equation** is a number sentence where one side is equal to the other side.

Finding missing values in an equation is called **solving** an equation.

You can solve an **equation** by writing it as a **function machine** and using **inverse operations**.

Chapter 17 Algebra

Example

Solve the equation $f + 5 = 12$.

The equation $f + 5 = 12$ can be represented in a function machine:

$f \rightarrow \boxed{+5} \rightarrow 12$

The inverse of $+5$ is -5.

$f = 12 - 5$

$ = 7$

Exercise 2

1) $m - 7 = 18$

   a) Copy and complete the function machine representing the equation $m - 7 = 18$.

   b) Copy and complete:

   $m = 18 +$ ____

   $ =$ ____

   $m \rightarrow \boxed{} \rightarrow 18$

2) Draw a function machine to represent each equation. Use it to solve each equation and find the value of x each time.

   a) $x + 9 = 25$ b) $x - 11 = 5$ c) $x + 2 = 19$
   d) $x - 1 = 27$ e) $x + 19 = 103$ f) $x - 54 = 62$

$4m$ means $4 \times m$. $\dfrac{n}{4}$ means $n \div 4$.

Forming and solving one-step equations

3) Solve the equations to find the value of y.

    a) $4y = 12$ y → × 4 → 12

    b) $10y = 450$ y → × 10 → 450

    c) $\dfrac{y}{5} = 9$ y → ÷ 5 → 9

    d) $\dfrac{y}{11} = 7$ y → ÷ 11 → 7

4) Solve the equations:
    a) $2m = 28$ b) $\dfrac{t}{5} = 7$ c) $y + 9 = 23$
    d) $r - 14 = 1$ e) $50y = 350$ f) $m - \dfrac{1}{2} = 9$

5) Grace and Bryan are solving the equation $10 - x = 4$.

Grace
$10 - x = 4$
$x = 4 + 10$
$ = 14$

Bryan
$10 - x = 4$
$x = 6$

    a) Who is correct?
    b) Explain how this equation is **different** to the equations in questions 1 to 4.

6) In your jotter, write down the value of g in each of these equations. Do not use a function machine for these; think carefully about your answers.
    a) $20 - g = 6$ b) $100 - g = 13$ c) $73 - g = 19$

Chapter 17 Algebra

☀️ **7)** Solve the equations.

a) $\frac{1}{2}m = 20$

b) $\frac{p}{5} = 0.4$

c) $17 = m - 11$

d) $0.2b = 20$

e) $14.5 - z = 7.9$

f) $19.2 + p = 105.4$

Forming equations

💡 I will learn to form an equation.

Remember, remember

$5m$ means $5 \times m$.

$\frac{m}{3}$ means $m \div 3$.

Forming an **equation** can help you to solve a mathematical problem.

When forming an equation, use a **letter** to represent the **unknown number**.

Example

Write an equation to represent the function machine:

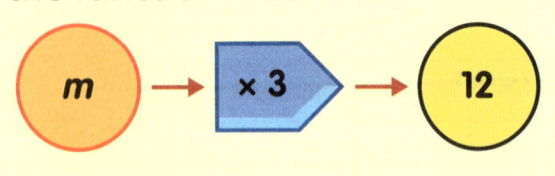

$m \rightarrow \times 3 \rightarrow 12$

$3m = 12$

Example

These scales are balanced:

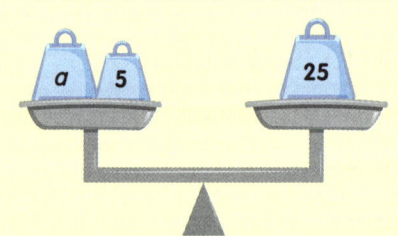

a, 5 | 25

Write an equation to represent the scales.

$a + 5 = 25$

Forming and solving one-step equations

Exercise 3

1) a) In your jotter, write an equation to represent each function machine.

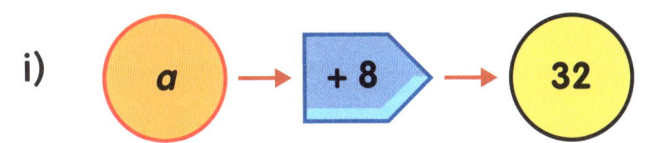

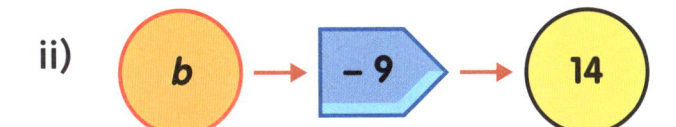

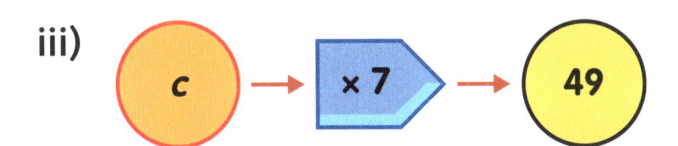

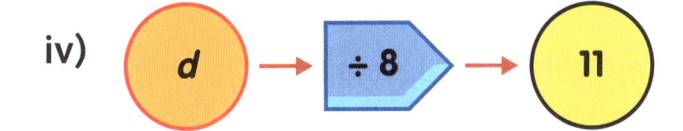

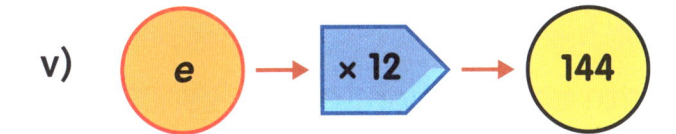

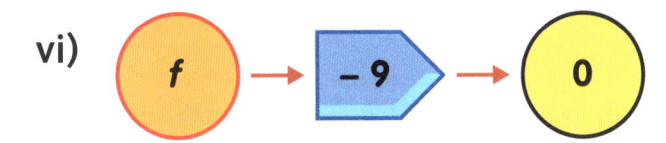

   i) $a \to +8 \to 32$

   ii) $b \to -9 \to 14$

   iii) $c \to \times 7 \to 49$

   iv) $d \to \div 8 \to 11$

   v) $e \to \times 12 \to 144$

   vi) $f \to -9 \to 0$

   b) Solve each of the equations in part **a**.

2) a) In your jotter, write an equation to represent each balance.

   i) $a + 6 = 13$

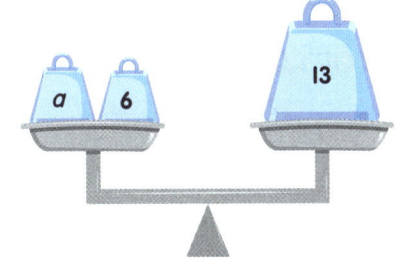

   ii) $b + 7 = 22$

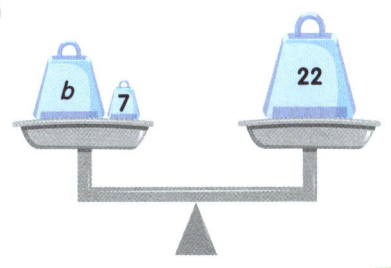

Chapter 17 Algebra

iii) [balance: 2 weights labelled c, c = weight labelled 20]

iv) [balance: 4 weights labelled d = weight labelled 36]

v) [balance: 3 weights labelled e = weight labelled 120]

vi) [balance: weight f + 25 = 45]

b) Solve each of the equations in part a.

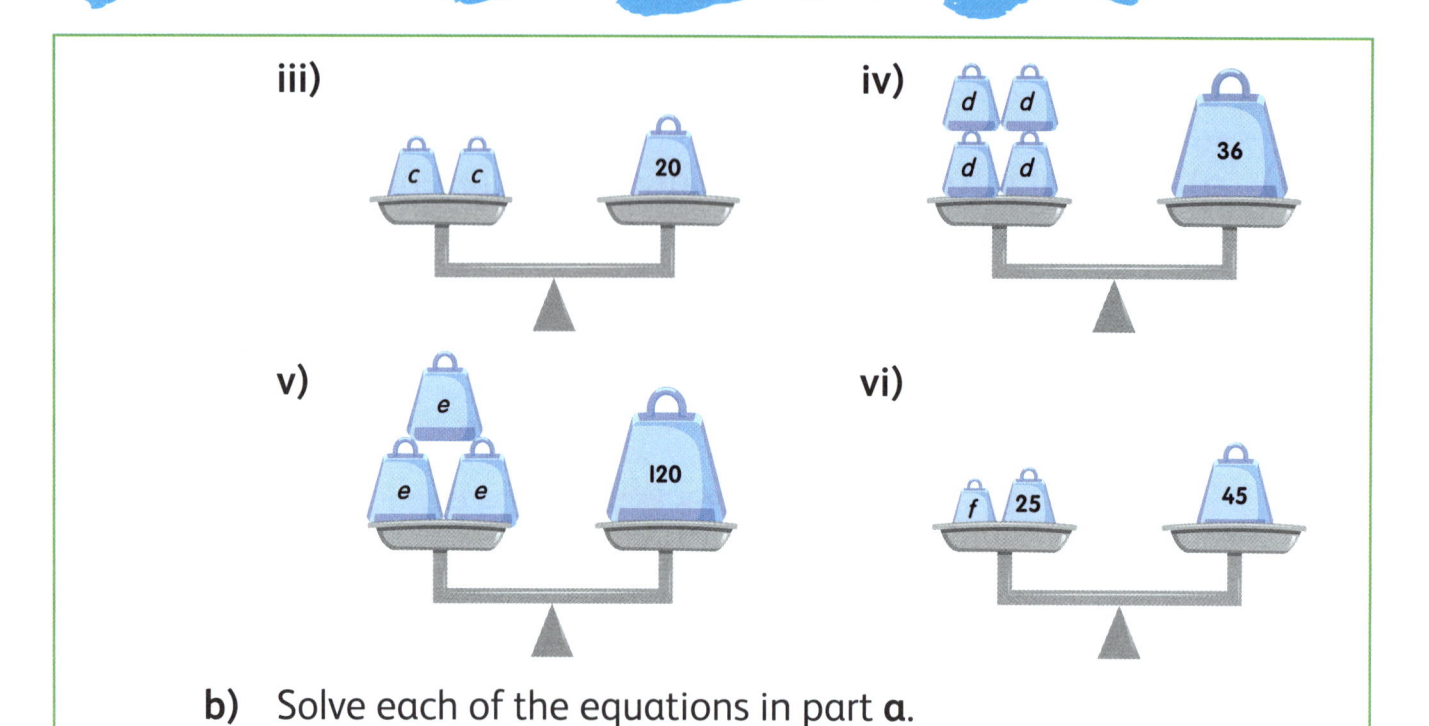

3) The combined age of Omar and Jen is 63.
Omar is 25.
a) Use j to represent Jen's age.
In your jotter, write an equation to represent the problem.
b) Solve the equation to work out Jen's age.

4) The total cost for 4 adults to fly to Prague is £1000.
a) Use p to represent the price of one adult ticket.
In your jotter, write an equation to represent the problem.
b) Solve the equation to work out the price of one adult ticket.

5) 240 grams of soup are served from a pot.
965 grams of soup are left in the pot.
In your jotter, write an equation and solve it to work out how much soup was in the pot originally.
(Choose a letter to represent the amount of soup in the pot.)

Forming and solving one-step equations

6) Josh shares his sweets equally between 4 people.

Each person receives 12 sweets.

In your jotter, write an equation and solve it to work out how many sweets Josh has to share.

7) When some balloons are shared equally, Kelly, Fran and Ali each get 16 balloons.

In your jotter, write an equation and solve it to work out how many balloons there are **altogether**.

Now try this!

I think of a number, divide it by 4 and get 7.

This can be written as an equation:

$\frac{x}{4} = 7$

What number was I thinking of?

Work in pairs.
- One person designs an 'I think of a number …' problem like this one.
- The other person writes and solves an equation to find the number.

Revisit, review, revise

1) What is the output of this function machine?

$56 \rightarrow \div 8 \rightarrow -3 \rightarrow$ Output

2) What is the input of this function machine?

Input $\rightarrow \times 3 \rightarrow +5 \rightarrow 29$

Chapter 17 Algebra

3) Solve the equations:

   a) $x + 3 = 11$
   b) $x - 5 = 5$
   c) $x + 15 = 25$
   d) $x - 7 = 0$
   e) $2x = 22$
   f) $\dfrac{x}{5} = 12$

4) In your jotter, write and solve an equation to represent each of these function machines:

   a) $t \rightarrow \times 9 \rightarrow 72$

   b) $z \rightarrow \div 10 \rightarrow 54$

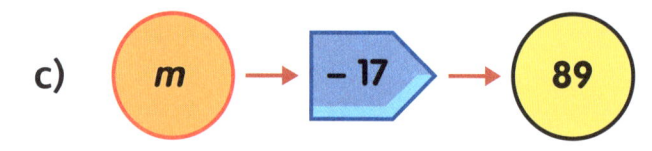

   c) $m \rightarrow -17 \rightarrow 89$

5) In your jotter, write and solve an equation to represent the set of scales.

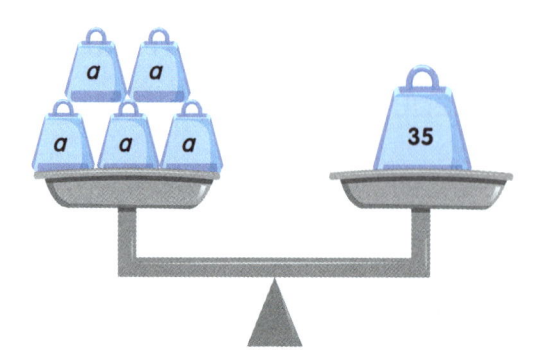

   (Scales: 5 weights of a balance a weight of 35)

6) Two dogs, Dinkie and Jinkie, have a combined mass of 55 kg. Dinkie's mass is 16 kg.

   a) Use j to represent Jinkie's mass.
      In your jotter, write an equation to represent the problem.
   b) Solve the equation to work out Jinkie's mass.

18 More fractions, decimals and percentages

Changing between common fractions, decimals and percentages

Fractions, decimals and percentages

> 💡 I will learn how to change between simple and common fractions, decimals and percentages.

Remember, remember

$1\% = \frac{1}{100}$ = 1 part out of 100 **equal parts**.

One hundredth can be written as a decimal:

$\frac{1}{100} =$

Ones	.	tenths	hundredths
0	.	0	1

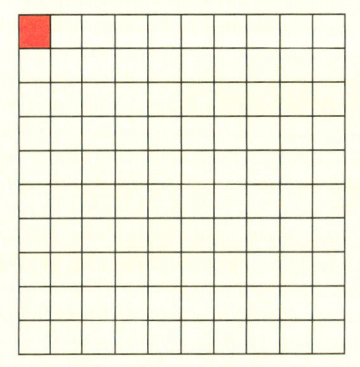

You already know how to find **equivalent fractions** with a denominator of 100 by **multiplying the numerator and denominator** by the same number.

For example:

$\frac{7}{50} \begin{array}{c}\times 2 \\ \times 2\end{array} = \frac{14}{100}$ $\frac{9}{25} \begin{array}{c}\times 4 \\ \times 4\end{array} = \frac{36}{100}$ $\frac{3}{20} \begin{array}{c}\times 5 \\ \times 5\end{array} = \frac{15}{100}$

You also already know that finding $\frac{1}{100}$ (one hundredth) is the same as **dividing by 100** and that when you divide by 100, digits move **2 places right**.

For example:

$\frac{14}{100} = 14 \div 100 =$

Tens	Ones	.	tenths	hundredths
1	4	.		
	0	.	1	4

185

Chapter 18 More fractions, decimals and percentages

This square is divided into 100 equal parts.
29 parts out of **100 equal parts** are orange.
This is 29% or $\frac{29}{100}$

$\frac{29}{100} = 29 \div 100 = 0.29$

So, 29% = $\frac{29}{100}$ = 0.29 of the square is orange.

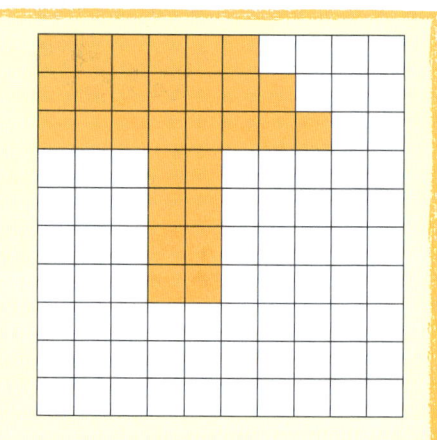

- You can write a percentage as a fraction or a decimal.
- You can write a fraction as a percentage or a decimal.
- You can write a decimal as a fraction or a percentage.

Exercise 1

1) This square is divided into 100 equal parts.
   a) What **percentage** of the large square is green?
   b) In your jotter, write the percentage as a **decimal**.
   c) Write the **fraction** of the large square that is coloured green.

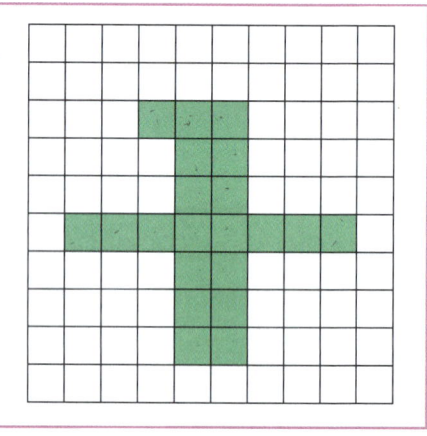

2) Copy and complete each equivalent fraction, decimal and percentage:
   a) 27% = $\frac{\square}{100}$ = 0.$\square\square$
   b) 53% = $\frac{\square}{\square}$ = 0.$\square\square$
   c) $\square$% = $\frac{61}{100}$ = 0.$\square\square$
   d) $\square$% = $\frac{\square}{100}$ = 0.79

3) In your jotter, write each percentage as a fraction.
   a) 87%   b) 33%   c) 51%   d) 19%

Changing between common fractions, decimals and percentages

4) In your jotter, write each percentage in question 3 as a decimal.

5) In your jotter, write each fraction as a percentage.

   a) $\dfrac{17}{100}$ b) $\dfrac{93}{100}$ c) $\dfrac{49}{100}$ d) $\dfrac{3}{100}$

6) In your jotter, write each fraction in question 5 as a decimal.

7) In your jotter, write each decimal as a percentage.

   a) 0.13   b) 0.71   c) 0.97   d) 0.39

8) In your jotter, write each decimal in question 7 as a fraction.

9) Copy and complete this table of fractions, decimals and percentages:

	Fraction	Decimal	Percentage
a)		0.57	57%
b)	$\dfrac{23}{100}$		
c)			99%
d)		0.07	

10) In your jotter, write each of these fractions with a denominator of 100:

    a) $\dfrac{1}{10}$ b) $\dfrac{1}{20}$ c) $\dfrac{1}{2}$ d) $\dfrac{1}{4}$ e) $\dfrac{3}{4}$

Chapter 18 More fractions, decimals and percentages

☀ **11)** Use your answer to question 10 to copy and complete this table showing the decimal and percentage equivalents of common fractions:

	Fraction	Decimal	Percentage
a)	$\frac{1}{10}$		
b)	$\frac{1}{20}$		
c)	$\frac{1}{2}$		
d)	$\frac{1}{4}$		
e)	$\frac{3}{4}$		

Solving fraction, decimal and percentage problems

💡 I will learn to solve fraction, decimal and percentage problems.

Sometimes you have to decide whether to work with a fraction, decimal or percentage when solving a problem.

Exercise 2

1) Here are a fraction, a percentage and a decimal:

$$\frac{1}{10} \quad 50\% \quad 0.25$$

a) In your jotter, write this list so that they are all percentages.

b) Use your answer to part **a** to write the original list in order, from **smallest** to **largest**.

Changing between common fractions, decimals and percentages

2) Here are a percentage, a decimal and a fraction:

   29%   0.21 $\frac{1}{4}$

   a) In your jotter, write this list so that they are all fractions with a denominator of 100.
   b) Use your answer to part **a** to write the original list in order, from **largest** to **smallest**.

3) Here are a decimal, a fraction and a percentage:

   0.09 $\frac{1}{100}$ 5%

   a) In your jotter, write this list so that they are all decimals.
   b) Use your answer to part **a** to write the original list in order, from **largest** to **smallest**.

4) Here are a fraction, a decimal and a percentage:

   $\frac{3}{4}$ 0.70   72%

   In your jotter, write the list in order from **smallest** to **largest**. First, write them all as percentages, decimals or fractions with denominator 100. You choose!

5) Jarek splits a square into 100 equal smaller squares.
   He colours 0.3 of the large square yellow.
   a) What fraction is this?
   b) Jarek says he has coloured 3% yellow.
      Is he correct? (Yes or no)
   c) If you answered no to part **b**, write in your jotter the correct percentage of the square that is coloured yellow.

Chapter 18 More fractions, decimals and percentages

6) A $\frac{1}{5}$ of £60   B 50% of £40   C 0.75 of £20   D 20% of £50

Which of these calculations gives the **most** money?

Show your working.

7) 40% of the animals on a farm are sheep.

$\frac{1}{2}$ of the animals on the farm are cows.

The rest are chickens.

What percentage are chickens?

Now try this!

Match the fractions, decimals and percentages in the grid.

25%	0.5	0.8	0.3
20%	$\frac{1}{2}$	70%	80%
	$\frac{2}{5}$	0.7	
30%	10%	$\frac{1}{4}$	

Make your own grid showing matching fractions, decimals and percentages.

Swap your grid with a partner.

Work out their matches.

Changing between common fractions, decimals and percentages

Revisit, review, revise

1) In your jotter, write:
   a) 0.09 as a fraction and a percentage
   b) 37% as a fraction and a decimal
   c) $\frac{59}{100}$ as a decimal and a percentage.

2) In your jotter, write:
   a) 0.25 as a fraction in its **simplest form** and a percentage
   b) $\frac{1}{2}$ as a decimal and a percentage
   c) 10% as a fraction in its **simplest form** and a decimal.

3) Which is smaller:
   a) 0.41 or 40%
   b) 71% or $\frac{7}{10}$?

   Show your working.

4) In your jotter, write these lists in order from **smallest** to **largest**.
   (First write them all as percentages, decimals or fractions with denominator 100.)
   a) $\frac{1}{2}$, 0.51, 49%
   b) 11%, 0.12, $\frac{1}{10}$
   c) 0.34, $\frac{3}{4}$, 43%

5) 40% of entertainers in a show are jugglers.
   $\frac{1}{4}$ are dancers.

   Are there more jugglers or dancers in the show?
   Show your working.

6) Which is more:
   a) 10% of £30 or $\frac{1}{3}$ of £6
   b) 0.5 of £18 or $\frac{1}{4}$ of £28
   c) 75% of £20 or $\frac{2}{5}$ of £30?

19 Measurement
Length, volume, capacity and mass

Length

> 💡 I will learn to measure, estimate and convert between units of length.

Remember, remember

Length can be measured in **kilometres**, **metres**, **centimetres** and **millimetres**.

$$1\,km = 1000\,m$$
$$1\,m = 100\,cm$$
$$1\,cm = 10\,mm$$

To convert between units of length, multiply or divide:

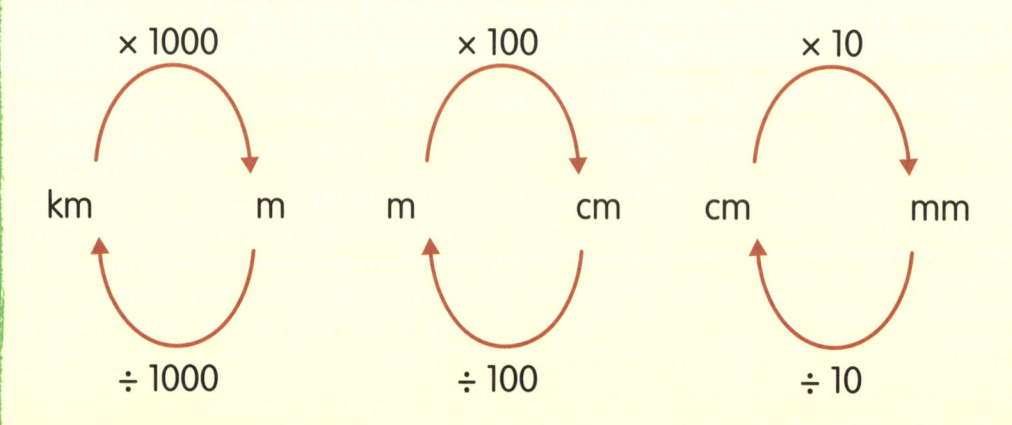

×1000	×100	×10
km → m	m → cm	cm → mm
÷1000	÷100	÷10

To compare lengths, write them all in the **same units** first.

An **estimate** of the length of a line is the **approximate** length.

Length, volume, capacity and mass

km, m, cm and mm are **metric** units of length.
These units are usually used in Europe.
In the United Kingdom, we sometimes use **imperial** units:
1 mile ≈ 1.6 km
1 foot ≈ 30 cm
1 inch ≈ 2.5 cm.

≈ means 'is approximately equal to'

To convert between **metric** and **imperial** units of length, multiply or divide.

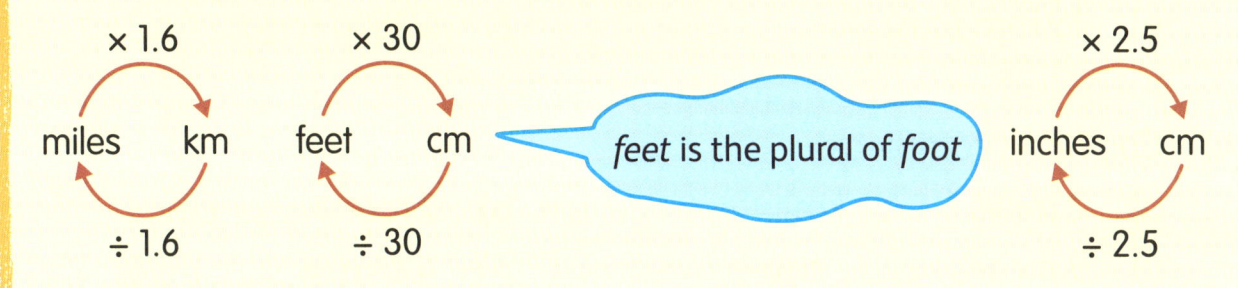

× 1.6   miles ⇄ km   ÷ 1.6

× 30   feet ⇄ cm   ÷ 30

feet is the plural of *foot*

× 2.5   inches ⇄ cm   ÷ 2.5

Example
Convert 4 feet into **metres**.
1 foot ≈ 30 cm
4 feet ≈ 4 × 30 cm = 120 cm = 1.2 m

Example
Convert 15 cm into **inches**.
1 inch ≈ 2.5 cm
15 cm ≈ 15 ÷ 2.5 inches = 6 inches

Exercise 1

1) a) Estimate the length of these lines in centimetres:
   i) _____
   ii) _____
   b) Measure the lines and write down the lengths in your jotter in:
   i) cm
   ii) mm.

193

Chapter 19 Measurement

2) a) In your jotter, draw a line 10.7 cm long.
    b) Then, draw a line 69 mm long.
    c) Which line is longer?

3) Convert these lengths to the units in brackets:
   a) 15 cm (mm)
   b) 4.5 m (cm)
   c) 9.2 km (m)
   d) 5600 m (km)
   e) 19 mm (cm)
   f) 526 m (cm)

4) Copy and complete:
   a) 2 miles ≈ ___ km
   b) 7 feet ≈ ___ cm
   c) 9 inches ≈ ___ cm
   d) 4.8 km ≈ ___ miles
   e) 180 cm ≈ ___ feet
   f) 20 cm ≈ ___ inches

5) A marathon is a race that is about 26 miles long.
   How far is this in kilometres?
   You may use a calculator.

6) Marika swims 32 lengths of a 25-metre swimming pool.
   a) How far does she swim in metres?
   b) How far is this in kilometres?
   c) How far is this in miles?

7) Ruben is 4 feet tall.
   Ami is 1.35 metres tall.
   a) How tall is Ruben in cm?
   b) Who is taller and by how many cm?

Length, volume, capacity and mass

8) Write these lengths in order from **shortest** to **longest**:

| 95 cm | 3 feet | 0.92 m | 850 mm |

(Hint: Convert all the lengths into cm first.)

Now try this!

To convert from km to cm you could × 1000 and then × 100.

If you wanted to do this in one step, what could you multiply by?

Copy and complete these diagrams:

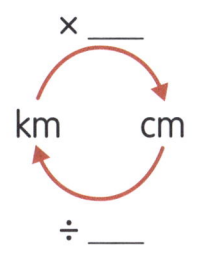

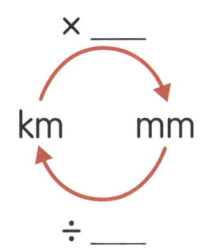

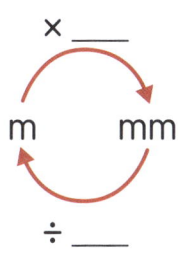

×____   ×____   ×____
km ⟶ cm   km ⟶ mm   m ⟶ mm
÷____   ÷____   ÷____

Volume and capacity

💡 I will learn to measure, estimate and convert between units of volume and capacity.

Remember, remember

Volume is a measurement of how much space is taken up by a 3-dimensional (3D) shape.

Volume can be measured in **cubic centimetres** (cm³) or **cubic metres** (m³).

Chapter 19 Measurement

Volume of a cuboid = **length × width × height**

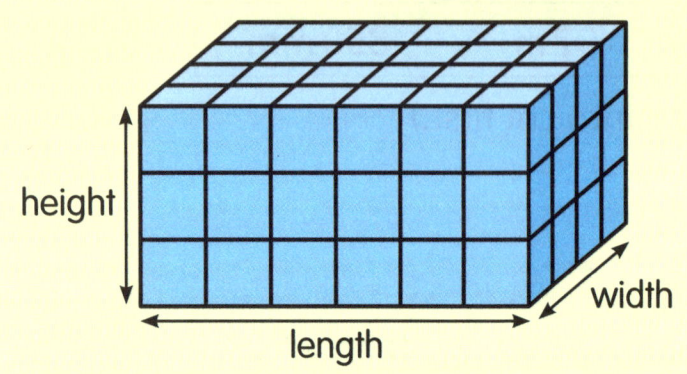

Capacity is another word for volume.

It is often used to describe liquids.

Capacity is usually measured in **litres (l)** or **millilitres (ml)**.

1 litre = 1000 millilitres

Capacity can also be measured in cm³ or m³.

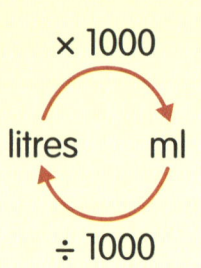

It is easy to convert between millilitres and cm³:

1 millilitre = 1 cm³

Litres (l), millilitres (ml), cm³ and m³ are **metric** units.

These units are usually used in Europe.

In the United Kingdom, we sometimes use **imperial** units:

1 pint ≈ 570 millilitres

1 gallon ≈ 4.5 litres

To convert between **metric** and **imperial** units of capacity, multiply or divide.

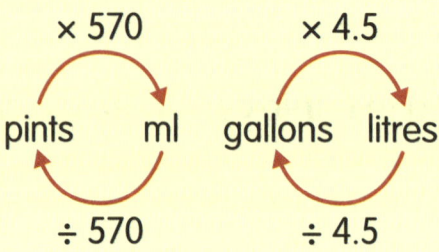

Length, volume, capacity and mass

> **Example**
> **Convert** 5 litres into cm³.
> 5 litres = 5000 ml = 5000 cm³

> **Example**
> **Convert** 900 litres into gallons.
> 900 ÷ 4.5 ≈ 200 gallons

Exercise 2

1) Put these shapes in order, starting with the one which has the **smallest** volume:

   | jug | teacup | bucket | swimming pool | bath |

2) a) In your jotter, write down the volume of liquid (in millilitres) in this jar of juice.
   b) How many litres is this?
   c) How many cm³ is this?

3) a) Calculate the volume of these cuboids in cm³:
   i) 6 cm, 4 cm, 5 cm
   ii) 2 cm, 10 cm, 12 cm

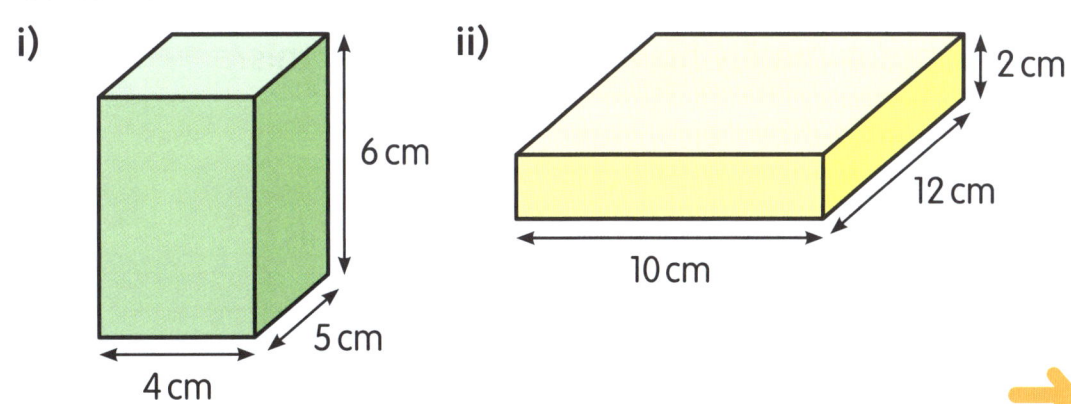

Chapter 19 Measurement

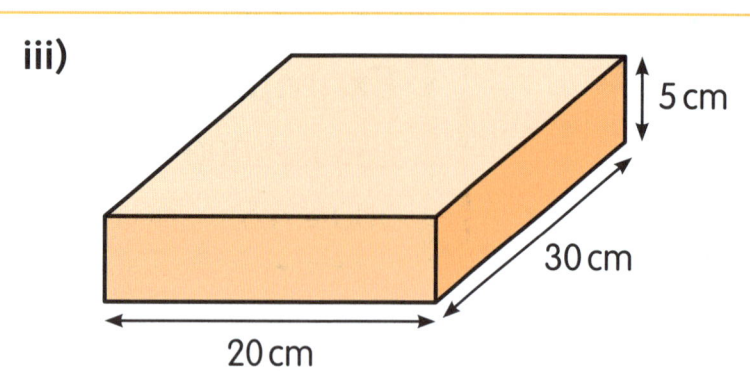

iii)

5 cm
30 cm
20 cm

b) Convert the volumes of the cuboids into:
i) millilitres
ii) litres.

4) Copy and complete (you may use a calculator):
a) 12 pints ≈ _____ millilitres
b) 30 gallons ≈ _____ litres
c) 3990 millilitres ≈ _____ pints
d) 2700 litres ≈ _____ gallons.

5) Copy and complete (you may use a calculator):
a) 3 pints ≈ _____ millilitres = _____ litres
b) 2 gallons ≈ _____ litres = _____ millilitres
c) 11 pints ≈ _____ millilitres = _____ litres
d) 14.2 gallons ≈ _____ litres = _____ millilitres.

6) Layla drinks $\frac{1}{2}$ a pint of water.
Approximately how many millilitres is this?

7) A car's petrol tank holds 63 litres.
Approximately how many gallons is this?

8) A bottle contains 2 litres of milk.
Approximately how many pints is this?
Round your answer to 1 decimal place.

Length, volume, capacity and mass

> **Now try this!**
> Work in a pair or group.
> In your jotter, write a list of all the liquids you know which are measured in:
> a) pints b) litres c) gallons.

Mass

💡 I will learn to estimate mass and convert between units of mass.

Remember, remember

The **mass** of an object is how heavy it is.
Mass can be measured in **grams (g)** and **kilograms (kg)**.

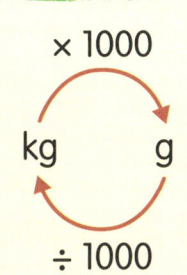

$$1\,kg = 1000\,g$$

× 1000
kg ⇄ g
÷ 1000

Grams (g) and kilograms (kg) are **metric** units.
These units are usually used in Europe.
In the United Kingdom, we sometimes use **imperial** units.

$$1\text{ stone} \approx 6.4\,kg$$
$$1\text{ pound} \approx 454\,g$$
$$1\text{ ounce} \approx 28\,g$$

Stone is sometimes written **st**.
Pound is sometimes written **lb**.
Ounce is sometimes written **oz**.

199

Chapter 19 Measurement

To convert between metric and imperial units of mass, multiply or divide.

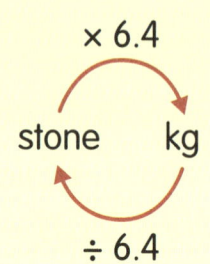

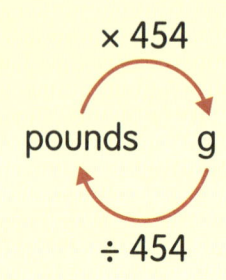

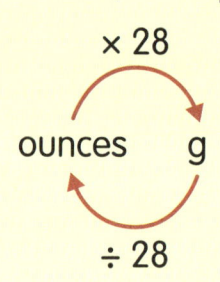

× 6.4   stone ⇌ kg   ÷ 6.4

× 454   pounds ⇌ g   ÷ 454

× 28   ounces ⇌ g   ÷ 28

Exercise 3

1) List the following fruit in order, from **lightest** to **heaviest**:

| apple | pineapple | plum | watermelon | grape |

2) Convert these masses into grams:
   a) 3 kg
   b) $\frac{1}{2}$ kg
   c) 16.5 kg
   d) 1 kg 200 g
   e) 5 kg 15 g
   f) $2\frac{3}{4}$ kg
   g) 3.05 kg
   h) 0.9 kg
   i) 102.7 kg

3) Convert these masses into kilograms:
   a) 3000 g
   b) 12 500 g
   c) 250 g
   d) 6400 g
   e) 5030 g
   f) 1050 g

4) Copy and complete (you may use a calculator):
   a) 3 st ≈ ___ kg
   b) 5 lbs ≈ ___ g
   c) 15 oz ≈ ___ g
   d) 128 kg ≈ ___ st
   e) 4086 g ≈ ___ lb
   f) 196 oz ≈ ___ g

Length, volume, capacity and mass

5) A recipe for a cake is given in ounces:

Convert the masses into grams.

Recipe
- 3 eggs
- 6 oz butter
- 7 oz sugar
- 5.5 oz flour

6) Copy and complete:

$\frac{1}{2}$ stone ≈ ____ kg = ____ g

7) In your jotter, write these masses in order from **heaviest** to **lightest**:

1 oz, 1 g, 1 kg, 1 st, 1 lb

8) Which is **lightest**: five 2 kg bags of flour or one 10 st bag of potatoes?

Revisit, review, revise

1) Copy and complete:
   a) 14 cm = ____ mm
   b) 230 m = ____ km
   c) 45 cm = ____ m

2) Copy and complete:
   a) 3 miles ≈ ____ km
   b) 9 feet ≈ ____ cm
   c) 4 inches ≈ ____ cm
   d) 32 km ≈ ____ miles
   e) 210 cm ≈ ____ feet
   f) 50 cm ≈ ____ inches

1 mile ≈ 1.6 km
1 foot ≈ 30 cm
1 inch ≈ 2.5 cm

Chapter 19 Measurement

3) Work out the volume of this cuboid in:
   a) cm³
   b) ml
   c) litres.

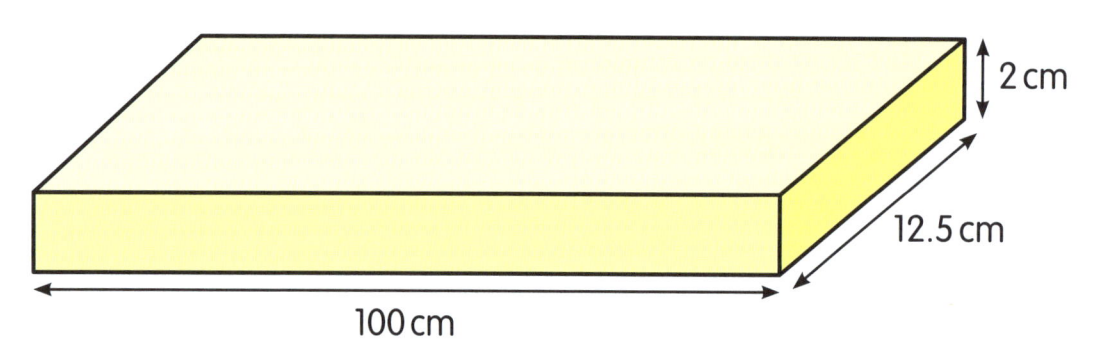

   2 cm
   12.5 cm
   100 cm

4) Copy and complete (you may use a calculator):
   a) 7 pints ≈ ____ ml = ____ litres
   b) 19 gallons ≈ ____ litres
   c) 2.25 litres ≈ ____ gallon
   d) 1.14 litres = ____ millilitres ≈ ____ pints

   1 pint ≈ 570 millilitres
   1 gallon ≈ 4.5 litres

5) Copy and complete:
   a) 7.2 kg = ____ g
   b) 195 g = ____ kg

6) A car has a mass of 1500 kg.
   What is the weight in stone? Round the answer to the nearest whole number.

7) Put these in order from **heaviest** to **lightest**:
   18 lbs, 2 st, 10 kg.

8) A recipe for pancakes needs 8 oz of flour.
   What is the mass in grams?

   1 ounce ≈ 28 g
   1 stone ≈ 6.4 kg
   1 pound ≈ 454 g

20 Numbers and sequences
Identifying number types and patterns in sequences

Types of number

> 💡 I will learn to recognise types of number.

Remember, remember

Numbers in times tables are called **multiples**.

(Non-zero) multiples of 10 are 10, 20, 30, 40, …

Numbers that divide exactly into another number are called **factors**.

The factors of 10 are 1, 2, 5 and 10.

Square numbers are found by multiplying a number by itself:

$1 \times 1 = 1$ $2 \times 2 = 4$ $3 \times 3 = 9$ $4 \times 4 = 16$ $5 \times 5 = 25$

Triangular numbers are found by adding whole numbers:

1     $1 + 2 = 3$ $1 + 2 + 3 = 6$ $1 + 2 + 3 + 4 = 10$ $1 + 2 + 3 + 4 + 5 = 15$

A **Fibonacci sequence** can be found by starting with the terms 1, 1. You find each following term by **adding** the previous two terms:

1, 1, 2, 3, 5, 8, …

Numbers in the sequence are called **Fibonacci numbers**.

Chapter 20 Numbers and sequences

Exercise 1

1) In your jotter, write down the first five (non-zero) multiples of 13.

2) In your jotter, write down **all** the factors of 30.

3) In your jotter, write down the first 10 numbers in the Fibonacci sequence that begins 1, 1, 2, …

4) Choose all the numbers from the cloud which are:
   a) multiples of 2
   b) factors of 20
   c) square numbers
   d) triangular numbers
   e) Fibonacci numbers.

   1   2   3
   5   10   16   20   25

5) a) Copy the Venn diagram. Add the numbers 1 to 20 to your diagram. The first few have been done for you.

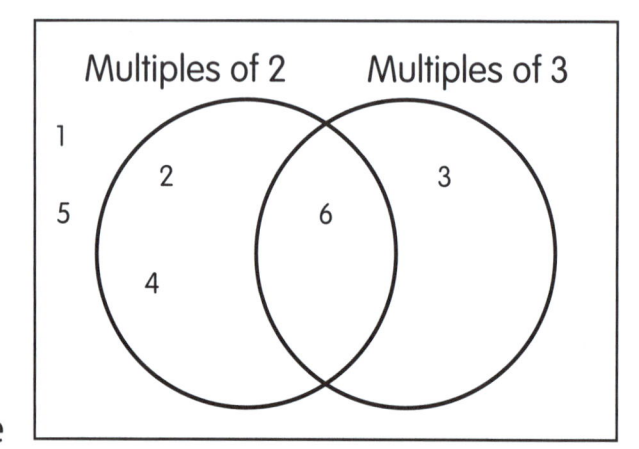

   b) What do you notice about the numbers in the overlapping section of the Venn diagram? Explain why this is.

   Multiples of 2   Multiples of 3
   1
   5   2   3
          6
          4

Identifying number types and patterns in sequences

6) Which numbers are multiples of 5 **and** factors of 30?

7) a) In your jotter, write down the first 10 square numbers like this:
1 × 1 = 1, 2 × 2 = 4, …
   b) Which square numbers are odd?
   c) Which square numbers are even?
   d) What do you notice?

8) In your jotter, write down a square number which is also a factor of 20.

9) Here are the first five triangular numbers:
1 = 1, 1 + 2 = 3, 1 + 2 + 3 = 6, 1 + 2 + 3 + 4 = 10, 1 + 2 + 3 + 4 + 5 = 15
   a) Will the next triangular number be odd or even?
   b) Which triangular numbers are odd?
   c) Which triangular numbers are even?
   d) What do you notice?

Now try this!

The triangular numbers are found using addition:

1st	2nd	3rd	4th	5th
1	1 + 2	1 + 2 + 3	1 + 2 + 3 + 4	1 + 2 + 3 + 4 + 5

a) What is the 6th triangular number?

b) Ahmed works out the 10th triangular number by adding pairs:
1 + 2 + 3 + 4 + 5 + 6 + 7 + 8 + 9 + 10 = (1 + 10) + (2 + 9) + (3 + 8)
                                                              + (4 + 7) + (5 + 6)
= 11 + 11 + 11 + 11 + 11
= 5 × 11
= 55

Chapter 20 Numbers and sequences

Use this method to work out the:
- 20th triangular number
- 50th triangular number
- 100th triangular number.

Sequences

💡 I will learn to find patterns in sequences and identify a rule to extend the sequence.

Remember, remember

A **sequence** is a list of numbers, letters or objects in a given order. Each number, letter or object in the sequence is called a **term**.

To find the next few terms in a **sequence**, look for a **rule** connecting the terms, or look for familiar sequences.

Exercise 2

1) In your jotter, write down the next **two terms** in each sequence:
   a) 7, 14, 21, 28, …
   b) 100, 95, 90, 85, …
   c) 11, 17, 23, 29, 35, …
   d) 23, 34, 45, 56, 67, …
   e) 19, 16, 13, 10, …
   f) 52, 43, 34, 25, …

2) Fill in the gaps in the sequences:
   a) 2, ___, 6, 8, 10, ___
   b) 77, 70, ___, ___, 49, 42
   c) 40, ___, 48, 52, 56, ___, 64
   d) 10, 19, ___, ___, 46, 55

Identifying number types and patterns in sequences

3) In your jotter, write down the next **two terms** in each sequence:
   a) −2, −4, −6, −8, −10, …
   b) −1, −3, −5, -7, …
   c) 1, 4, 9, 16, 25, …
   d) $\frac{1}{4}$, $\frac{1}{2}$, $\frac{3}{4}$, 1, $1\frac{1}{4}$, …
   e) 1, 3, 6, 10, 15, …
   f) 1, 1, 2, 3, 5, 8, …
   g) 1, 2, 4, 8, …
   h) 0.7, 1, 1.3, 1.6, 1.9, …

4) In your jotter, write down the next **three terms** in each of these Fibonacci-style sequences:
   a) 2, 2, 4, 6, …
   b) 0.5, 0.5, 1, 1.5, 2.5, …
   c) 0.1, 0.1, 0.2, 0.3, 0.5, …
   d) $\frac{1}{4}$, $\frac{1}{4}$, $\frac{1}{2}$, $\frac{3}{4}$, $1\frac{1}{4}$, …

5) Find the **10th term** of each of these sequences:
   a) 10, 20, 30, 40, …
   b) 1, 4, 9, 16, 25, …
   c) 90, 88, 86, 84, 82, …
   d) 91, 81, 71, 61, 51, …

6) A sequence of numbers starts:
   4, 7, 10, 13, 16, …
   Do you agree with Sam?
   Explain your answer.

   The 5th term in the sequence is 16, so the 10th term must be 2 × 16 = 32.

7) In a school the desks are set out as shown:

   1 table
   8 children

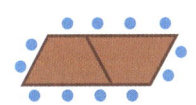

   2 tables
   12 children

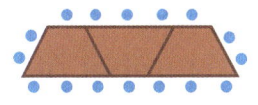

   3 tables
   16 children

Chapter 20 Numbers and sequences

a) In your jotter, draw the next picture with 4 desks.
b) Copy the table and add the **missing** numbers.

Number of desks	1	2	3	4	5
Number of children	8	12	16		

c) For every **extra** desk, how many more can be seated?
d) Copy and complete:
Number of children = ___ × number of desks + 4
e) How many children can sit at 20 desks?

8) A fence is made using posts and panels.

2 posts
3 panels

3 posts
6 panels

4 posts
9 panels

a) In your jotter, draw the next picture with 5 posts.
b) Copy the table and add the **missing** numbers.

Number of posts	2	3	4	5	6
Number of panels	3	6	9		

c) For every **extra** post, how many more panels are needed?
d) How many panels will you need with:
  i) 7 posts   ii) 8 posts   iii) 10 posts?
e) Copy and complete:
Number of panels = ___ × number of posts − ___

Identifying number types and patterns in sequences

Revisit, review, revise

1) In your jotter, write down all the factors of 25.
2) a) In your jotter, write down the numbers from 1 to 20.
   b) Put a **circle** around the multiples of 3.
   c) **Underline** all the square numbers.
3) Choose all the numbers in the cloud which are:
   a) square numbers
   b) triangular numbers
   c) Fibonacci numbers
   d) factors of 20
   e) multiples of 4.

   1 2 4 6 7 8

   (You may use the numbers more than once.)
4) In your jotter, write down the next **two terms** in each sequence:
   a) 12, 24, 36, 48, …
   b) −5, −10, −15, −20, …
   c) 100, 81, 64, 49, …
   d) 2, 2, 4, 6, 10, 16, …
5) Work out the **8th term** of the sequence which starts 5, 8, 11, 14.
6) A sequence is made with wooden bricks.

   3 bricks   5 bricks   ___ bricks   ___ bricks

   a) Copy the table and add the **missing** numbers.

Term	1st	2nd	3rd	4th	5th
Number of bricks	3	5			

   b) How many **extra** bricks are needed each time?
   c) Copy and complete:
   Number of bricks = ___ × term number + 1

21 Probability
Calculating and simplifying probabilities

Probability

> 💡 I will learn to use the language of probability and calculate simple probabilities.

Remember, remember

The **probability** of something happening is the mathematical chance of it happening.

We can use these words to describe probability:

certain, **likely**, **even chance**, **unlikely**, **impossible**.

The **mathematical probabilities** of the outcome of an event are usually given as **fractions** or **percentages**.

Probability is given on a scale of 0 to 1.

- If an outcome is **impossible**, then the probability is **0**.
- If an outcome is **certain**, the probability is **1**.
- If an outcome has an **even chance**, the probability is $\frac{1}{2}$ = **50%**.

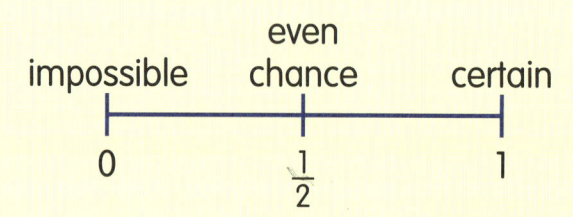

```
impossible    even chance    certain
    |-------------|-------------|
    0            1/2            1
```

If all the outcomes of an event are equally likely then:

$$\text{probability of event} = \frac{\text{number of times it can occur}}{\text{total number of outcomes}}$$

Calculating and simplifying probabilities

Example

A fair dice numbered 1 to 6 is rolled.
What is the probability of rolling the number 1?

If a dice is fair it means every number has the same chance of being rolled.

There is one number 1 on the dice and there are 6 different outcomes.

Probability of rolling 1 = $\frac{1}{6}$

Exercise 1

1) A ball is picked at random from this set:

   | certain | likely | even chance | unlikely | impossible |

   Use a word or phrase from the box to write down how likely it is that the number on the ball is:

   a) 12
   b) 13
   c) a whole number less than 13
   d) an odd number.

2) Fatima flips a £2 coin.
   What is the probability that it will land showing tails?

3) Lisa plays the game Rock, Scissors, Paper.
   What is the probability that she will show rock on her next turn?

Chapter 21 Probability

4) A jar of sweets contains the same number of red, yellow, orange and purple sweets.

Davina chooses one without looking.

What is the probability she chooses:
- a) a yellow sweet
- b) an orange sweet
- c) a red sweet
- d) a purple sweet
- e) a blue sweet?

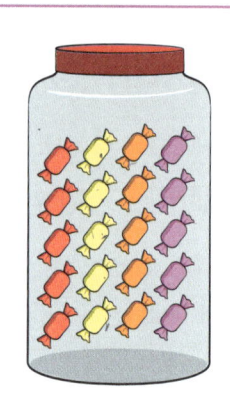

5) Three bags contain counters numbered 1 or 2.

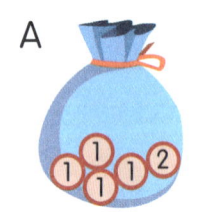

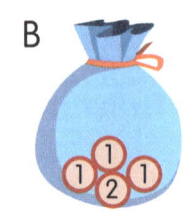

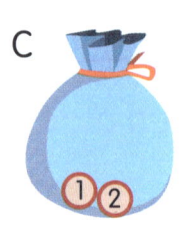

A   B   C

Dale and Matt pick a counter from a bag without looking.

a) The probability of Dale picking a 2 is 50%.

Which bag does she pick from?

b) The probability of Matt picking a 2 is 20%.

Which bag does he pick from?

6) Here is a fair spinner.

What is the probability of spinning a 3?

Give the answer as a fraction and a percentage.

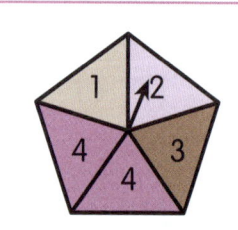

7) Here is a fair spinner.

Each section of the spinner has the letter A or B written in it.

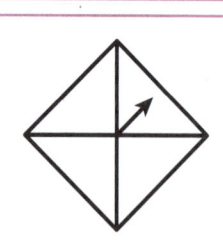

Copy the spinner.

Write the letters A or B in each section of your spinner so that the probability of spinning B is 25%.

Calculating and simplifying probabilities

8) A packet of sweets contains 10 coloured sweets.
How many red sweets are in the packet if the probability of picking a red sweet is:

a) 10%
b) 100%
c) 0%
d) 50%?

9) A bag contains 10 counters.
The counters have the letters A, B, C, D or E on them.
Copy the bag and counters.
Label the counters so that:

a) the probability of choosing A is 0
b) there are the same number of counters with the letters B and C
c) the probability of choosing D is 10%
d) the probability of choosing E is $\frac{3}{10}$.

Simplifying probabilities

I will learn to calculate and simplify probabilities.

Remember, remember

If all the outcomes of an event are equally likely then:

$$\text{probability of event} = \frac{\text{number of times it can occur}}{\text{total number of outcomes}}$$

A fraction can be simplified by dividing the numerator and denominator by the same number.

$$\frac{10}{12} = \frac{10 \div 2}{12 \div 2} = \frac{5}{6}$$

Chapter 21 Probability

If the number of times an event can occur is more than 1, the probability of an event may be a fraction which can be **simplified**.

In mathematics, a shorthand is used to write probability.

For example:
- **probability of 1** may be written **P(1)**
- **probability of blue** may be written **P(blue)**.

Example

A pencil case contains 10 blue pens and 2 red pens.
A pen is picked without looking.
What is:

a) P(blue)   b) P(red)   c) P(black)?

Answer

There are a total of 12 pens in the case.

There are 10 blue pens: P(blue) = $\frac{10}{12}$ = $\frac{5}{6}$

There are 2 red pens: P(red) = $\frac{2}{12}$ = $\frac{1}{6}$

There are no black pens: P(black) = $\frac{0}{12}$ = 0

Exercise 2

1) A bag of marbles contains 3 blue and 7 red marbles.
   Lydia picks a marble without looking.
   What is:
   a) P(blue)   b) P(red)?

Calculating and simplifying probabilities

2) This fair spinner is spun.
   What is:
   a) P(red)
   b) P(blue)
   c) P(yellow)
   d) P(black)?

3) There are 12 sheep in a field.
   Six are brown and six are white.
   A sheep is selected at random.
   What is:
   a) P(white)
   b) P(brown)
   c) P(pink)?
   Simplify the fractions if possible.

4) The letters in the word SYMMETRY are written on cards.

   S Y M M E T R Y

   The cards are shuffled and a card is chosen without looking.
   What is:
   a) P(S)
   b) P(M)
   c) P(A)?
   Simplify the fractions if possible.

5) A fruit bowl contains 4 apples, 6 oranges and 2 bananas.
   Jenna chooses a piece of fruit at random.
   What is:
   a) P(apple)
   b) P(orange)
   c) P(banana)
   d) P(pear)?
   Simplify the fractions if possible.

Chapter 21 Probability

6) Dev is asked to write down what month he was born.
What is P(July), the probability that he was born in July?

7) A fair 6-sided dice is rolled.
What is:
a) P(1)
b) P(even number)
c) P(number smaller than 7)
d) P(9)
e) P(factor of 6)
f) P(multiple of 3)?

8) The sections of a fair spinner are numbered so that:
- P(1) = P(2)
- P(3) = 50 %
- P(4) > P(2).

Copy the spinner and write a number in each section.

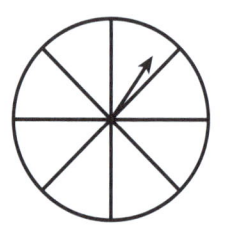

9) Here are two bags of balls, A and B.
Each bag contains green balls and yellow balls only.
Matthew chooses a ball from each bag without looking.
From which bag is he more likely to choose a green ball?
Explain how you know.

A: 7 green and 11 yellow

B: 9 green and 13 yellow

Calculating and simplifying probabilities

Experimental probability

> 💡 I will learn to work out experimental probability.

If a dice is rolled, the probability of rolling a 4 is $\frac{1}{6}$.

Does this mean that if you roll the dice 6 times, you will get one 4?

Try rolling the dice 6 times.

What do you find?

Experimental probability is found using the results of an experiment.

$$\text{experimental probability} = \frac{\text{number of times outcome occurs}}{\text{total number of trials}}$$

Example

Shabana drops a piece of buttered toast 20 times.

It lands butter side down 11 times.

What is the experimental probability of it landing butter side down?

Answer

Experimental probability of toast landing butter side down = $\frac{11}{20}$.

Exercise 3

1) Ari records the colours of cars going past his house.

   Of the 20 cars he counts, 7 are blue.

   What is the experimental probability of a car passing Ari's house being blue?

Chapter 21 Probability

2) A factory makes lightbulbs.
One day it makes 2500 lightbulbs.
3 are broken.
What is the experimental probability of a bulb being broken?

3) 20 customers in a café order a drink.
12 of them order tea.
What is the experimental probability that a customer orders tea?
Simplify the answer.

4) A gardener plants 50 seeds.
35 of the seeds grow into seedlings.
What is the experimental probability that a seed will grow into a seedling?
Give the answer as a:

   a) fraction   **b)** percentage.

5) A bag contains coloured counters.
Rose picks a counter, records the colour and puts the counter back.
She does this 15 times.
She picks 3 blues, 7 yellows and 5 reds.

   a) What is the experimental probability she chooses:

      i) blue   **ii)** yellow   **iii)** red   **iv)** black?

   b) Do you agree with Rose? Explain your answer.

I did not pick any black counters, so there cannot be any black counters in the bag.

Calculating and simplifying probabilities

Example

The probability of rolling a 5 on a dice is $\frac{1}{6}$.

How many times will a 5 occur if you roll a dice 12 times?

Answer

$\frac{1}{6} \times 12 = 2$

5 should occur twice.

6) You will need a dice.

   a) Roll the dice 12 times.

   Did 5 occur twice?

   b) How many times would you expect 5 to occur if you roll the dice 60 times?

7) You will need a dice.

   Work in pairs.

   a) Copy the tally chart.

Score	Tally	Frequency
1		
2		
3		
4		
5		
6		

Chapter 21 Probability

b) Roll the dice 60 times and record the scores in the tally chart.

c) From the tally chart, work out the experimental probability of rolling a:

    i) 1   ii) 2   iii) 3

    iv) 4   v) 5   vi) 6

d) Are your answers to the questions in c) all $\frac{1}{6}$?

8) Polls suggest that 7 in 10 people will vote for Teresa Snaple in an election.

45 000 people vote.

How many votes do you expect will **not** be for Teresa Snaple?

Now try this!

Two dice are rolled together.

The score is found by adding together the numbers on the dice.

Score = 5 + 6 = 11

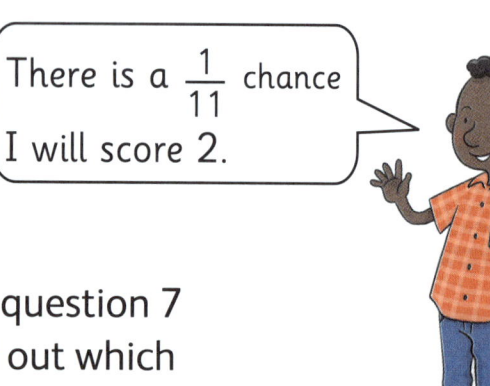

There are 11 different possible scores.

a) In your jotter, write a list of all the possible scores.

There is a $\frac{1}{11}$ chance I will score 2.

b) Do you agree with Mo?

Explain your answer.

c) Draw up a tally chart like the one in question 7 and carry out an experiment to find out which scores are most likely.

Try to explain any patterns you notice.

Calculating and simplifying probabilities

Revisit, review, revise

1) In a box of ice lollies there are 5 orange lollies and 1 green lolly.
   What is the probability of taking out the green one without looking?

2) Copy the bag and counters.
   Colour the counters so the probability of picking a green counter is 20%.

3) The letters in the word MATHEMATICS are written on cards.

   | M | A | T | H | E | M | A | T | I | C | S |

   The cards are shuffled and one is chosen without looking.
   What is:
   a) P(H)   b) P(M)   c) P(vowel)   d) P(Y)?

4) A bag contains 12 sweets:
   1 strawberry, 2 lemon, 3 apple, 6 orange.
   Match the probability to the correct fractions or percentages:

P(strawberry)	P(lemon)	P(apple)	P(orange)	P(lime)
$\frac{1}{2}$	$\frac{1}{4}$	$\frac{1}{12}$	0	$\frac{1}{6}$

5) Omar bakes cakes.
   One day he bakes 7 cakes; 1 does **not** rise.
   a) What is the experimental probability that Omar's cakes do **not** rise?
   b) In a month Omar bakes 84 cakes.
      How many does he expect to **not** rise?

22 End-of-year revision

1) In your jotter, write down a number between 40 and 50 that is a multiple of 9.

2) In your jotter, write down all the factors of 12.

3) Work out:
   a) 18 − 8 × 2
   b) 32 ÷ 4 + 1
   c) 48 − 8 ÷ 2

4) A pack contains 8 thank you cards.
   Bobby has 3 packs.
   He writes 7 thank you cards.
   a) In your jotter, write the calculation you would use to work out how many thank you cards Bobby has left.
   b) How many thank you cards are left?

5) A pack of paper contains 500 sheets.
   How many sheets of paper in 5 packs?

6) What numbers are **missing**?
   a) 20 × ___ = 800
   b) 600 × ___ = 42 000
   c) ___ ÷ 30 = 20
   d) ___ ÷ 900 = 40

7) Work out **mentally**:
   a) 0.7 × 4
   b) 0.04 × 2
   c) 4.9 ÷ 7
   d) 0.56 ÷ 8

End-of-year revision

8) A sheet of cardboard is 0.3 cm thick.

What is the **total** thickness of 9 sheets of cardboard?

9) Work out:
- a) 0.95 − 0.37
- b) 0.426 + 0.59
- c) 30.9 × 4
- d) 561.9 ÷ 3

10) What is one fifth of 917.25?

11) A children's charity raises £647.14 in June and £581.29 in July.
- a) How much do they raise **in total** in June and July?
- b) What is the **difference** between the amount they raise in June and the amount they raise in July?

12) Sammy earns £22.60 per hour.

He works 8 hours.

How much does he earn?

13) Three office printers cost £782.25.

What is the cost of 1 office printer?

14) Which box of apples is better value?

8 apples — £6.48

6 apples — £4.98

Show your working.

Chapter 22 End-of-year revision

15) You can use a debit card or a credit card to make payments.
In your jotter, write down **one** thing that is **different** about these cards.

16) Work out:
- a) 10% of 40 m
- b) 50% of 70 km
- c) 20% of 90 litres
- d) 25% of £240
- e) 75% of 500 litres
- f) 1% of £8 (give your answer in pence)

17) A weekday ticket to a show costs £30.
A weekend ticket to the same show costs an extra 5%.
How much is a weekend ticket to the show?

18) In your jotter, write:
- a) 0.01 as a fraction and a percentage
- b) 37% as a fraction and a decimal
- c) $\frac{89}{100}$ as a decimal and a percentage.

19) In your jotter, write this list in order from **smallest** to **largest**.

$\frac{1}{20}$ 0.25   15%

20) Work out:
- a) $2\overline{)93}$
- b) $5\overline{)64}$
- c) $8\overline{)150}$
- d) $4\overline{)1385}$

Give your answers as decimal fractions.

21) What is the temperature on this thermometer?

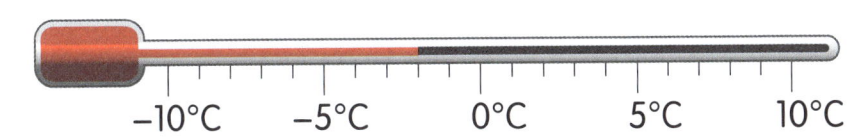

−10°C   −5°C   0°C   5°C   10°C

22) Here are the temperatures recorded at night in the Cairngorms for one week:

Monday	Tuesday	Wednesday	Thursday	Friday	Saturday	Sunday
−5°C	−3°C	−1°C	−2°C	−4°C	−6°C	−3°C

Which night was the **warmest**?

23) What is the **missing** number on this number line?

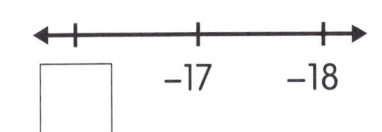

☐   −17   −18

24) a) In your jotter, write down the:
   i) diameter
   ii) radius
   of the circle.

12 cm

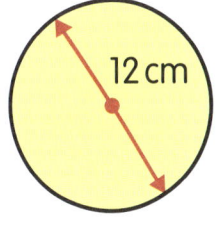

b) Use a pair of compasses to draw a circle with diameter 10 cm.

Chapter 22 End-of-year revision

25) In your jotter, write down the names of these shapes:

a) 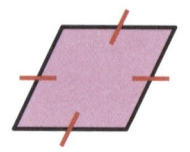   b) 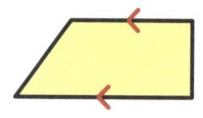   c)

d) 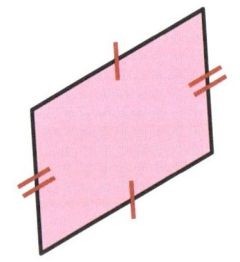   e) 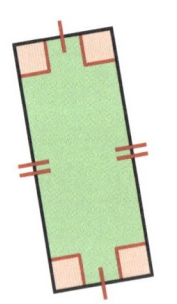   f)

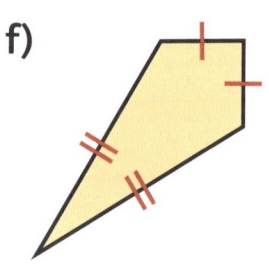

26) What is the name of a seven-sided polygon?

27) Calculate the area of these shapes:

a) 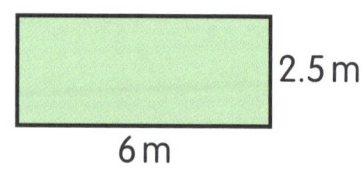 2.5 m, 6 m

b) 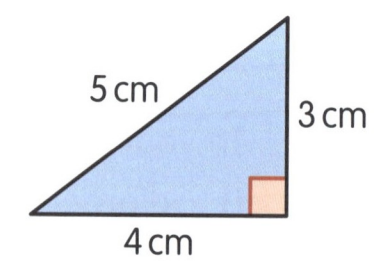 5 cm, 3 cm, 4 cm

28) Draw and label two different rectangles with perimeter 20 cm.

29) 300 golfers were asked which was their best shot.
The pie chart shows the results. 
   a) What fraction chose driving?
   b) How many chose driving?
   c) What percentage chose putting?
   d) How many chose putting?

End-of-year revision

30) Pupils take a maths test and an English test.
The marks are shown in the line graph.

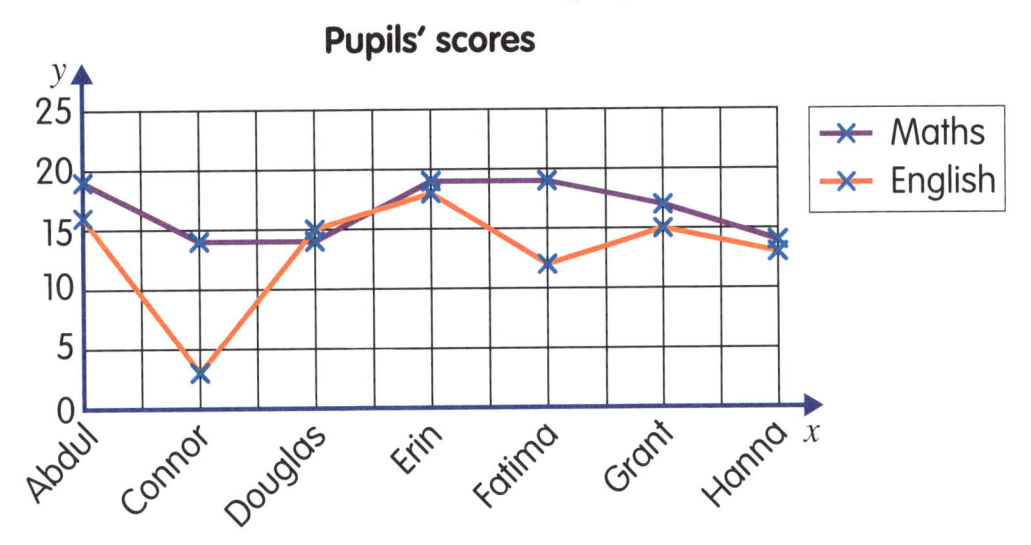

Pupils' scores

a) Who achieved the highest score in:
   i) maths
   ii) English?
b) Which pupil has the **greatest difference** between their two scores?
c) The marks for the two tests are added together.
   Who has the **highest total** score?

31) Copy these shapes onto squared paper.
   a)
   b)

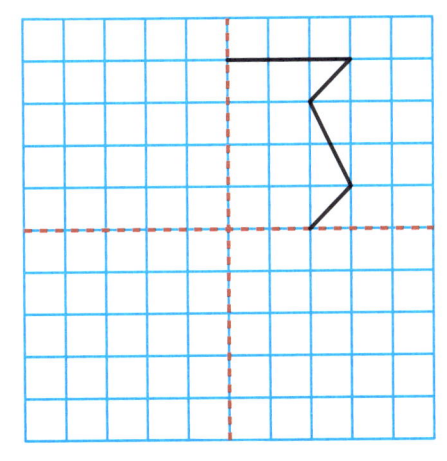

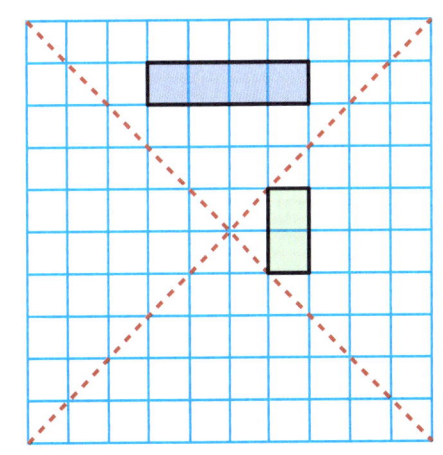

Complete and colour the shapes so the dashed lines are lines of symmetry.

Chapter 22 End-of-year revision

32) a) In your jotter, write down the coordinates of point **A**.

b) **ABCD** is a square.

What are the coordinates of the point **B**?

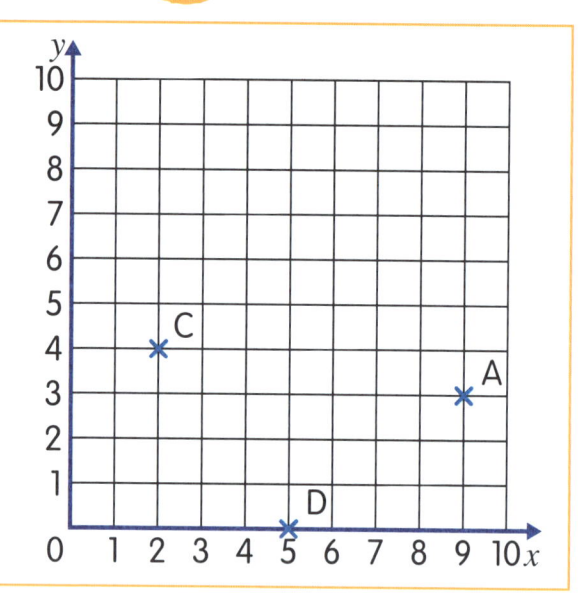

33) What 3D shapes will these nets make?

a)

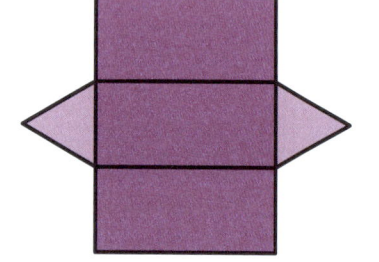

b)

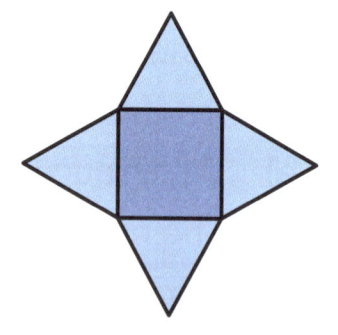

34) The stopwatch shows the time in minutes and seconds for the winner of an 800-metre race.

a) How long did the winner take to finish the race?

b) Round the time to the nearest:

i) minute

ii) second.

The stopwatch shows 2:03:55.

35) a) How many seconds in 5 minutes?

b) How many minutes in $3\frac{1}{4}$ hours?

c) How many hours in 2.5 days?

End-of-year revision

36) a) Barbara walks for $3\frac{1}{2}$ hours at 7 km per hour.
How far does she walk?

b) A train travels at 50 miles per hour.
How long will it take to travel 375 miles?

37) Calculate the size of angles *a*, *b* and *c*.

a) 47°, *a*

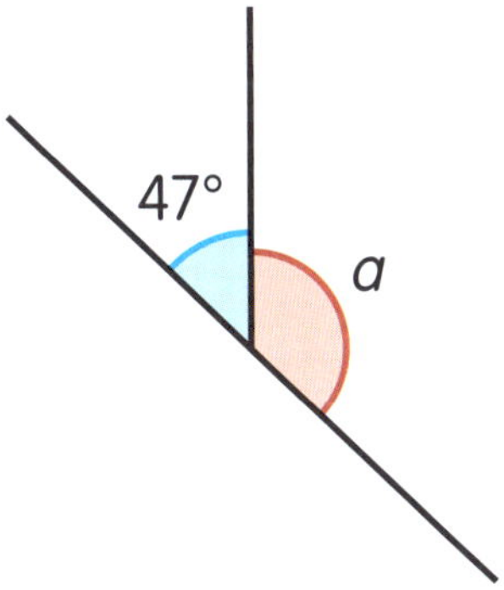

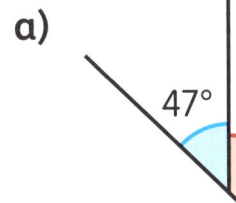

b) 295°, *b*

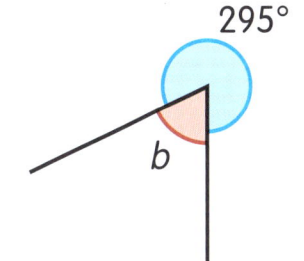

c) 90°, *c*

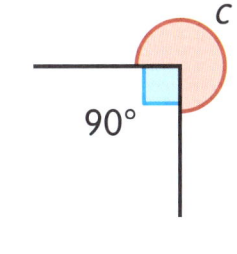

38) Arun is facing NE.

He turns 90° clockwise.

Which direction is he now facing?

39) This spear has been drawn to a scale of **1 cm = 12 cm**.

a) What is the length of the **real** spear?

The same scale is used to draw a diagram of a shield which is 0.96 m tall.

b) How tall is the shield **in the diagram**?

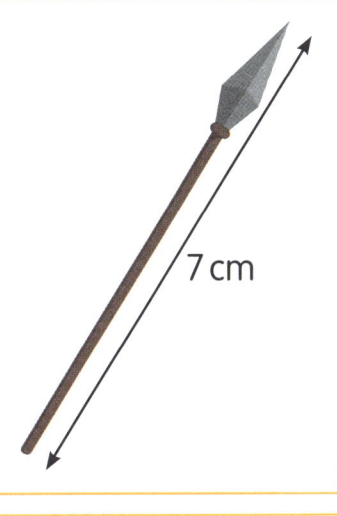

7 cm

40) What is the input of the function machine?

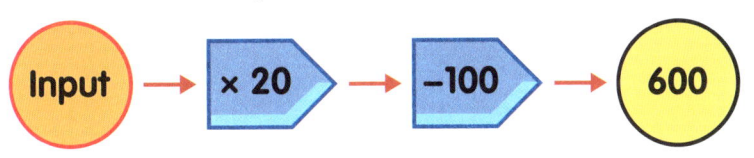

Input → × 20 → −100 → 600

Chapter 22 End-of-year revision

41) Solve the equations:
  a) $x + 5 = 12$
  b) $3x = 24$
  c) $x - 7 = 20$
  d) $\dfrac{x}{6} = 11$

42) In your jotter, write and solve an equation to represent the set of scales:

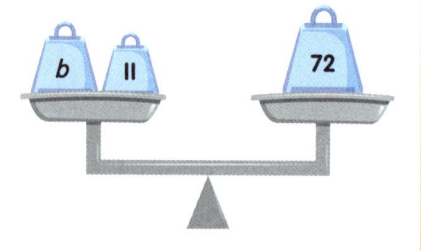

43) Copy and complete:
  a) 18.2 cm = _____ mm
  b) 9.5 m = _____ cm
  c) 45.2 km = _____ m

44) Copy and complete:
  a) 3 miles ≈ _____ km
  b) _____ feet ≈ 210 cm
  c) _____ inches ≈ 15 cm

  1 mile ≈ 1.6 km
  1 foot ≈ 30 cm
  1 inch ≈ 2.5 cm

45) a) Calculate the volume of this container in cm³.
  b) How many litres will the container hold when full?

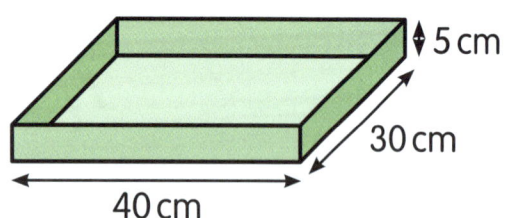

  5 cm
  30 cm
  40 cm

46) 1 stone ≈ 6.4 kg

A lion has mass 25 kg.

Use a calculator to convert this into stones.

Round your answer to the nearest whole number.

47) Which of the numbers in the cloud are:
 a) square numbers
 b) factors of 6
 c) multiples of 3
 d) Fibonacci numbers
 e) triangular numbers?

1, 8, 9, 15, 14, 3, 12, 7, 2, 13, 10, 6, 11, 5, 4

48) What is the **10th term** in the sequence 5, 8, 11, 14, …?

49) A player wins a game if a multiple of 3 shows when they roll a 12-sided dice (numbered 1 to 12).

What is the probability of winning the game?

Simplify your answer.

50) The age of patients visiting a doctors' surgery is recorded one morning.

72 patients are adults and 48 are children.

A patient is selected at random.

What is the experimental probability the patient is a child?

Simplify your answer.